A CALL FROM HOME

A CALL FROM HOME

Armenia and Karabagh
My Journal

BY

Carolann S. Najarian, M.D.

ARPEN PRESS

CAMBRIDGE, MASSACHUSETTS

A CALL FROM HOME
Armenia and Karabagh, My Journal

Published by
Arpen Press
P.O. Box 400135
Cambridge, MA 02140

Jacket and book design, typography and electronic pagination by
Arrow Graphics, Inc., Cambridge, Massachusetts

Printed in the United States of America

Publisher's Cataloging-in-Publication
(*Provided by Quality Books, Inc.*)

Najarian, Carolann S.
A call from home : Armenia and Karabagh my journal /
by Carolann S. Najarian. — 1st ed.
p. cm.
Includes bibliographical references.
Preassigned LCCN: 98-093280
ISBN: 0-9664985-0-X

1. Disaster relief—Armenia (Republic). 2. Najarian, Carolann S.—
Journeys—Armenia (Republic) 3. Earthquakes—Armenia (Republic)
4. Nagorno Karabakh Conflict, 1988–1994—Civilian relief.
5. Armenia (Republic)—History. 6. Physicians—Massachusetts—Biography.
7. Women physicians—Massachusetts—Biography. I. Title.

HV555.A76N35 1998   363.34'8'094756'0973
                            QBI98-833

To my husband George
who has patiently endured and lovingly encouraged me through
my years in medical training and medical practice, my long
absences while in Armenia, and the writing of this book

Contents

Foreword

This fascinating book recounts the odyssey of an accomplished American physician who has dedicated herself to improving health care for Armenians afflicted by overwhelming tragedies: a devastating earthquake, a major war, blockade, famine, and pestilence.

Herself a descendant of survivors of the Armenian Genocide early in this century, Carolann Najarian provides a poignant account of her own efforts to deal with the medical needs of this population. She captures the sadness and despair of the people. The heart-wrenching accounts of sick children in hospitals without heat, food, or medical equipment will touch every reader.

But the book also engenders hope and optimism for the future as it chronicles the slow but steady improvement of conditions in Armenia and portrays the great dignity and inner strength of the people, their resourcefulness, and their strong determination to survive.

Aram V. Chobanian, M.D.
Dean, Boston University School of Medicine

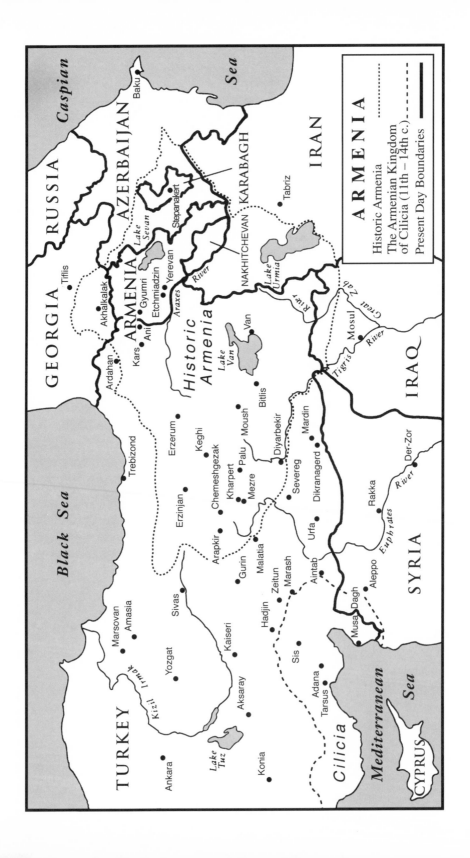

Acknowledgments

My deepest thanks to:
My friends in Armenia and Karabagh, whose lives are the substance of this book.

My sister-in-law Anne Merian, who spent countless hours editing the many drafts of this manuscript, quieting my fears, and encouraging me to continue writing. Without her tireless effort this book would not have become a reality. I will be forever grateful to her.

Stella Grigorian, Ph.D., Claire Panosian, M.D., and my aunt, Hassie Yankelovich, and my sister, Rose Munch, for their input and suggestions that helped me shape the direction of my writing.

My friends Frances and Burton Herman, who not only read the manuscript but helped with the title while we were on vacation; to Judge André and Renalde Gelinas, who read the manuscript in its various stages and encouraged me to continue.

Dr. Charles Hatem, mentor, physician, and friend, for reviewing the manuscript's medical references and for his encouragement over the years regarding the worthiness of this project.

Professor Gourgen Melikian for teaching me so much over the years about life in Armenia as reflected in this book and for reviewing the manuscript for historical accuracy.

Ara Ghazarians for checking the accuracy of the historical data, advising on transliterations, and assisting with the selection of maps; Vahé Ghahramanian, of Northeastern University's

Department of Civil Engineering, for providing technical data on the December 7, 1988 earthquake; Marie Ghahramanian for researching the 40-day traditions; the Zoryan Institute and Julie Bailey for details on the Armenian Legionnaires.

Alvart Badalian and Aramais Andonian of Arrow Graphics for working so congenially with me, and for the care with which they have approached the production of this book.

All the volunteers, lay and professional, who have given of their time and expertise, who have made the work of the Armenian Health Alliance, Inc., possible. Special thanks to Nancy Asbedian, Dr. Vatché Seraderian, Anne Vartanian, Dr. Elizabeth Gregory, Boris and Fred Tahmassian, Anita Edgarian, Esther Stepanian, Iris Tatian Kassabian, Dr. Krikor Shoghikian, Arminé Koundakjian, and Michael Najarian. And the Armenian Health Alliance committee in California headed by Lilit Marzbetuny and Tamar Mahshigian, who organized the Adopt-A-Sister project for the women of Gedashen .

Sonya Nersessian, Esq., whose upbeat attitude and encouragement continue to keep me buoyed through the difficult times and without whom the Armenian Health Alliance would never have been.

And, my appreciation to the Ministry of Health of Armenia and of Nagorno-Karabagh for their ongoing assistance and support of our work.

Prologue

On December 7, 1988, at 11:41 a.m. the seismically active fault under the northern regions of Armenia shifted, causing an earthquake that destroyed most of northern Armenia and the lives of tens of thousands of men, women, and children. For twenty terrifying seconds the noise of the quake thundered throughout the region as the great plates separated and moved, pushing and rising over each other. Four minutes and 20 seconds later, in a great aftershock, the noise thundered again as the earth shook a second time with terrifying ferocity, wreaking its full destruction. Survivors would recall its shattering noise over and over again.

In those few minutes an earthquake that registered 6.9 on the Richter scale destroyed the cities of Leninakan and Spitak along with scores of villages and caused major structural damage to the towns of Ashotsk, Kirovakan, and Stepanavan. The dead were officially numbered at 26,000 by the Soviet government, a figure that Armenians have never accepted. The real number will probably never be known. Some estimates put the number between 40,000 and 50,000 but the people who live in the earthquake region believe it to be closer to 80,000. The injured were in the tens of thousands; of that there could be no dispute, and the homeless simply numbered the entire population of northern Armenia, close to one million people.

When the black dust settled the extent of the destruction became evident: few homes were left, all factories had been destroyed, and the schools, hospitals, cinemas, and shops had crumbled to the ground. Whole communities, where everyday life unfolded, had vanished. For the survivors, life was a living death as they tried to organize themselves to preserve whatever and whoever was left. Public health issues were paramount: clean water, food, protection from the cold, prevention of epidemics, and the nightmare of finding, identifying, and burying the dead. Hundreds of children who had survived orphaned, injured, or unable to find their families in the confusion were sent by train to other republics of the Soviet Union. Many never returned to Armenia.

The magnitude of destruction and the resulting needs were far beyond Armenia's, and even of the then Soviet Union's ability to handle. Within hours of the catastrophe the call for help resounded throughout the world.

The earthquake occurred in the midst of an ongoing political crisis that eventually played a role in the downfall of Communism and the dissolution of the Soviet Union: the struggle for freedom by the Armenians of Mountainous Karabagh, a little known enclave within Azerbaijan.

Now, ten years later, the story of what happened in that seemingly insignificant part of the world, as I saw it and witnessed it, needs to be told. It is a story of survival, of faith, and of hope. In the end, it is a story of victory and courage. It is a story about all humankind.

My story begins in a time and place long before these events, before I was born, in a land I have never seen, called Anatolia, a part of ancient Armenia.

· PART I ·

OUT OF THE ASHES

*Mount Ararat towers over Khor-Virab, a monastery built during
the Middle Ages on the site of a second century prison. Ararat's
smaller peak is hidden behind the clouds. Armenia 1993.*

*Armenian Empire (c. 80 B.C.) extended from
the Mediterranean to the Caspeian Sea.*

CHAPTER 1

My Roots, Our History

At one time, about two thousand years ago, ancient Armenia encompassed an area of 140,000 square miles, with the Ararat plateau its center and bounded by the Caucasus and the Mediterranean and Caspian seas. Slowly over the centuries that followed, it lost most of its land to the warring nations that rose up around it: Persia, Greece, Rome, and finally the Ottoman Empire. It was no small feat that despite being ravaged over and over again, the Armenians retained their identity and their nation state until the 15th century when the Ottoman Turks conquered them as they marched to Byzantium. The major part of Armenia's ancient homeland came under Turkish rule and became the eastern part of modern-day Turkey.

In 301 A.D. Armenians adopted Christianity as their national religion, the first nation to do so, even before the Romans. The Armenian language, its roots in the Indo-European family of languages, has its own distinctive alphabet created in 404 A.D. for the specific purpose of translating the Bible into the Armenian language. Thus, the Armenians were set apart, forever, from their neighbors and from their conquerors.

This was the land of my ancestors, the land of the great mountain Ararat with its twin snow-covered peaks. It is on this mountain, according to the legend, that Noah's Ark landed. And according to the old Armenian legend, the Armenians are descended from *Haik*, a descendant of Noah's third son *Japheth*, born after the Ark rested on Mt. Ararat. However, historians are more likely to agree that the Armenians emerged as a mosaic of the many tribes that settled in this region more than three thousand years ago. The last of this amalgamation took place among the Urartians (who gave the mountain its name), the Armens (who gave us our name), and the Hayasas (who most likely gave us the name we call ourselves, *Hai)*. In 500 B.C. the Armenians, a separate ethnically identifiable people, were recorded in history as a nation living on these lands that are the crossroads between the East and the West.

It is here, deep within the interior of ancient Armenia, modern-day Turkey, that my story begins, in the region called Kharpert, where my parents' ancestors had lived for centuries.

My mother, Arpen, was born in 1912 in a place called Arapkir, not too far from my father's village. Her parents were Rosa Massoumian and Kegham Kaboolian. In a picture taken on their wedding day Rosa is standing tall next to my grandfather, her arm passed through his, poised for the camera. She wore a long dress made of white brocade that she had embroidered with shiny beads that can still be seen in the faded photograph. A necklace of gold beads hung around her neck; bracelets most likely of gold, as well, adorned her wrists. An ornate belt made of silver, typically Armenian, had been placed around her waist, probably by her mother. Her hair, which remained full and black up to her death, was pulled back that day just the way I remember it. I remember how she would comb her hair in long strokes after a bath, and then, with a few quick movements would roll it into a bun and pin it above the nape of her neck.

In the photograph my grandfather looks as carefully prepared for the wedding as my grandmother. He has on a well tailored dark suit, with slightly tapered shoulders, and sleeves adjusted to the right place at his wrists. His white shirt, with its decorative laces in place of buttons, has a high, stiffly starched collar that reaches almost to the line of his jawbone. His tie appears to be made of silk and falls in a soft bow around the high collar. Someone had placed a small flower in his lapel. My grandfather was a handsome young man with a broad face, a thin mustache, dark eyes, and a head of perfectly groomed thick black hair.

My grandmother and grandfather are not smiling in this photograph; they appear to be worried. Their dark eyes, set far apart, are staring straight at the camera. The lines of their mouths point downward, not at all the way I remember them when I was growing up. Maybe my grandmother is not smiling because she is being married to a man she hardly knows; it was my grandfather who had seen her and had sent his family seeking her hand in marriage. Or maybe they were already concerned about what the future held for them.

They were right to worry. Shortly after the birth of my mother, it was decided that Kegham should go to America to work with his uncle, who had been living in New York City for several years. He left his wife and daughter in the care of her family, promising to return as soon as he could with enough money to guarantee their future. He never came back.

My father, Avedis, was born in a village not too far from my mother's, called Sheikh Hadji, a few years before my mother. He was the second of three children born to Sahag and Elizabeth Abrahamian. In 1908, just a few months after their daughter Araxie was born, Sahag went to America. Elizabeth had agreed that he should go, but not for more than three years. Upon his return he planned to start a small business. In fact, he too, like Kegham, would never again see his homeland.

It was not unusual for men to leave their villages to find work elsewhere, and those who had the opportunity, like my grandfathers, even went to the United States. There were non-economic reasons for the men's departure as well. The Turks had begun to persecute their non-Moslem minorities, the Greeks, the Assyrians, and Christian Syrians, again. The wholesale massacres that had taken place in the late 1890s in the interior of Turkey, savagely killing more than two hundred thousand Armenians, was still fresh in the minds of Armenians. Then in 1909, in the city of Adana, more than 30,000 Armenians were brutally massacred. A period of relative calm followed, but by 1913 reports of isolated "incidents" were filtering through from village to village.

Armenians, like my grandparents, expected that these pogroms would pass. It would have been impossible to convince them otherwise. In fact, some Armenian political parties in the United States were actively trying to get immigrant Armenians to return to Turkey to help build the new modern Turkish nation being promised. Even when villagers themselves brought news of the atrocities and deportations being carried out in neighboring regions against other Armenians, they simply could not believe that their Turkish neighbors would carry out such things against them. In 1915, however, when in my father's village, as in hundreds of other villages, their very own Turkish *Agha* read the decree in the village square that all arms were to be turned in, that the men were to present themselves in the square that night, and that everyone would be leaving the village in the morning, did people begin to think that something awful might be happening to them. Even when the men who went to the square did not return, those who were left did not understand that the others had been murdered.

My grandmothers expected to wait for my grandfathers' return from America and to continue their lives in the land their forefathers had inhabited for 3000 years. But in 1915 a new agenda was adopted by the Turkish government; it was to annihilate the Armenians. Villagers, like my grandmothers, did not realize until it was too late for most of them that this was to be the 20th century's first organized attempt at genocide. The eyewitness accounts of non-Armenian missionaries, of travelers through the region, and of men like Henry Morgenthau, the then United States ambassador to Turkey, corroborated the accounts of the Armenians who survived.

The fish in the river Euphrates must have choked on the blood that flowed through it. And the sheep and the goats that covered the countryside would have laid down and wept if they could when they saw what was being done. A great sadness must have fallen upon those who were left; a great curse must have settled on those lands, a curse that the wind and the rain can never remove.

This was the land my mother left when she was two years old, and my father as a boy of nine. Their mothers fled their homes carrying whatever they could on their backs, their children in hand. The vast majority of these villagers never made it to a safe haven, but those who survived the hunger and thirst, the rapes and the killings along the way, to reach safety, became the builders of the Armenian nation in exile. It is thus that the Armenian Diaspora was born, out of the ashes of the ancient homeland.

Both my grandmothers traveled on foot. After leaving Sheikh Hadji, Elizabeth went to Mezre, then to Erzerum, Tiflis, the port city of Novorossik on the Black Sea, and to Armavir. It was in Armavir that she met another group of refugees, among them, Rosa and Arpen. My two grandmothers became friends there as did the two little girls, Arpen and Araxie. But they parted ways for reasons unknown to us; Elizabeth eventually reached Istanbul after crossing the Black Sea by boat and Rosa made her way to Marseilles, France. Their stories of their survival were filled with acts of bravery and more than one miracle as they made their journey.

My grandfathers were living in New York City, and each, like other Armenians in America, searched for their relatives' names on the lists of survivors regularly published by Near East Relief. This humanitarian organization, based in the United States, was working to save the Armenians coming out of Turkey and had raised some twenty million dollars to support that effort. Near East Relief's slogan "Remember the starving Armenians" became so well known that parents commonly used it to admonish their children to finish their dinner, even decades later when few remembered who the Armenians were or why they were starving.

Luckily, my grandfathers found Rosa and Elizabeth on the Near East Relief lists and through the organization arranged for and paid for their families' passage to America. In 1921, with hundreds of other immigrants packed in the hulls of ships from

Marseilles and Istanbul respectively, my grandmothers embarked for America, crossing the Atlantic, leaving behind them, as best they could, the nightmare of the genocide and the years of uncertainty, the years of living like nomads. They had been torn from the loins of the earth that gave them life, from the sweet air and the sun that ripened the apricots and the grapes they loved so much. Now, America would give them the opportunity to build new lives, thousands of miles away from the lands that were once theirs.

In New York my mother and Araxie met again and became close friends. Araxie introduced her brother Avedis to Arpen; they fell in love and married. *Avedis* means good news or "the gospel" in Armenian, but as a young man my father was an atheist. This created a big problem when it came time for Kegham, my mother's father, to give his consent to their marriage. My father refused to be married in a church or by a clergyman. My devoutly Christian grandfather would not consent to a civil marriage ceremony. Pressure was brought on both men to compromise and on April 28, 1935, Avedis and Arpen were married in Avedis' parents' living room by Reverend Antranig A. Bedikian, the well-known Protestant clergyman who was minister to both families. Following Armenian tradition, the event was recorded in our family Bible next to my mother's birth record. It was the Bible my grandmother managed to carry with her all the way from Arapkir that we still have.

That is how I came to be born in New York City at the Wadsworth Hospital, just off St. Nicholas Avenue, in the Washington Heights area of Manhattan, an area where Armenian immigrants were settling. My sister Rose had arrived four years earlier, named for the grandmother whose birthday she shared, but who unlike any Armenian any of us knew, had flaming red hair and blue eyes. World War II was beginning and the Great Depression was coming to an end, but not for my family.

We lived in the West Bronx, in a house owned by my grandfather Sahag. It was a two family house not far from the Heights, where my mother's family lived.

Araxie, now married too, lived in the first floor apartment with her family. It was one of those wood frame houses seen in old photos, with crooked stairs going up the front and double doors of half glass and half wood. It was a "cold-water flat," without central heating or hot water. We relied heavily on the pot-bellied stove in the kitchen.

We were, I suppose, poor, but I don't remember ever being hungry. When I look back on the photos from that time, I now have to wonder why my father was so thin, and my mother slender. My clothes were almost always hand-me-downs except when my mother or my aunt Araxie sewed a new dress just for me. Mom was strict regarding when my sister or I could wear our new clothes, those few precious garments were to be saved for special occasions, like the first-day-back-to-school or Easter Sunday. To this day I am unable to break the habit, saving new clothes sometimes for years before allowing myself the luxury of wearing them. This trait, I have come to understand, is not only rooted in the poverty of those early years, but in the uncertainty about life, having spent their childhood trying to survive.

In 1944 my grandfather decided to sell our house and invited us to move to a much better house, in a much better neighborhood in the East Bronx where he and my grandmother were already living. The new house was brick, one of many that lined each side of our new street, Ellis Avenue. We lived at number 1954, my grandparents on the first floor; my parents, Rose, and I lived upstairs. We had heat and hot water and a real refrigerator. Life was civilized and orderly and safe.

What did my immigrant family think about when they got into warm beds at night, tucked safely under their *vermags*, their homemade quilts of lamb's wool sewn exactly as they were in the "old country"? What did they do with their memories? How did they hold back from yelling out to their new neighbors, "Do you know what horrors I've been through? Do you know what horrors I've seen?"

My father and his brother, Abraham, owned a paint and hardware store named Arox, not too far from where we now lived. In the 1960s, if you dropped by the paint store you might have been invited to the back room for a cup of instant coffee and a discussion about whatever book he was reading or about an article in *The New York Times* that day. Despite the fact that he had little formal education, he was an avid reader and loved to talk about history and philosophy.

I remember long before Vietnam was recognized as a real war, when events there were reported on the back pages of the Times, he was already worried about Vietnamese villagers being uprooted and forcibly deported to other regions of their country, and about the young Americans, called "advisors," who were sent there.

"This is what the Turks did to the Armenians, this is what happened in my village. The Western powers turned their backs on us, they knew what was going on and did nothing. Now the same thing is happening to these poor people," I remember my father saying. He pleaded with anyone willing to listen, and sometimes those who did not care to, that they pay attention to what was going on in Vietnam, warning that America would pay dearly for supporting such folly. To him the news reports were ominous and frightening and aroused great concern in those early years, long before the anti-war movement surfaced.

I never knew why my father became a Christian in his later years, or why he was an atheist in his youth for that matter. Maybe it was because of the awful things he saw happening to his people and the things that happened in his village that convinced him that there is no God. He believed that religion and nationalism were the two most dangerous forces in the world, and that these forces led to greater loss of human life and suffering than anything else. It was hard to argue otherwise.

My father's generosity of spirit must have come from his early experiences in his village. A few years before his death he wrote in his memoirs:

"There was no poverty whatsoever in our village. It was primitive, but there was no poverty. Those who did not have it, and by that I mean food and the other necessities of life, received it from those who had it.

Giving was voluntary because it was considered a moral obligation. If a family did not have a father and had a child or children to support, the family was well provided for. When the wheat was harvested, they received a portion of the wheat. When syrups were made or honey collected from the hives, they got a portion of whatever was collected. As a result, there was no poverty. There were beggars who went around the village begging for food, but they were not our villagers because we took care of our own. We gave food to the beggars just as we gave food to our own villagers who were in need."

My father and mother worked hard to support us. In addition to running the paint store during the day with Abraham, my father contracted to paint restaurants in downtown New York at night. He was gone when my sister and I got up on school days, and often came home after we had gone to bed. My mother did intricate bead-work on consignment until my sister and I were both in school, after which she went to work for Macy's Department Store in the Bronx. With the additional money these jobs brought my parents paid for extras like the gigantic set of the Encyclopedia Britannia that sat in a prominent place in the center of our apartment, a used Steinway upright piano that cost $150, and piano lessons for my sister and me at $5 per week.

The best gift my father ever received was his High School Equivalency Diploma, which arrived on his 60th birthday. He proudly told everyone how, when he entered the room where the exam was to be given, the other people taking the test thought he was the official administering it. What a thrill for him! What could be more satisfying than to have been mistaken for a teacher? "There is nothing in this world that you cannot do if you want to. Everything is possible," he regularly preached. Without doubt his words echoed in my ears as I tackled organic chemistry and filled out medical school applications when I was 35 years old.

My father had a dignified but warm appearance. Except for being taller than most, he looked typically Armenian: smooth olive complexion, dark hair, a big nose and big dark brown eyes. Once when I was living in Greenwich Village, I took my parents to a nightclub on Eighth Avenue that featured belly dancing, which is not a part of the Armenian tradition. My father was a little embarrassed and shy about being in a place like that, especially with me, his youngest daughter. He seemed so uncomfortable after the dancer began her rhythmic undulations that I began to wonder whether I had made a terrible mistake. My father could not quite bring himself to look at the dancer's half clad body, and the sexuality of the dance itself, in his mind, was inappropriate in a public place. I became even more tense when the dancer started to move through the audience, stopping at each table in turn, twirling her veil around one or the other of the men admiring her performance. When she came to my father she stood perfectly still in front of him, put her hands on her hips, looked straight into his eyes and said something in Turkish, the language he had learned to speak as a child in his village of Sheikh Hadji.

My heart nearly stopped; what had she said to him? She hesitated a moment. A smile passed across his face and then she resumed her dance and moved on to the next table. A moment had passed between them, a moment in which he did not seem to be with us, as his eyes met hers, and they shared something, this belly dancer and my father. She had touched him somewhere deep inside of him quite unexpectedly. After the music stopped he told us this story:

"It was after my mother was forced to leave Sheikh Hadji and we had taken refuge in Mezre, a larger town a few hours away. We were living with my uncle in the German orphanage there. I was about 8 years old. The only way we had of making money was for Araxie and me to peddle little cakes that our mother baked. We didn't have a license and this was forbidden. One day I got caught and what seemed to me the biggest Turkish policeman in Mezre grabbed me by the throat and started yelling at me. Then he looked into my eyes and said, 'What beautiful black eyes you have. Get out of here and don't let me catch you again!' I had forgotten about this until this very moment. The dancer used exactly the same Turkish words. God help me."

Under his thick dark brows, his beautiful black eyes glazed over as he went back in time to Mezreh and his other life in the heart of ancient Armenia, his home. He must have thought of the other stories too, the ones that he had told me as a child, the ones I had heard all my life.

I was about seven years old when my father began to tell me stories about his childhood. I listened mesmerized, wanting to hear more and more, yet wishing I had not heard any of it. Night after night he would tell me the awful tales: how, while the family watched, his beautiful cousin took poison rather than submit to the local Turkish ruler; how his beloved village became a death trap for the Armenian men; how the deportation of the men first, then the women and children started and what he, as a little boy saw along the way; how my grandmother bore up under the burden of getting her three children to safety; how he saw the feet first and then looked up to see the bodies of men he knew hanging in the village square; how they had escaped traveling at night through the mountains, never knowing what fate awaited them. I asked him to repeat the stories over and over again, even though night after night I cried myself to sleep. Sometimes he and my mother would come to me and comfort me. Mother would say to him, "Stop telling her these stories. She is too young, look at what is happening to her." But the stories had to be told. My father told me too about the Turks who risked their lives to save them; there would have been many more he believed, had the penalties for hiding or assisting an Armenian not been so harsh.

My grandmother Rosa also told us her stories of how she and my mother escaped from Turkey. She, like many survivors it was recently pointed out to me, told the same stories over and over again, making us impatient with her, unable to understand her need to do so. Some people in our family never talked about their experiences until life was almost over for them. Abraham, my uncle and Elizabeth, my father's mother, were among them. Maybe I would have known my grandmother better if I could have understood her prayers. When I would come home from school I could hear my grandmother's voice through the glass door that led to her apartment, crying out to her God. She prayed this way for hours at a time, in the afternoons, there on Ellis Avenue, in the Bronx. It must have been to God only that she poured out her heart and sought comfort and protection for her family, even then, when they were safe from the Turks. Sometimes, she would interrupt her prayers when she heard me and would open her door. "Hi Ma," I would say. She would always smile, her dress immaculate and neat, her white hair tinted with blue and would ask, "*Inch bes es?*" (How are you?) and then she would invite me in to share a grapefruit! We would talk about the neighbors and their kids.

The Armenian families from the interior of Turkey were dominated by women, remnants of the ancient Armenian family as they fled eastern Turkey in 1915. I learned that many of the women in my family had been educated at Euphrates College in Kharpert. Some of them had been taken into Turkish harems and later escaped. I found it unimaginable that these meek-seeming women in their dark-colored dresses, their hair pulled back and rolled into buns like my grandmother's, could have survived such dramatic events. How daring and clever they must have been to have escaped. These were the women I knew growing up. They had earned the loyalty, love, and respect given to them.

My mother was too young to remember her journey to America. But, somewhere in her subconscious those experiences lay waiting to surface and haunt her. One morning, years later, when she lived in a residence for the elderly in New York, my mother appeared at the front desk crying and screaming, "The Turks have set my house on fire. Help me! Help me! Get everyone out." She was more than eighty years old.

While instilling in us a deep sense of gratitude and allegiance to the country that provided them protection and the opportunity for a new life, my family also passed on a pride in being Armenian, and a sense of responsibility that came with that. To dishonor oneself in any way was to dishonor our ethnic heritage; the converse was equally true.

The family remained tightly knit. Our traditions were perpetuated. And our families took part in the establishment of new Armenian community life in America. My sister and I traveled one hour each way by subway, every Sunday, to the only Armenian Protestant church in New York City. (The vast majority of Armenians belong to the Armenian Apostolic Church; only a small percentage are Protestant or Roman Catholic.) The church was, and still is, on 34th Street. When I was a junior in high school, in a desperate attempt to become more American, I declared my intention to join a local church some of my friends attended. It caused a family crisis. When my mother and father were unable to dissuade me, they called my grandmother Rosa. She got right on the trolley for the one hour trip from Washington Heights to our home in the East Bronx. She was standing in the kitchen when I got home from school to personally inform me that nothing of the kind would be tolerated. "You are Armenian and to our Armenian church you will go." I had never seen my grandmother quite as angry as she was that day. Her hands shook as she pointed her finger at me. It was as if I was deserting the Armenian nation. She exacted the promise that I never would.

*One of the few churches that remain of the ancient Armenian capital
of Ani, the city of 1001 churches. This territory was given to Turkey
by the Treaty of Moscow, 1921. Photo taken from the Armenian
side of the border using a telephoto lens, 1992.*

CHAPTER 2

Soviet Armenia

T here was another part of Armenia's ancient land, not much bigger than the State of Maryland, that Turkey did not control. It lay to the east of where my parents were born, along Russia's southwest border. This Armenian territory, part of the region called Transcaucasia, came under the control of the Russian Czars during the early 19th century. Then, after the Russian revolution of 1917, Armenians saw the opportunity to form an independent state and declared the first Republic of Armenia in 1918. Its existence was immediately threatened. As part of its World War I offensives, Turkey advanced its army against Armenia, reaching Alexandropol (later known as Leninakan, and then Gyumri). But fortunately, the war ended and Turkey withdrew. The threat to the new republic was averted.

Despite the fact that Turkey was defeated by the Allies, it received favorable treatment in the treaties made with the West and with Russia, both for economic and strategic reasons. Armenia did not fare as well. President Woodrow Wilson, sympathetic to the Armenian cause, was unable to obtain support for his proposal to redraw Armenia's boundaries, including portions of its historic lands and access to the Black Sea. The United States mandate he had promised Armenia failed too. Congress was understandably reluctant to take responsibility for a small country without strategic importance and fraught with problems.

Turkish armies marched against Armenia a second time. Armenia, left with no other option, turned to Russia's new Communist rulers for protection. In 1921, Armenia relinquished its independence and became one of the new Soviet Socialist Republics (SSR) of the Soviet Union. Armenian SSR was even smaller than the independent Armenia of 1918–1921. The Treaty of Moscow signed on March 16, 1921, gave Turkey the fertile plains around Mt. Ararat, including the great mountain itself, the ruins of the ancient Armenian capital Ani (called the city of 1001 churches), and the region of Kars. In return, Armenia was assured that its southern half, Zangezour, would remain Armenian.

For the next seventy years, until independence was declared for a second time, Armenia remained closed to the West and to the three million Armenians of the diaspora who were scattered all over the world.

This Armenia held little interest for me. My heritage, the land I thought of as "Armenia," was the region that today is part of the modern Turkish state. Armenians who had come out of Turkey, like my parents, were cut off from the new Armenian SSR, isolated behind the Iron Curtain. My interest in Soviet Armenia surfaced a little when Anastas Mikoyan, the Armenian member of the politburo who had managed to survive the reigns of Stalin, Khruschev, and Brezhnev was in the news, or when the chess champion, Gary Kasparov, also a Soviet Armenian, won another world tournament.

With the rise of Gorbachev and the beginning of *glasnost* ("openness," implied to the West), however, the republics of the Soviet Union started to attract the attention of Americans. In the mid 1980s a group of citizens from Cambridge, Massachusetts, applied to the Sister City International Association for one of the first affiliations with a soviet city. Yerevan, the capital of Armenia, was chosen. The group went to work immediately, putting together contacts and developing a relationship with Yerevan, and officials on both sides made exchange trips within the first year.

Armenia began to be in vogue and traveling there was no longer an extraordinary thing to do. My husband, George, made his first visit with a group of Armenian-Americans from Worcester, Massachusetts, in 1987. He saw it as a pilgrimage not only for himself, but for his father, Neshan. In 1916 Neshan was living in Boston, safe from the threat of genocide, when he responded to the call to arms made by the French Foreign Legion: to fight during WWI against the Turks. Neshan, 19 years old, enlisted along with 4000 other Armenian men from all over the world and was inducted into the French army. They trained in Cyprus and at Port Said, Egypt, and went forward, hoping to stop the ongoing slaughter of the Armenians in that region. They had been promised a free Armenia by the English and the French at the end of the war.

The politics of the times was extremely complicated and, unfortunately, none of their aspirations was realized. Those who survived were bitter at what they saw as a betrayal by the Allies, who left them without food, arms, and other support. Neshan returned home and was never quite able to recover from the disappointment of that experience. On his deathbed nearly 70 years after these events, the only visitors he seemed to see were in visions: the people he had encountered during those years, especially the young women he saved, including a young girl who would later become his wife.

George understandably had a great desire to see Armenia, his mind filled with the imagery his father had described of the territory he had fought in, not far from present day Armenia. His first trip did not disappoint him. When he returned, he was full of enthusiasm for the place he now called his ancestral homeland. He had seen mountains and villages, just as Neshan had described. He had even seen caves dug into the sides of the mountains where Armenians hid during times of war and massacre. For George there was no longer any difference between the two parts of Armenia; they had merged in his thinking. He tried hard to convince me to go see for myself, but I remained unconvinced. My medical practice kept me busy, and I had no time to make the arduous trip for what I viewed as nostalgia for an imagined homeland.

However, early in 1988, a dramatic change took place in my feelings. This was when I first learned about an enclave of Armenians within Azerbaijan who lived in a place called Nagorno-Karabagh, translated "mountainous black garden"; they were being threatened with ethnic-cleansing by their overlords, the Azeris, close kin to the Turks. Fear was aroused in all of us who heard their story.

Karabagh, a territory of less than 2000 square miles and less than an hour from Armenia by helicopter, has been identified by historians as "Armenian" since the time of Christ. The enclave, perhaps because of its mountainous terrain or the strong will of its people, had always been granted a measure of self-rule by those who conquered it. At the end of World War I, when the Allies were settling regional issues in the Caucasus, the British, who were in Baku and eyeing the oil fields there, handed Karabagh to Azerbaijan, despite promises to the Armenians that this would not be done. When the Communists came to power, and Azerbaijan and Armenia became Soviet republics, the issue of Karabagh was again addressed; Stalin's advisors recommended that Karabagh be returned to Armenia, but Stalin reaffirmed the status quo, leaving Karabagh under Azeri domination.

During the ensuing seventy years, the people of Karabagh suffered despite proclamations that they were to retain their "autonomous" character. Official use of the Armenian language was forbidden, ties to Armenia were severed, roads were left in disrepair, hospitals allowed to crumble, schools were neglected. The policy, it was hoped, would drive the Armenians out of Karabagh, just as it had in another territory on Armenia's southwestern border, Nakhichevan, that was also under Azeri rule.

Time and time again, the Karabagh Armenians petitioned the Soviet central government for reversal of Stalin's decision. In 1987, with Gorbachev in power promising *glasnost* and *perestroika* (reconstruction), the people of Karabagh began the petition process once again. Gorbachev made promises to them, sharply raising expectations in Armenia and Mountainous Karabagh; but he never fulfilled these promises.

In February 1988 the parliament of Mountainous Karabagh voted for separation from Azerbaijan SSR and for official merger with Armenian SSR, a move that was made out of desperation and frustration. No one thought that this move would put Armenians living within Azerbaijan SSR in danger. However, in response, angry mobs in the port city of Sumgait, deep within Azerbaijan, countered with a terror and violence against the Armenians living in that city reminiscent of the Turkish atrocities of 1915. Hundreds of Armenians were rousted out of their homes and savagely beaten; and at least thirty-five were murdered, many slashed with knives, tortured, and then burned alive; women, naked, were dragged through the streets, and raped. While some Azeris helped hide and save their neighbors, many looked the other way or even helped the mobs. For three days the nightmare continued unchecked.

Armenians around the world were stunned by these events, but none more than the Armenians living within the Soviet Union. How could this unbridled savagery take place, they demanded to know, within their own country, where theoretically they had the protection of the Soviet government?

There was strong evidence that this was not a random act of violence, but a carefully planned, centrally sanctioned attack. The mobs' leaders had official residential lists of Armenians, identifying even those whose names had been changed. Soviet soldiers had mysteriously disappeared from Sumgait, returning only after the brutality was in its third day. Even the city's location, in a remote area of Azerbaijan on the Caspian Sea, was suspiciously favorable for "uncontrollable" riots.

The sentiment began to develop among some Soviet Armenians that Gorbachev was in fact fueling the situation, using Karabagh as a way to pit one faction of the Moscow leadership against the other in order to maintain his own power. Gorbachev, they felt, could have brought the issue to an equitable resolution long before the sides hardened against each other, before thousands gave their lives, thousands more were injured, and yet more thousands became refugees, fleeing the vast lands laid waste by war on both sides of the issue.

In Armenian SSR, to show solidarity with the Armenians of Karabagh, a group of important intellectuals, writers, and scientists formed the Karabagh Committee. They became the spokespeople for Karabagh with the Soviets and with the West.

The Communists' hold over the minds of the Armenian people began to weaken. Privately at first, and then more openly among friends, and finally at mass rallies in the streets, the party minions started to question the system. In Armenia, people like Andrei Sakharov, who challenged the system, became openly proclaimed heroes of the day, replacing Lenin and Marx.

And so, early in 1988, not long after the Sumgait massacres, when the Cambridge-Yerevan Sister City Association announced a trip to Armenia, I was finally interested in going. My feelings about Armenia had a new perspective. It was no longer an issue of whether this was the same land from which my ancestors had been purged. It was about the line of Haik, from whom all Armenians were descended, who were now suffering what my father and mother had suffered. The plight of the people of Nagorno-Karabagh had changed my feelings about Armenia, and I knew that it was time to see it and experience it for myself.

It was May of 1988.

Armenia was a hotbed of unrest due to events in Karabagh and the recent pogroms in Sumgait. Yerevan was simmering with agitation, but as official guests of the city our days were filled with official visits to schools and hospitals, meeting with our professional counterparts, special luncheons, and very long speeches. Everything was new for us. We were aware that we were being watched, but we did not know who the KGB agent was or whether our rooms were bugged. We were careful not to step out of line: we wanted to make certain that if we applied for visas again, Moscow would consider us welcome, and even more important, we did not want to get any of our new Armenian friends into trouble, like Gulnara Shahinian who worked in the Foreign Relations Office of the City Council of Yerevan, and was the liaison for the project between Cambridge and Yerevan. We were careful not to be too friendly, not to ask too many questions, to listen politely, and to remember that there were ears everywhere. We were tolerated, if not completely welcome, guests.

None of these considerations, however, prevented us from sneaking off to Opera Square, where the rallies of the Karabagh Committee were taking place. The square was surrounded by Soviet troops, but no one seemed to care. Speaker after speaker stood on the Opera House steps and addressed the crowd, using a microphone that enabled their amplified voice to boom across the large imposing square. Some speakers would get everyone's full attention, signifying to us that they were people of importance. But when others spoke, the crowd would break up into smaller, less attentive groups, humming with conversation. We would move among them, sometimes talking with individuals, sometimes drawn to the edge of a small knot in hot debate. At times there were wave-like movements as people joined hands and chanted, "*Karabagh-a-mern-e*" (Karabagh is ours), over and over again.

Night after night, thousands of people filled the square. They brought their children, some even pushed baby carriages. They were ordinary middle class people, and we marveled that so many of them dared to come out to protest the Soviet policy toward Karabagh despite the presence of tanks and soldiers.

Our efforts not to attract attention were futile. The minute we approached the square, people would turn to look at us. At first, they addressed us in Russian, the language they would normally use with a stranger. When we responded in Armenian a group would gather around us. "What are people thinking in America?" "What are non-Armenians thinking?" We tried to explain that most people in America knew very little about Karabagh. This was incomprehensible to them. How could it be that the issue dominating their lives so totally was barely known in the outside world? As we talked we constantly looked about to see if we were being watched. It was a very uneasy feeling.

The troops surrounding the square stood with their backs turned to the crowds. They tried to look stern, but most of them were just young boys, probably homesick and bored. The yellow color of their skin and the almond shape of their eyes told us that most of them were from far away republics, like Mongolia. Since many of the speeches were in Armenian, they understood little of what was being said.

Over the course of the next several months, an interesting phenomenon took place. The people befriended the soldiers, bringing them yogurt and bread and other food from their homes when they came to the square at night. Thus, the regiments had to be changed every few months; the commanders feared that the troops would not be capable of carrying out harsh orders against these friendly people. Fortunately, no such orders ever were forthcoming. Given the charged atmosphere in the Opera Square, it was quite remarkable that there never was any violence or confrontation between the soldiers and the crowd.

Since Yerevan was under curfew, we made sure we were back at the hotel early. We would gather in one of our rooms to talk about what we had seen during the day. Fearful of "bugs," we played a radio loudly and talked softly, hoping our conversation would be unintelligible to anyone who might be listening. One of the members of the group had special contacts with the Karabagh Committee and was privy to their secret meeting. Each night he would give us the latest information on what was transpiring within the inner circles of the movement. We tried to figure out what it all meant and what Moscow would do. Would violence erupt? The troops we saw in the streets were not armed, but we had heard that others kept out-of-sight were armed. We knew we were witnesses to something really big, though we did not realize this was the beginning of the disintegration of the Soviet Union.

After returning from Armenia, George and I became involved with the Zoryan Institute in Cambridge, Massachusetts. Its purpose was to chronicle contemporary Armenian history and was a natural gathering place for many of us who had never been involved in any Armenian organizations. In 1988, Armenians were once more being slaughtered and persecuted. But unlike 1915 when Near East Relief acted virtually alone, there was now a large diaspora that could help the Armenians living in Karabagh. The genocide of 1915 had created us; it was imperative that we prevent it happening again.

Initially our activities centered around the media and Congress. We wrote letters to our congressman and to the President. We called newspaper editors when we saw unfavorable or, even worse, uninformed press. What I had told the people in the Opera Square was true: few people in the outside world knew anything about Armenia or Nagorno-Karabagh. We tried to educate reporters and politicians on the issues as we saw them and to provide them with verifiable historical facts.

Early in the Fall of 1988, Andrei Sakharov came to Boston for medical treatment. George's brother, Michael, made contact with Sakharov's family, and despite his ill health, Sakharov agreed to meet with a group of us. Six of us, including the director of the Zoryan Institute, Jirair Libaridian, attended a meeting that went on for several hours. Sakharov was clearly very concerned about evolving events regarding Karabagh. He was in telephone contact with his wife, Elena Bonner, in Moscow; she reported events taking place in Kirovabad, Azerbaijan, where Armenians were being forced from their homes and were again being subjected to unthinkable atrocities. He encouraged us to be active and to persist in educating the media and the general public on the issues regarding the Armenians and Karabagh. After he returned to Russia, Sakharov would travel to the Caucasus to show his concern and solidarity with the people of Karabagh in an attempt to draw world attention to the situation.

In October 1988, thousands of diasporan Armenians marched up New York City's Third Avenue to the Soviet Embassy, hoping to influence Moscow's Karabagh policy. Nothing changed. When we learned that Gorbachev was going to make his first visit to the United States in December, the Armenian community moved into high gear with plans for more rallies and newspaper ads on behalf of Karabagh. This burning issue of survival for us was still seen as an insignificant internal struggle by most politicians and media people. We hoped to change that.

Then on December 7, 1988, the unthinkable happened.

A church destroyed by the earthquake. Gyumri, 1989.

CHAPTER 3

The Earthquake

Early that morning we learned that a great earthquake had shaken northern Armenia. As the day unfolded, we were paralyzed by the awfulness of the reports we were receiving over the networks and by telephone from friends in Armenia. The irony was hideous: in the midst of the political turmoil to free the people of Karabagh and prevent another genocide, tens of thousands of Armenians die in a natural catastrophe.

To this day, most people in Armenia believe the earthquake was not a coincidence. They assert that the Soviets fired missiles known to be stored in silos under the Armenian city of Spitak, causing instability of the faults and resulting in the earthquake. Nothing any scientist says can remove this conviction from their minds and souls.

On December 8 Gorbachev hastily returned to Moscow and traveled from there directly to Armenia. In the mangled ruins of Leninakan he stood among the survivors of the quake. Gorbachev had barely begun to talk with the people surrounding him when someone asked him a question not about the earthquake or about Leninakan, but about Karabagh. The man wanted to know when Gorbachev was planning to grant the people of Karabagh the right of self-determination. Gorbachev went into a rage, shaking his finger at the crowd. He could not believe the question nor would he ever understand it. Despite the enormous catastrophe that had just befallen them, for the people of Leninakan, Karabagh was a more pressing issue. The threat of another genocide was more terrifying to Armenians than the horror of the earthquake.

For the first time in 70 years the Soviets immediately asked the West for emergency assistance after acknowledging that a disaster had occurred within their borders. To Gorbachev's credit, the doors to Armenia were opened wide: visas for relief workers were waived; air corridors were cleared for the cargo planes carrying humanitarian aid; landing rights were granted instantly; and customs regulations were ignored. Travel restrictions requiring special papers to move from city to city within Armenia, in effect up until that time, were terminated and never reinstituted. Perceived by the non-Communist world as a unique opportunity to gain access to one of the Soviet republics, the 1988 earthquake in Armenia gave rise to a relief effort so massive that it, in itself, became a breaking news story.

Within 48 hours of the disaster newspaper and television corps from America and Europe were in Armenia. In the earthquake zone the major networks set up satellites with the ability to send on-the-spot reports of the relief effort. Vivid and heart-wrenching photos from Armenia covered the front pages of America's newspapers. On the nightly news, we saw teams of dogs sniffing for survivors, surgeons setting up field hospitals, Soviet soldiers digging through the rubble, and dazed survivors roaming aimlessly, holding onto a child or huddled around an outdoor fire.

Governments around the world, including the United States, France, Germany, China, Japan, and Israel, announced they would be sending aid to Armenia. Internationally known humanitarian organizations, such as the Red Cross and Ameri-Cares, called for donations. Long lists of addresses to which donors could send contributions appeared in newspapers and were scrolled across our television screens after the evening news. People responded overwhelmingly, and money started to pour in. Some organizations collected close to 100 million dollars for Armenia.

For the Armenian diaspora, the call for help was the most compelling we had ever heard. Within a few hours of first hearing the news of the earthquake, a small group gathered in our home to make preliminary plans for obtaining donations of clothing and medicine to take to Armenia as fast as we could get there. By the ninth of December our telephone had already begun to ring with calls from people who wanted to help. It was clear that the relief effort was going to turn into something very big and that we would have to be better organized than our little group had naively intended. In an effort to coordinate activities in the Boston area, a meeting was held, inviting all Armenian organizations, including the church leaders, to discuss how this should be done. It was agreed that a coordinated effort for the collection of relief donations would be best, and the offices of a prominent local Armenian businessman became its headquarters. An account was opened at the Bank of Boston and a post office box was obtained, to which the general public could send their donations.

We did not have time to think about what to do or how to do it. We were hit by a tidal wave of relief in the form of money and in-kind donations. Some volunteers handled the bank deposits and formal acknowledgments to donors. Others manned the telephones, which never stopped ringing. Still others worked on obtaining donations of food, clothing, and medical supplies, and networking with other groups around the country. The community also had to learn how to work with those who held political office, because we relied heavily on them for support: Boston's Mayor Ray Flynn, Massachusetts Governor Michael Dukakis, Speaker of the Massachusetts House George Keverian, Senator Edward Kennedy and later Congressman Joseph Kennedy. Without their ongoing cooperation and the assistance of their staffs, none of what we accomplished could have been possible.

Everyone involved in the effort put their life on hold. There were no parties, no vacations, no movies, no dinners out, no friends over for an evening of idle chit-chat. We did not have time to clean or cook, sometimes not even to eat. We scanned newspapers and magazines for articles on Armenia; there was no time for whatever else was going on in the world. Some of the organizers of the relief effort worked as many as fifteen hours a day under extreme pressure. At times individuals clashed and tempers flared as each of us had our own way of doing things and ideas about how the campaign should be carried out or how we should interact with the public. But we all knew that we shared the same objective, that of helping victims of the earthquake, and so we managed to overcome these difficulties.

On leave from my practice at the time, and having been to Armenia once, it was natural that I take responsibility for the medical aspect of the relief effort in our area. By the end of the second day at the headquarters I realized that I would do my job better from home. George arranged for additional telephone lines to be installed and rented fax and copy machines, turning our once-quiet house into a small relief center itself. Volunteers, too numerous to name, came daily to help with the work of answering the telephones and following up on leads for donations.

The world of medical relief was more complicated than I could have imagined.

I was anxious to go to Armenia, and along with hundreds of American doctors and nurses I registered with the Federal Emergency Management Agency (FEMA). This US government agency for coordinating disaster response, announced the formation of medical teams that would go to Armenia, similar to the ones that had helped after Mexico's earthquake. I hoped to be included in one of the teams. Dr. Richard Aghababian, Chief of Emergency Medical Services at the University of Massachusetts in Worcester, formed his own team, including non-Armenian physicians and nurses as well. We all obtained the necessary vaccinations and were on standby, with our bags packed, ready to leave at a moment's notice. We waited for FEMA to call, but none of us was included. It became clear that Armenian physicians were deliberately being excluded. FEMA officials informed us that we would be too emotional to work effectively once in

Armenia and would not be sent. Neither was Dr. Aghababian's team sent, despite being fully equipped through donations and monies raised in the Worcester area. (Eventually, two Armenian surgeons were included by FEMA to complete other teams going to Armenia.)

Disappointed and angry, confused and feeling wrongfully left out, we wondered whether there was an underlying political issue here. Had the Soviet Embassy asked FEMA not to include Armenians on the relief teams? Would there be too much contact with ordinary citizens whose language we spoke? We never found out.

Despite our disappointment at not being called, we were in touch with FEMA at least once a day to see how we could be most helpful and to keep up with events as they evolved. The officials there discovered that the Armenian diaspora could be useful in filling special needs and solving problems for them because we were willing to work night and day. They asked us to find a surgeon for one of the teams going from Oregon: the surgeon could be Armenian. Working with Medical Outreach For Armenians founded by Dr. Vartkes and Mary Najarian (no relation) on the West Coast, we found the kind of surgeon they wanted in less than 24 hours. Next they requested five pharmacists who spoke either Armenian or Russian to help sort through and organize the drugs to be sent to Armenia. We had only 48 hours to find them and we did.

In the meantime there was plenty of work to do at home. Calls were coming in from all over: manufacturers of drugs and medical equipment, humanitarian organizations, religious groups, political people, doctors and nurses and hospital administrators, and individuals who had things in their homes that they wanted to donate. Each call required time to find out what exactly the caller was offering or what information they were seeking.

If the caller had a non-monetary donation we were going to accept, the real work started for coordinating the delivery of the shipment. One of the women in our group volunteered to be a dispatcher of sorts, working with the truckers delivering donations to a vacant TWA hanger at Logan International Airport, on loan to us for use as a warehouse. Consistency and continuity were critical, so that we would not inadvertently cause problems at the gates to the airport's cargo area, where entry is restricted. All we had to do was to tell Nancy, our "dispatcher," when a donation was expected and to notify the cargo area at the airport. Sometimes one of the volunteers from the main headquarters or from the group working at our house would forget and a trucker would appear at Logan unexpectedly. All hell would break loose!

The work of explaining the needs, reviewing our procedures, networking with other organizations, checking and rechecking on information and donations that were promised, and coordinating with other volunteers at other locations around the country went on and on. We were exhausted, but happy to carry on and thankful that offers of help and donations were still being made.

Millions of dollars worth of antibiotics, intravenous fluids, bandages, antiseptic solutions, needles and syringes, crutches, blankets, and even Belmont Springs Water were among the tons of needed relief supplies donated by major corporations and individuals. Doctors sent us EKG machines and blood pressure cuffs; hospitals offered used dialysis equipment and supplies; major pharmaceutical companies gave generously. Non-Armenian humanitarian organizations and religious groups made donations; many offered to help with warehousing the relief donations and even offered to go to Armenia. School children collected food, wrote letters, and sewed quilts for the orphaned children. Others spent weeks creating origami birds, the birds of peace and friendship, to send to school children who had survived. Help was coming from every sector of American life, and the Armenian community came together, working night and day, sorting and labeling supplies, clothing, medicines, soap and food, preparing them for shipment.

At first we accepted all donations offered to us. However, we soon learned that some donations were given solely for tax write-offs; they included useless items such as medicines that had long since expired and equipment that was damaged or had missing parts. We began to question donors more carefully, while trying not to appear ungrateful.

Newspaper and television reporters with their photographers and camera crews came to our home frequently for updates on this news story. Radio stations called for live interviews. Giving interviews became a normal part of our day's work and we quickly learned that the media is not always friendly. Reporters often tried to get us to say things against the Soviets. They would start with a question like "Are you satisfied with the rate of progress of the relief effort?" and then begin to press us for a negative statement. We were very careful not to say anything to antagonize the Soviet government. Armenia, the relief effort, and Karabagh were all in jeopardy. The doors of Armenia were open, but would they remain open? Would we be barred from returning at some point? On December 10, two days after the earthquake, orders were given to begin arresting the Karabagh Committee members, and by early January eleven had been moved to Moscow and jailed; we were put on alert that extreme caution was wise.

While all of this was taking place, we began to face the logistics of getting the donations we had received to Armenia, nearly 8000 miles away. At first we had assumed that our donations would be shipped on the large cargo flights being sent by the United States government in cooperation with the Soviet Embassy in Washington. However, when the list of acceptable items was circulated, medicine and medical supplies, like the ones we had at the TWA hanger, were not on the list. These flights were only for food and items such as clothing, thermal garments, gloves, shovels, flashlights, and tents.

Large established humanitarian organizations were willing to arrange shipment of our donations, but they acknowledged that once the shipment arrived in Armenia, they lost control over it. In addition, the Soviet authorities were forcing many relief planes headed for Armenia to stop in Moscow first, unloading thousands of pounds of relief supplies before the plane was allowed to continue on to Yerevan. In one such incident dialysis equipment needed to treat crush injury patients was removed from the aircraft. The Soviets argued that Russians were taking care of many victims of the earthquake and that they too needed these supplies. They had a point. After that, one entire shipment sent by a group of Armenian organizations went directly to Moscow in an effort to foster good relations. The Soviet Embassy in Washington expressed its gratitude.

There were also problems on the ground in Armenia, where officials not only had to deal with the disaster, but with the aid that was now pouring in. Stories filtered back to the United States about supplies left on the tarmac at Yerevan airport where they were pilfered or ruined by the snow. Others reported that drugs and medical supplies were piled into hospital warehouses and left never used. Nowhere in the world had so much relief aid arrived in so little time after a disaster.

Although we were anxious for our relief supplies to get to Armenia, we also wanted to be sure that they were put to good use. We decided not to send anything until we could be certain that it would reach the earthquake region. Finding a way to get them there became George's job. He contacted various carriers but was quoted prices from $90,000 to $120,000. Finally, the West Coast Najarians contacted the Armenian owner of a Florida-based aviation company who agreed to donate a plane for the flight. However, we would have to cover the cost of the fuel: $25,000. The Armenian Missionary Association of America, based in New Jersey, agreed to cover this cost. It looked like we would soon be on our way!

A few days before the flight, the aviation company notified us that two passengers could accompany the flight. This was an unexpected bonanza. It was agreed that I should go, along with another doctor. On December 30, 1988, I called Dr. Richard Aghababian, the doctor who had organized an emergency medical team that never got sent by FEMA to Armenia. He agreed to join me.

Two days before our scheduled departure, I went to a sporting goods store to purchase a coat for the trip. Quite unexpectedly, I started to sob when the sales girl asked me something about what the coat was for and where I was going. Only then did I realize how filled I was with emotion, anticipation, anxiety, and even fear over the commitment I had made. It seemed that my whole life was in preparation for this moment, and yet now that it was here, the truth was, I was terrified!

The empty cargo plane arrived from Florida on January 2, 1989, at about 11 a.m. The 80,000 pounds of cargo had been neatly stacked on huge pallets borrowed from the airport with the promise that they would be returned. The contents of each pallet had been wrapped round and round with large sheets of plastic. The young volunteers, who had been working night and day, now carried out the actual loading of the aircraft. As they pushed each of the pallets out onto the tarmac, people from the community who had started to gather for the send-off applauded and cheered. Each pallet in turn was pushed onto the hydraulic elevator, slowly raised up, and pulled off the lift by others at the aircraft's open doors. Then, as each pallet disappeared into the belly of the plane, more cheers erupted from the crowd.

It seemed that every Armenian who lived in or around Boston was present for the send-off. After all, this was what they had worked so hard for from the day we received the call for help, and now it was finally happening. In the hour before flight time, a press conference was held with Governor and Mrs. Michael Dukakis, Senator Edward Kennedy, Speaker George Keverian, and Mayor Ray Flynn, all of whom had been extremely helpful and worked hard behind the scenes to help solve problems. The clergy from the Armenian churches were present as well as representatives from various Armenian political parties.

The speeches were short, but to my ears, eloquent: praise for all the volunteers, commitments for future assistance and cooperation, and of course, God's blessing for a safe trip. The Governor's wife, Kitty Dukakis, and I had a few moments together in our makeshift office after the press conference. She expressed her admiration for what the community had done for Armenia and promised to help in any way she could. Her warmth was touching. Senator Kennedy asked me to give him an eyewitness account upon my return.

The send-off was a major event. Caught up in the excitement of preparing for the trip, we did not have time to give much thought to what lay ahead.

Our pressing need to get to Armenia with the cargo did not allow us to consider the possibility that we were putting ourselves in a dangerous situation. Two cargo planes had already crashed in the mountains outside of Leninakan. One from Yugoslavia was filled with relief workers, the other with Soviet soldiers being sent to help dig survivors out of the rubble.

We had to set our feelings aside in order to get the job done. This was the first of many cargo flights that I would make, and it was similar to the rest. The cockpit had five seats. Dick and I sat up front with the crew. Inside the cockpit, my fear of flying vanished. On takeoff, it seemed that the plane rose up right out of the water, with Boston falling off under us. Later I would learn that the ground crew, which had come to the edge of the runway to wave a final good-bye, feared for our lives; the plane lifted off with less than 25 feet of runway left. What I had seen from the cockpit as thrilling had in fact been quite dangerous. I'm glad that I didn't know then that our cargo plane did not meet FAA standards and had been allowed to fly only because of the emergency nature of the trip!

The flight went smoothly. We stopped for refueling in Shannon, Ireland. The crew had radioed ahead for steak dinners, which was a nice surprise for Dick and me; we had brought box lunches for everyone! There we waited until the tower received clearance for us to land in Armenia, a matter of weather conditions and landing rights. As soon as it came through, we were in the air again.

The landing in Yerevan held another kind of thrill. We flew over Turkey and entered Armenia's airspace. Through heavy static, the radio tower communication became clearer and clearer, giving the pilot landing coordinates.

It was dawn and Mt. Ararat loomed up in front of us, covered with snow, magnificent in the morning sun. With the landing field in sight, all we could think of was how far we had come, how long and hard we had worked to bring help to our people. We were convinced that despite the millions and millions of dollars of relief that had already come to Armenia, our contribution from Boston was needed too.

The contrast between my first visit to Armenia before the earthquake and this, my second trip, was dramatic. The first time we were "chaperoned" and taken care of. Now, Dick and I were here on our own, with no visas, no reservations, no vehicles for travel, 80 thousand pounds of cargo to distribute and no idea how we would return to Boston once we were done. At that moment, though, the only thing that seemed important was that we and the cargo had arrived in Yerevan: the next step, we hoped, would somehow take care of itself.

From the cockpit we could see many other cargo planes lined up on the tarmac. It took nearly a half hour before stairs were rolled into place and the aircraft's hydraulic door was opened. A blond-haired soldier with fair skin and a machine gun slung over his shoulder marched up the stairs, gave a slight nod of greeting, and then issued orders in Russian that clearly meant we were to remain in the aircraft. He was followed by several stern looking men, some in uniform, others in civilian clothes. After a brief discussion with the crew, they asked for and took our passports. They left the aircraft as sternly as they had boarded, assigning one of the soldiers with a machine gun to remain on board.

Dick and I were nervous. Despite the winter temperature, which had now penetrated the plane's cabin, I could feel the sweat dripping down my back. Could something go wrong at this point? Would we be denied entry for some reason? We waited.

One of the officials eventually returned. Our visas were stamped on our passports. All was well. A guard remained in the aircraft to prevent stowaways. Dick and I made our way down the stairs and touched Armenia's soil. For Dick it was the first time. For me it was as if it were my first time. Our eyes filled with tears, but there was no time to savor our emotions. The soldiers were motioning us forward; decisions regarding the cargo had to be made immediately.

Meanwhile the crew informed us that as soon as the plane was unloaded they would be taking off, anxious to head back to Europe before nightfall. The unloading of the cargo, all 80,000 pounds of it, however, had to be done manually, a slow and tedious process, because Yerevan's airport had no hydraulic fork lifts at that time. As the work progressed, the pallets slowly being lined up on the tarmac, Dick and I kept pressing for the cargo to be removed from the pallets. But soon it became clear that there was not sufficient manpower to do this as well. In the midst of all the frenzy around us, all I could think of were the last words my husband, George, whispered in my ear as we left Boston (after saying "I love you"), "Be sure the pallets return with the plane!" But nothing Dick or I could do would make that happen now and I knew that the pallets would never get back to Boston as promised.

Soviet soldiers proceeded with unloading the plane and then, after the plane left, with dismantling the pallets and loading the cargo onto waiting trucks. Our cargo, which had been so lovingly and gently prepared and packed for shipment, was now thrown every which way, one box on top of the other, medicines mixed with food, equipment mixed with clothing, and bales of blankets piled on top despite Dick's and my protests.

Our adventure had begun. I did not realize then that this would be the longest journey of my life, one that would last ten years.

· PART II ·

AFTERSHOCKS
1989–1991

Map of Armenia: the shaded area shows the earthquake region, 1988.

*Dr. Richard Aghababian and me in front of the boy's school
on the church grounds. Etchmiadzin, January 1989.*

CHAPTER 4

The First Trip
After the Earthquake

Janaury 1989
For the next two weeks Dick
and I were thrust into the
relief scene on the ground in Armenia, visiting hospitals in the
earthquake zone and in Yerevan, meeting with doctors, taking
care of patients, and distributing our supplies. We even went to
Idjevan, a region of Armenia on the border with Azerbaijan.

A man named Avedis, a laboratory technician from Michigan
who was somehow connected with the Florida air cargo company, had met us at the airport and was now making all of our
arrangements. Under his direction the cargo was taken to Etchmiadzin, the seat of the Armenian Apostolic Church, thirty minutes outside Yerevan. There, the church school for boys had been
turned into a warehouse. With classes canceled because of the
earthquake, the students were free to help with the unloading of
cargo, truck by truck, bit by bit, all through the night and into
the next morning. Dick and I spent our first night at the Hotel
Armenia, then moved to the quiet and comfort of the church's
guest house, just across the quadrangle from the boy's school.

That next morning the church grounds at Etchmiadzin were
as we would see them every day for the next two weeks, overrun
with trucks and people. An office of sorts had been set up in the
back of the school building, on the first floor. Avedis introduced

us to the man who was in charge of running the warehouse. He was not a priest, but was closely associated with the church. With these formalities over, and having obtained permission to go anywhere in the building, we started room by room to search for our cargo, which was mixed in with donations from other organizations. The rooms themselves were grand, with cream colored walls, impressive marble floors, ornate moldings along the ceilings, and velvet drapes that framed the long windows. It was hard to see how beautiful the rooms really were through the stacks and stacks of boxes haphazardly piled high everywhere.

Most of the general relief supplies were stored on the first floor; medicines were upstairs in locked rooms where classes were usually held. Crates of medicines that had been sent in bulk quantities were neatly stacked, but thousands of sample drugs, sent packaged two or three tablets to a box, were scattered around. Armenians had never seen "sample medicines" and could not understand why so much packaging was devoted to so few tablets.

At Etchmiadzin there was a microcosm of the relief effort and we saw firsthand part of what was later documented: 500 tons of drugs and consumable supplies were sent to Armenia in the weeks following the earthquake, but only 30 percent were immediately usable, and 20 percent had to be destroyed because they were outdated or did not have understandable generic names. For example, antibiotics came with 238 different names, written in 21 languages, often unknown to the health care professionals on location. Even if they recognized the drug's generic name, they did not always know how to use it. Whenever Dick and I had free time, we would go into these rooms to sort through the drugs, putting like drugs together, hoping that in this way they would eventually be used.

But first, we found our cargo: the blankets, clothing, water, and medical supplies were on the first floor; the cases of drugs, including Rocephin and Bactrim, were upstairs under lock. Everything seemed to be in order, with one exception: two of the three EKG machines that we had brought appeared to be missing. (Eventually they were found in a corner of one of the rooms, the boxes open, but the machines intact.) We spent the first day sorting through the cargo and let it be known that we planned to oversee its distribution.

On our second day we were anxious to go to the earthquake zone. We had hoped to go to Spitak first, but were advised against it; relief workers, we were told, bringing food to the city, had been attacked by mobs. We had no way of knowing whether this was true, but decided to take the advice. Instead, we went to Leninakan, Armenia's second largest city that had been especially known for its architectural beauty and its people for their sense of humor.

It was a cold wintry day. Fortunately, there had not been any heavy snowfalls and the roads were clear. On the approach into the city there were a series of railroad tracks that ran parallel to the left of the road. As we got closer, we saw that the freight trains stopped on the tracks were filled with relief supplies. Crowds of people were trying to get close to the open doors of the boxcars, pushing forward with their arms and hands stretched toward the workers standing in the boxcars, hoping to catch one of the bags being thrown down at them. What was in the bags-flour? sugar? or rice? Clutching their bags, they hurried away from the crowd to some safe place to inspect what they had caught. Some people huddled around open fires, looking over to the scene around the trains. It was very cold, and the only comment we could manage on the demeaning scene was that no one appeared to be wearing gloves. It was painful to watch these unfortunate people grappling for a handout. Painful for them too, we were sure.

Avedis drove slowly, almost reverently, as we passed these first scenes of tragedy on our way into Leninakan. The destruction began to come into full view; Dick and I fell silent. All that could be heard were our soft sobs.

Canvas tents were everywhere, dark green and khaki-colored, pitched along the road. Some of the people we saw looked as if they had something special to do, heading purposefully in this or that direction; others seemed to be just wandering around. We learned later that the main activity occupying these survivors was the search for their dead family members. We saw caskets, even very small ones, all simple and made of wood, lined up in several areas.

The streets of the city had been ripped apart by the earthquake and getting through was difficult. Most buildings lay in crumbled heaps on each side of the road and the few still standing tilted to one side or the other. Despite all that we had seen on our television news and in the newspapers, nothing could convey the awfulness of what Leninakan actually looked like, even now, three weeks later.

We found one hospital standing upright. It was called the "Railroad Hospital" because it had been intended for use by only railroad workers and their families. The hospital was technically under the jurisdiction of the Republic of Georgia because the railroad started in Georgia. Therefore, the doctors told us, they would not receive relief supplies from Armenian's Ministry of Health even though survivors of the earthquake, not just railroad workers, were being treated in the hospital.

Dick and I walked through the corridors overflowing with beds and patients. Upstairs, in an ordinary room, an operation was taking place. People were walking in and out of the operating room freely; the use of gowns and masks, scrubbing for the surgical team, and sterile techniques in general seemed to be ignored. The patient, anesthetized, could be seen through the glass doors, naked from the waist up but still with trousers and socks on, perhaps because the hospital was very cold. The patient's family was gathered around the glass door, peering in, sometimes opening the door for a better look. We did not ask what the operation was for or if it was related to an injury from the earthquake.

Later we met with some of the doctors working here as well as the Chief Doctor. They were visibly exhausted and complained about the lack of supplies, of medicine, and of help. We learned from them that the city had no water, gas, oil, or food. The hospital was cold and there was little food for the patients or the staff for that matter. We invited the chief to send a truck to Etchmiadzin on the following day; we would try to help them out. The chief insisted that we have some tea, a light brew, which she served in chipped cups. She begged our pardon.

We stayed in Leninakan for only two hours; it was all we could endure.

The farther away we got from the city, the less I was able to preserve the images of Leninakan in my mind's eye. Maybe it was just as well. How could anything so tragic be just two hours away? How could people go to work and carry on normal lives here in Yerevan and in Etchmiadzin while Leninakan lay destroyed? The contrast overwhelmed us and for a while after we returned, we retreated into our rooms, emotionally drained. Dick and I would talk later about what we had seen.

That night four men came from Spitak to Etchmiadzin for relief supplies. Dick had been in the back office with the man in charge of the supplies when they arrived. He called me to join them. The men looked as if they had just been let out of a prison: grim, unshaven, and haggard. The man who spoke for the group told us that the people left in their city were desperate for food, clothing, and medicine. We gave several hundred blankets donated by a Mennonite charitable organization to these men from Spitak. They had no water. We gave them tens of cases of Belmont Springs Water. When these cases of water had been unloaded into the school's storage area a day earlier, they sparked enormous interest; people thought they contained some kind of nutritional beverage. When they learned that these containers held ordinary water, the men working in the warehouse laughed at how stupid we were for bringing water to Armenia. The men from Spitak did not laugh. Months later we saw the gallon plastic containers being reused by people all over the earthquake region.

Many of the earthquake's uninjured survivors remained among the rubble of their cities and towns despite the hardships they encountered. They would not leave their dead. Many bodies still had not been recovered; others had not had proper burials; graves were not yet appropriately marked. As soon as they could, artisans, using photos retrieved from the rubble, etched portraits of the dead into granite slabs that became their headstones. It was so important to do this that some survivors used the money they were given for housing to pay for these etched stones. (I hope that now, ten years after the earthquake, I will be forgiven for openly discussing these most sacred matters.)

Later during that first week we traveled to an area of Armenia that was not in the immediate earthquake zone but had suffered damage to its small maternity hospital, the town of Idjevan, very close to the border with Azerbaijan. Azeri attacks on villages were expected to start soon, and the local hospital was short of supplies. Dick and I both felt it was important to help them and decided to include them in our distribution of supplies.

The chief doctor of the region and the Communist Party secretary showed their appreciation for our coming to visit them by first taking us to dinner and then giving us a tour of the carpet weaving factory. This was in the time when state owned factories like this were still able to operate. Women wearing blue smocks with blue scarves tied around their hair were seated at the looms weaving, while the men operated the larger pieces of equipment. These were commercial carpets that did not appear to be a very expensive type. Dick and the men had moved on ahead of me when a bell rang; it was break time and we were separated by a sea of women in blue. I was encircled, first by a few, then by seemingly a hundred or two. I could see Dick at the other end of the long factory building. He had turned and was looking toward me. I towered over the women who were now crowding in around me. The questioning started—"Are you American? Armenian? Are there others like you? How come you came?" Then, the questions stopped and the women echoed each other's sentiments, whispering, "Thank you, thank you; tell the others thank you. We need you. We need you."

Their warmth and eagerness to reach out to me, en masse, was overwhelming. I was unable to tell these women what was going through my mind as I looked down into their eyes, their big deep eyes, some smiling, some sad. They had tears, like mine. I kept turning from woman to woman, some were touching me, others were reaching out over the crowd. I didn't know to whom to respond; all I could say was thank you in return.

By the time I reached Dick, I could not hold my tears back; Dick understood completely and was as affected by the scene as I was. It was one of those moments neither of us would forget. (When Dick talked about it recently he said, "It was a picture etched in my mind forever.")

Back in Etchmiadzin word quickly spread that two American doctors were staying at the church guest house and people seeking help regarding their medical problems started coming to the church school looking for us. One young man, too shy to come into the warehousing area where we were working, kept walking back and forth around the church grounds. He had an obvious limp. Dick, suspecting that he had come to see us, approached him and learned that he had indeed needed to see us. He was a refugee from Azerbaijan.

We found a private place and Dick examined his leg. He had a deep wound oozing with pus. Despite our questions and his answers, we could not quite understand how he had received the wound or why he had not gotten any treatment for it. Dick cleaned it off, applied antiseptic ointment locally, and dressed it. But, a more thorough examination was needed to see if the infection involved the underlying bone. Dick explained and we directed the young man to the only orthopedic doctor in Armenia we knew at the time, the chief doctor of the Trauma and Orthopedic Hospital in Yerevan for whom we had brought nearly one million dollars worth of orthopedic supplies. We were sure he would help the young man if he gave our names.

❧

With Gulnara's help Dick and I were able to get appointments with Dr. Emil Gabrielian, the Minister of Health and with his deputy, Dr. Albert Khatchadurian.

The meeting took place on January 6, 1989. Both men were weary. Khatchadurian told us that for days after the earthquake they did not go home. Now, they worked from early in the morning until late at night, seven days a week. There were unending lines of people outside the Ministry offices, most of them the representatives of relief organizations, Armenian and non-

Armenian, from around the world. They had questions, required information, and made special requests that the Ministry officials had to help with to facilitate their relief work. He told us that they met daily with as many as fifteen different humanitarian organizations and an equal number of individuals. Working through interpreters, the Minister would update each on the medical conditions in the disaster zone and the problems of Yerevan's hospitals. "We have to go through the same things over and over again with everyone who enters this Ministry," Khatchadurian explained, "because we don't know who will actually do something here. There are many proposals and promises of projects, but we have no way of knowing which will actually be carried out."

I recorded directly into my journal what Gabrielian told us:

- *900,000 people were made homeless by the earthquake*
- *More than 1000 doctors came to Armenia from other republics of the Soviet Union and from other countries. (I wondered if they all had brought their own tents and food?)*
- *10,000 hospital beds were prepared in Yerevan for the injured*
- *19,268 ambulatory patients were seen in the first days*
- *11,831 patients were hospitalized with earthquake related injuries*
- *4,200 operations were performed in this first month*
- *414 patients died after surgery*
- *460 patients were sent to other parts of the Soviet Union*
- *800 people sustained crush injuries and lived*
- *60 kidney dialysis machines were sent to Armenia*
- *400 people had spinal cord injuries*
- *more than 400 people had lost one limb; 35 people lost both arms and both legs*
- *several hundred medical facilities, including hospitals, were destroyed*

Gabrielian went on to say, "*I can't say to you, 'Bring this or bring that.' This is your fatherland. You can help as you want. Mobile units will be very helpful. Computers will be needed to help us to maintain inventories. If we had satellites for communication and helicopters for emergency services, it would be very helpful. The offers of help that we are receiving are very generous. Right now we have enough of many things, enough to last for the next year. What we need are new hospitals. We need to install new equipment. The territory is very big."*

Doctors from another group who were in the meeting with us asked, "Do you need doctors or nurses?" Gabrielian said, "No. We need specialists in some fields: kidney dialysis and spinal cord injuries." (Dialysis was especially crucial, because the crush injuries to muscles sustained in the earthquake release a substance toxic to the kidneys.) But when we were in Leninakan the doctors there said that they need help badly. They were exhausted, working long shifts, without breaks, under difficult conditions. Doctors were needed, they had told us, to provide them with relief. Now we were being told that doctors were not needed; clearly, those in charge in Yerevan had a different set of priorities, based on their different responsibilities and perspectives.

Dick and I spent our days and nights at the church school overseeing the distribution of our supplies. Doctors, like the ones we met at the Railroad Hospital, sent their trucks to the school, as we had advised them, to pick up the relief supplies we promised them. Sometimes the drivers came alone, at other times the doctors we had met came with them. We tried to tailor what we gave to each hospital based on their needs and hoped that the medicines would be used correctly. If a doctor had come too, we explained in detail how the drugs were to be used; if not, we sent handwritten instructions with the driver. A complete manifest of the truck's contents also had to be prepared before the truck could leave the church grounds. It was a tedious but necessary process. Without the proper documents and stamps, the drivers could be arrested by the police, who stopped all trucks carrying cargo.

One day, an elderly man I had not seen before was walking around the first floor of the school. He started asking a lot of questions disturbed by the presence of a woman in the church school. Why is a woman in here? What is she doing here? Who let her come here? And so on. I moved away from him into one of the other rooms, annoyed by his attitude. Apparently someone took him aside and explained to him that I was an American doctor who had come to help them. With his eyes full of tears he found me, warmly took my hands in his, and simply said, "Thank you. I am sorry if I offended you."

We got a break in our work schedule when we were invited to dinner by Louise Simone (the daughter of the noted Armenian philanthropist, Alex Manoogian) who was heading the Armenian General Benevolent Union's earthquake relief effort. Zori Balayan, whom I had met on my trip to Armenia the previous May, was at the dinner also. When he learned that Dick and I had come to Armenia with a planeload of supplies for the earthquake zone, he asked if we would give some of what we had brought to him for shipment to Karabagh. The request presented us with a problem. Did we have the right to send supplies to Karabagh that had been collected for the earthquake zone?

Dick and I spent considerable time discussing the ethics of doing this. In the end, we reasoned that since we had already distributed huge quantities to the earthquake zone and to hospitals in Yerevan, and since a considerable amount was still left, it would be acceptable. A few days before we left Armenia, Zori came to the school late at night with his brother-in-law, Dr. Valerie Marutian, a surgeon from Karabagh's capital city, Stepanakert. They had two trucks that were going to Stepanakert that night and they said that they would take anything we were willing to give them; the need in Karabagh was very great. Blockaded for nearly two years, Karabagh did not have the medical supplies they would need if war came, as anticipated. We helped load the trucks with medicine and medical supplies and, as quietly as they had come, they pulled out of the church grounds in the darkness.

In Yerevan we visited several pediatric hospitals and the orthopedic hospital, where survivors of the earthquake were being treated. Each hospital had its own set of needs and long lists of requests. Most did not have basic equipment such as blood pressure cuffs, electrocardiogram machines, or cardiac monitoring equipment.

Dick and I also visited the dialysis units set up by the American and European doctors at several hospitals. The foreign teams of doctors, nurses, and technicians brought with them almost everything they needed to perform dialysis, but maintenance of the equipment presented many problems. The 220-volt current often surged to 240-volts or more, straining sensitive medical equipment; wiring was frequently inadequate; plugs were incompatible; special attention had to be given to grounding equipment; and replacement parts had to come from the United States or Europe. These were problems everyone who was bringing medical equipment to Armenia faced, not just those involved with dialysis. However, dialysis was more complicated and therefore presented more problems. In addition, if the equipment did not function properly, lives were immediately affected adversely.

By the time we left Armenia, Dick and I were both emotionally depleted and worn-out.

We flew home via Miami on a private aircraft.

The flight took about 13 hours. It gave Dick and me a chance to think about all we had seen and done, to compare notes, and to make some plans regarding the public statements we would make. We agreed that it would not be wise to talk about sending supplies to Karabagh; the Karabagh Committee members were still in jail, and if the Soviet Embassy got wind of it, they might not grant us visas again.

Once in Florida, we took commercial flights back to Boston. George met me at Logan airport for what was an emotional homecoming. When I came off the plane and saw him waiting with a bouquet of flowers in his hands I collapsed into his arms, exhausted and emotionally drained.

It was as if I had been catapulted through a reality-altering tunnel from one world to another, from one point in time to another. Armenia was so far removed from the world I had come back to, a world that was right-side-up with food, cars, telephones, water, and electricity.

But Armenia was real. I knew that as soon as I could I would have to go back. That spring, I had the opportunity.

Approach to the city of Ashotsk, April 1989.

CHAPTER 5

Flowers from the Children of Ashotsk

April 1989
Less than three months after returning from Armenia I was invited to join a team of mental health workers going to the earthquake zone. My contribution would be to advise the team on patients they saw who might need medication and to see medical cases that came to their attention. The team was the second one organized by Dr. Armen Goenjian of California at the invitation of the Minister of Education of Armenia, Dr. Ruben Sarkissian.

Reports of poor performance in school and various types of erratic behavior, both uncommon in Armenia's children, were reaching the Minister from schoolteachers throughout the earthquake region. Something was happening to these children, something unlike anything they had ever experienced. The Minister understood that this something was a direct result of the earthquake and that it was very serious.

It was a courageous leap in thinking and insight on the part of Dr. Sarkissian to know that he needed help and that the psychologists in Armenia (all of whom worked in the educational system and were under his jurisdiction) lacked the expertise to provide that help. He knew that he needed to go outside the Soviet system to get it. Not so long ago he might have lost his job for such a move or, worse, been sent to Siberia as his reward.

When we arrived in Yerevan, Dr. Sarkissian met us and settled us into the Hotel Armenia. The following morning he briefed us on the task ahead. We were divided into four teams, each to go to a different region within the earthquake zone. After two weeks we would meet again in Yerevan, discuss our experiences, and prepare a report for the next team Dr. Goenjian was already planning. The names of patients who needed medical consultation were to be given to me then. Since I was staying on in Armenia for an additional month, I could travel from region to region to do the follow-up work. However, until that time, I was teamed up with Garbis Moushigian, a psychologist from Connecticut who had no other partner. Although I was not a psychologist, Dr. Goenjian had felt that I had enough background to work with Garbis; as a practicing primary care internist I had some special training and experience in mental health.

Garbis and I were sent to the region of Ashotsk (called Ghoukassian before 1991), and, as it turned out, the epicenter of another earthquake that had occurred two weeks before our arrival. It was late in the afternoon when we finally arrived there, having first dropped off other members of the team in Talin and Leninakan. Ours was the last stop.

Ashotsk, on Armenia's northern border with Georgia, is a barren and cold place, known as the Siberia of Armenia. The people of Ashotsk will tell you, "Nothing grows here except weeds." Summer lasts less than a month, and in the winter the mountain roads are made impassable by the relentless snow that drifts over the mountains, completely cutting the region off from the rest of Armenia for weeks at a time.

It's not a place people visit unless they are on their way to the Republic of Georgia, nor does anyone voluntarily live in Ashotsk unless born there; others who come are assigned to work there by the government. The town, with the same name as the region, had a hospital, a grade school, a high school, and government administrative offices. There was no theater, cinema, or concert hall. The town had a tired, worn-out look without any obvious sense of order. Its houses and apartment buildings, built with Armenia's pink tufa stone, were not quite straight and in need of obvious repair. We wondered if the earthquake had caused them to look that way or if that was the way they had always looked.

In the region surrounding the town there were more than 50 villages, each with 500 or more inhabitants. The local farmers here were organized into cooperatives, but were allowed to do some private farming to provide extra food for their families and, theoretically, additional income from selling their surplus. But there was not much surplus in Ashotsk, because growing conditions were so poor.

All of the children of Armenia go to school, even in these remote regions, giving the country a literacy rate approaching 100 percent (UNESCO 1995). Therefore, as we expected, most villages had a grade school. Most had a medical post as well.

The first night Garbis and I spent in Ashotsk we stayed in the local hospital, which had suffered structural damage in the earthquake but was still standing. The chief doctor could not ask any of the staff to take us "home" since no one really had a home. It was a terrible night. I did not sleep, grappling with my own very real fears of another earthquake. We had a small wash basin in one of the rooms; we used the toilet once and knew we could never enter that room again. Without any running water in the hospital, the human waste had accumulated. The doctors had not wanted us to see these conditions, but there were no other facilities to offer us.

In the morning two young doctors, Ida and Tigran, rescued us. They were waiting for us with the chief doctor when we entered the doctors' room. "Tigran and Ida would like to take you to their home," he said. "They feel very bad about having left you here last night, but did not know if you would want to go to their home. This is no place for you to sleep." Garbis and I were delighted, though we tried not to show how uncomfortable we had been the night before by accepting their invitation too enthusiastically.

Ida, a general medical doctor, and Tigran, an ear, nose and throat physician, were married after medical school and were assigned by the Ministry of Health to work in the city of Leninakan. These work assignments after medical school were both a kind of internship and a payback to the system for their education. Tigran is from the Armenian village of Damala, in Georgia, where his family still lives, and Ida is from Yerevan, where her family lives. In Leninakan, unable to follow the usual Armenian custom of the couple taking up residence with the groom's family, housing became a major problem. The apartment they were given had to be shared with another newlywed couple, an intolerable situation. They decided to look for work elsewhere. They found it in Ashotsk, but before moving, written approval had to be obtained from the authorities, medical and civilian, in both cities. Without these papers, neither work nor housing would be given to them. Finally, one week before Leninakan was reduced to rubble, they moved to Ashotsk. It was a move that most likely saved their lives. The hospital they had been working in and the apartment they had been living in were both completely destroyed by the earthquake.

We spent a few minutes talking with our new hosts and later that day, after work, Tigran and Ida took us to their apartment, which was in one of the stone apartment buildings we had seen in the city. The building, damaged in the earthquake, had been slated for demolition by the authorities. The surface cracks visible along the stairwell walls, our hosts told us as we climbed to the third floor, were not the real problem. Structural damage to the foundation was what made the building unsafe. Most of the other tenants had vacated their apartments. Large padlocks had been placed on every door we passed.

Tigran and Ida had vacated too, taking up residence in a small boxcar called a *domic*. Thousands of these boxcars had been sent from other parts of the Soviet Union to temporarily house families made homeless by the earthquake. Their domic was conveniently placed in the yard alongside their apartment building. They continued to use their apartment's bath facilities but slept and cooked in their domic. Sarkis, a young surgeon at the hospital who had no other place to stay, was living with them in the domic. He and Tigran had become close friends in medical school and when Tigran moved to Ashotsk, Sarkis followed.

We entered the small apartment with some anxiety about its safety. It was sparsely furnished with the barest of necessities. There were two bedrooms, a living room, a bath, and a kitchen. The balcony, we were warned, had separated from the rest of the structure in the quake and was not safe. The apartment was clean and, surprisingly, had running water in the mornings. A hot water heater, fired by gas, allowed us to take showers on most days after we learned how to turn on the heater without causing an explosion.

After dinner on that first evening Ida and Tigran went down to their domic, leaving the apartment to Garbis and me. Ida had prepared our beds, one in each of the bedrooms, made up with crisp whiter than white sheets and topped with a *vermag*, just like the one I had back in the Bronx. Instead of being overcome by sleep, which I badly needed, I lay wide awake the entire night worrying: What if there is another earthquake? How would we get out? The next morning I told Garbis (who had not had any trouble sleeping) that we had to make a plan just in case there was another earthquake. First, we decided not to lock the front door: ever. We were the only ones in the building, and it seemed unlikely a thief would venture up to our third floor in the middle of the night. As for egress, Garbis thought the best route was via the metal ladder right outside the apartment door leading up to the roof. "It is the safest place in an earthquake," he informed me. But after studying the situation it was clear that if the building was shaking, I would run down the three flights of stairs and out the front door rather than negotiate the ladder, the more dangerous of the alternatives.

For the next two weeks I slept fully clothed and left a bag of necessary belongings next to the front door, which remained unlocked. We never shared our fears with Ida, Tigran, or Sarkis, not wanting to cause them any concern. We knew that they thought nothing could happen to us: we were special, we were from America.

These three young doctors are now among my close friends in Armenia. Not only did they share with us everything they had over those few weeks, but when I returned later to deliver medicine to their hospital, they said to me, "This is too much for us, take it to people who have less." I knew we would be friends forever!

Our living situation settled, Garbis and I were able to start working intensively. Visiting schools, including those in remote villages, to observe the children was our first priority. We talked with parents, teachers, and doctors as well as with the children. The Minister of Education's briefing had been accurate. Children were not sleeping. They were unable to concentrate and were doing poorly in school. It was no surprise that many children did not want to attend school: the earthquake took place while they were in school, and going there brought back all-too-vivid memories of the earth shaking. Parents and teachers recognized that the children were in trouble; they simply did not know what to do about it. These were the first signs of post-traumatic stress syndrome, the devastating psychiatric problem that continues to afflict the population of the earthquake zone.

The first village we visited was Medz Sepasar. Their new two-story school building had been severely damaged by the earthquake and classes were being held in an old one-story stone school building. We arrived in the morning as the children were filing into their rooms. Before speaking with them and their parents, we had a meeting with the teachers.

The principal, some of the older teachers and, of course, the Communist Party's representative (who was always with us) escorted Garbis and me into a small classroom. We sat in chairs behind a narrow wood table and the officials took their places on either side of us. The teachers began to cram into the room, taking up the other seats and then lining up along the walls, packed in as tightly as possible. After a few introductory remarks by the principal and the Party representative's welcome, Garbis and I each spoke. Garbis took the lead—not only because he was the psychologist, but also because his Armenian was fluent and mine was still faltering. He briefly explained who we were, why we had come, and what we hoped to accomplish. I added that there were many others in America who would have come if they could and emphasized a point that Garbis had already made: we had come to work with them, not "tell" them what to do. Then we asked the teachers to tell us about the children, their problems, and anything else that was pertinent. We were also open to suggestions, Garbis said, as to how to proceed over the next two weeks.

In the presence of the Party representative we were afraid that the teachers would not speak truthfully about what was going on with the children, since standard Soviet practice was to cover up all problems. However, they knew that the Minister of Education had organized our visit and the First Secretary of the Communist Party in the Ashotsk region had also given it his blessings. But would that be enough to overcome reservations they were sure to have about talking with foreigners? This meeting was unprecedented, a fact everyone was keenly aware of.

The teachers proved to be very willing to speak with us, the only people who have come to their village after the earthquake and the only foreigners they had ever seen. We were profoundly moved by their response to our presence. One of the first teachers to speak said, "Just the fact that you have come all the way here, all the way to Ashotsk, is enough. We will find a way to survive." Others talked about what problems the children are having in school. Then they revealed their own fears—not only of the possibility of another earthquake, but for the safety of their families, still living in houses that had been badly damaged by the quake.

Emotions that had nothing to do with the earthquake charged the room. This was the first contact the people of Ashotsk had ever had with Armenians from abroad, Americans at that. From time to time during the meeting, eyes clouded over with tears, theirs and ours. Garbis and I answered questions about ourselves: where we were from, where our parents came from, how Americans—including non-Armenians—had reacted to the earthquake, how everyone came together to get help to them. Our emotions got the better of us too. Garbis' eyes had filled with tears as he explained why we had come to Armenia. I heard his voice quiver and halt. I completed his sentence and continued. A few minutes later he had to rescue me.

During this first meeting we began to understand the extent to which this community was gripped by fear and how its isolation, even from the rest of Armenia, contributed to their psychological paralysis in the face of multiple traumas. Over and over the teachers verbalized the same thought: that our coming has made an enormous difference to them. They were surprised to learn that there were people outside of Ashotsk, outside of Armenia, who were thinking about them and trying to find ways of helping them. One woman said that we are the only people she has come in contact with since the earthquake who were not terrified also.

The teachers confirmed what Dr. Sarkissian had told us about the children. They added that the children no longer spent any time playing. They seemed inactive, listening, waiting for the earth to shake again.

The meeting lasted for several hours. We were exhausted and happy for the break when the principal called the meeting to a close and announced that lunch was served.

During lunch the school's principal started to talk about the Voice of America radio programs they listen to almost every day. Several of the teachers had heard an interview with a Dr. Goenjian, they thought, describing a mental health project in Armenia. They were delighted to hear that it was the same Dr. Goenjian sponsoring our trip; somehow that gave more legitimacy to our presence. Then the principal reached into his jacket's inside pocket, brought out a yellowed newspaper clipping and handed it to me. It was a *New York Times* article written about Alex Manoogian, the Armenian philanthropist. There in Medz Sepasar, one of the most remote areas of Armenia, behind the Iron Curtain, in the Soviet Union, this man had obtained and carried with him a *New York Times* article—not a copy of but the actual article. How did he get it? I never found out. But I had no difficulty understanding; in their near-total isolation, this piece of paper brought the world to their village. The article had been translated into Armenian and all of the teachers admitted to having copies. The Communist Party representative had not stayed for lunch so she missed this revelation!

After lunch we visited the classrooms for the first time. The children stood in unison when we entered each room and presented us with bouquets of small yellow crocuses, the first ones of spring they had picked from the fields. They sang songs, and some students rose to recite poetry. In one class a young girl sang a long song that she wrote about the earthquake. Garbis then told the children why we had come and invited them to talk with us.

Slowly at first, but then quite openly, the children began to talk. They told us they read the same page in a book over and over again and still did not know what it said. They all thought about the earthquake all the time, even dreaming about it. One of the teachers pointed out that in Ashotsk there were usually three or four minor earthquakes a year and said that everyone who lived here was accustomed to experiencing tremors; no one had been afraid like this before. One of the children mentioned a rumor he had heard that the end of Armenia was imminent; other children indicated they had heard the same thing. We seized the moment to dispel the rumors, taking advantage of our status as authority figures. With all the authority we could muster we told the children that we had not heard any such thing, that it simply was not true.

We visited classes in several villages and heard of the same problems everywhere. All of the children agreed they would rather not be in a school building, but out-of-doors. They all wanted to be near the windows or near the exit door. No one would go up to the second floor of any building. The older children seemed to be more depressed than the younger children and the boys look sadder and more withdrawn than the girls. Later we wondered if the boys were indeed having a harder time, trying to be more "manly," less able to accept their fear than the girls were.

Parents were asked to bring their children for individual sessions if they were having special problems; the teachers were also asked to identify the children they thought were particularly troubled. With Garbis taking the lead, we met with these families to try to help them. Uninterrupted quiet time was needed, with both the adults and the children, in order to learn what was going on. Initially we met with the parents and the children together. However, like anxious parents the world over, they would answer the questions addressed to their child or the anxious child would look to the parent for cues on how to answer. It became clear that some sessions had to be held without parents present. It was hard enough to explain what it was that we were doing; it was even harder to explain why we had to do it in private.

Privacy is not a right in the Soviet system, but a hard won luxury. The doctor-patient relationship is not a private one. Consultations are held in rooms that seem to have no doors or walls. The sessions in Ashotsk were my first experiences in trying to obtain privacy in a professional setting, but they were not the last. While having a medical consultation with a patient, people thought nothing of walking in, without knocking, looking for someone, wondering when we would be finished, or whether I could see them. These intrusions were always a shock to me and made me angry, but my patients never seemed to mind. Since they had never had any privacy, they did not expect it.

The problem of getting the privacy we needed was not easily solved. We first tried putting signs on the doors requesting that no one intrude. These were ignored. Then one of us would simply stand against the door to prevent it from being opened. (We could not lock the doors. Many children in Leninakan died because classroom doors had been locked from the outside that morning, an unfortunate coincidence, thus preventing their escape when the earthquake occurred. The children here knew that.) Little by little, parents, teachers, and administrators (even the KGB watchman) realized that we meant to keep the sessions private. The intrusions stopped.

For the first time children were being asked what they thought, what they felt, what they feared. They had been told, "Don't cry," "Don't be afraid," "There won't be any more earthquakes." The adults could not understand why the children continued to be afraid despite these assurances. But the fact was, there would be more earthquakes. Strong tremors had occurred again on January 4 and 9, again on February 23, and, most terrifying of all, on March 30, when Ashotsk was the epicenter of a small earthquake. The children knew that the adults around them were as terrified as they were. They also knew that many children had been orphaned, and that was their worst fear: the earthquake would come again and they too would be orphaned!

We began to learn why there was so much terror among people in a region where only buildings had been damaged and where no deaths had occurred, unlike the city of Leninakan, where tens of thousands of people had died.

On December 7 when the earthquake shook the ground and the buildings of Ashotsk rumbled, people ran to the school, got their children, filled available cars, and drove over the mountains to Leninakan, just 45 minutes away. Leninakan was the center of the Shirak region within which Ashotsk is located. It was where people went for all their special needs, from shopping to medical care. And now, they looked to Leninakan for safety from the tremors. How could they know they would find scenes of horror that would forever be etched in their minds.

The sky over Leninakan was still filled with black smoke when the people of Ashotsk arrived; it was early afternoon, but it seemed like midnight. Driving through the streets torn up by the earthquake was nearly impossible. They saw human limbs hanging from concrete slabs, on the floors, and from ceilings of the city's high rises. Everywhere were twisted forms and bizarre shapes of vaguely familiar things. Screams came from the injured and dying. Thousands of survivors were running throughout the once beautiful city, many lost because nothing familiar remained.

These were the images these innocents drove into. The realization that Leninakan had been destroyed was stunning. The people of Ashotsk were the first outsiders to reach this city. Not even the authorities in Yerevan knew what had happened at this point.

Had they stayed in Ashotsk, their children would have never seen these ghastly sights that haunted them now. "*Yerani, yerani . . . ,*" "if only, if only," we heard over and over again. "If only we had not gone to Leninakan our children would have been spared."

The stories kept coming from family after family, child after child: Marina, 7-years old, was brought by her mother because she started crying at any loud noise or sudden movement. The family lives on the second floor of a damaged house. Seventeen relatives died in Leninakan.

A 50-year-old woman came alone. On March 30 she told her children to run out of the house, but she then went into a seizure-like trance and was unable to move for some hours. She has been unable to work or sleep since then and cries all the time. She too had gone to Leninakan and had seen the body of her sister's crushed child in their mangled apartment building. Maybe this was the end of the world. There was no faith any more. (Her mental state was serious. We made arrangements to speak with her polyclinic doctor about starting her on antidepressant medication as well as psychotherapy. We could give her the medicine but had no idea who would provide the badly needed therapy after we left.)

A 41-year-old woman brought her son. He drew while his mother talked. They lived on the fifth floor of a damaged apartment building. None of her children wanted to come home after school, but there was no other place for them to live. The children talked in their sleep and cried a lot. Ten members of their family were killed in Leninakan. They too had gone there and had seen the destruction. Her son drew a picture of a large single-story house, with large windows and a roof clearly made of wood. He told us that it was a safe house ("*abahov dun e*"). Then the mother unwittingly solved her own problem when she told us that her parents lived in a nearby village. Why not go to live with them for a while? It seemed an acceptable solution.

Another mother came with her three children: Gariné 10, Hratchic 8, and Hasmig, 6 years of age. On March 30 when the tremors started her husband did not let the children run out of the house. ("If we are not afraid, why should you be?") We explained to the mother that this made children unable to tell their fears to anyone; we asked if she and her husband could return without the children. These children's drawings were of small stick figures, without any embellishment, stark and cold. We asked Gariné what she would wish for if she had three wishes. After careful consideration she said, "First, to have water all of the time. Second, to have the sun so that there will never be any darkness. Third, peace everywhere." This was not the first time a child had mentioned peace when Garbis had asked for their three wishes. The violence against Armenians in Sumgait was on children's minds too.

One of the many reasons these children were so terrified was that they never got a chance to forget. The horror of the earthquake was reinforced nightly on television where scenes of earthquake-devastated regions were shown again and again, accompanied by funereal music. Adults, too, talked of almost nothing else. Over and over, the earthquake was relived in front of the children. New and fantastic rumors spread wildly through the towns and villages, fantastic stories not only about the next great earthquake but also, as we had already been told, about the end of Armenia and even the end of the world. No wonder the children were frightened. As one mother had told us, no one knew if they would live or die.

The children drew many pictures: airplanes with big red crosses and nurses coming to help; black skies and destroyed buildings; new houses with big windows and big doors. Many of their drawings depicted flowers, which Armenians give to each other for special occasions, to mark events and anniversaries, or just when visiting someone's home. Tradition has it that odd numbers of flowers are given to a living person, even numbers to commemorate the dead. These children drew flowers in vases and in gardens, in the hands of stick figures and in the air, and the number was always even: 2, 4, 6. The flowers were always for the dead.

Garbis and I worked long hours every day. He was leading individual therapy sessions with the more severely affected children and adults, while I was seeing medical patients, some with the local doctors or alone. Each night, after dinner, we stayed up late to review what we had done and to make our plans for the next day. We also worked on a set of recommendations we would make to the community.

During our last few days in Ashotsk we met again with groups of teachers and parents in each of the school districts. The rooms were packed with people eagerly looking to us for recommendations. First we confirmed that all of the symptoms their children were demonstrating were a reaction to the trauma of the earthquake called post-traumatic stress syndrome (PTSS). Even giving it a name seemed to help by letting them know that other people in other places had experienced the same thing.

Although Garbis and I were far from experts on PTSS, we were able to make some simple observations and offer suggestions to break their cycle of fear and prevent the syndrome from becoming chronic.

First we explained that fear is not necessarily a bad thing. If it appropriately warns you of impending danger, it enables you to protect yourself. Only if it prevents you from taking appropriate action is fear bad. Then it must be brought under control. We encouraged teachers and parents not to deny their own fears so adamantly and let the children talk about what was frightening them. We suggested that the adults emphasize positive things: that no one in Ashotsk died in the earthquake, that the damaged buildings were being repaired; and that the unsafe schools had been abandoned. Community meetings should be held at which the latest series of rumors could be openly discussed and dispelled.

Finally, we told them to make plans: unlock all windows, especially the school windows, and leave them slightly open. Remove flower pots from windowsills so that these will not be an obstacle to jumping out. Allow the children to have frequent rest periods. Conduct weekly earthquake drills to practice evacuation through windows and exits, just as they do in countries like Japan.

At home, put together a bag of warm clothes and a favorite toy for each child. Put the bag next to the predetermined escape route. Plan the escape route and practice it. Point out changes that have been made at home to make the children's sleeping place safer.

But most of all, we again emphasized, the children needed to talk freely about their fears to sympathetic listeners, their parents and their teachers. Only then would the children be free to be normal children again.

We explained that all of these recommendations were designed to bring "fear" out in the open and to do something about them. The community was very thankful that we had come. They admitted that at first they could not understand what we were going to do. After all, more earthquakes were sure to come, and since we had no power to change that, they could not see how talking about it was going to help. However, some of the children were already better and the adults were feeling a sense of relief at being able to express their own fears as well. It was a new kind of psychology for them and they liked it. Our suggestions, we reiterated, were just a start and we hoped that they would add their own for the healing process to continue.

After we left Ashotsk, our recommendations were printed in the local newspaper, point by point, which pleased us greatly.

As planned, the team came together in Yerevan at the end of the second week. We discovered that everyone had the same experiences, although those who had gone to Leninakan found problems among the children and the adults to be much more serious than elsewhere. Our final report confirmed that Leninakan needed more mental health workers who could provide continuity of care by staying for at least one month at a time.

Page after page of my journal is filled with notes about the patients I saw during the next six weeks. Many of them were patients the other members of the team had seen in Leninakan, in Talin, in Artik, and in Yerevan. Others were brought to me at the Hotel Armenia, friends of the desk clerks or the housekeepers and people who had come to Gulnara's office seeking help. Still others were refugee families from Sumgait living in hotels and hostels around Yerevan; all were in desperate condition, survivors of one catastrophe or another.

George joined me in Armenia at the end of April. As promised, I returned to Ashotsk to check on some of the more seriously ill children and adults Garbis and I had seen and to give the doctors some of the medicine George had brought with him. My first stop was at the town's administrative offices to check in with the First Secretary of the region and his deputy, who had accompanied Garbis and me most of the time. She was delighted to see me again and once more accompanied me to the hospital and to two of the schools while I distributed the medicines and checked up on our patients.

At the end of the day, bouncing around in the back seat of the jeep, she turned and, taking me completely by surprise, said, "We would like to give you a gift of a baby. Would you like to adopt a baby from Ashotsk? There is a baby we know of who has just been born into a very large family. The family is poor and the child is not wanted. We can arrange for you to adopt this baby."

Now I understood why she had asked me so many questions about whether I had children, wanted children, how long George and I had been married. I thought she was simply exhibiting the usual curiosity Armenians have about these things and their lack of reticence in asking about them.

I had viewed her as an adversary, the party watchdog, the person that I was least connected with. Now, in this barren place where nothing grew, she was offering me a baby, the most precious gift of all.

My heart stopped. Unexpectedly and uncontrollably, the buried pain of never knowing motherhood welled up inside of me, choking my insides. With great difficulty I managed to find my voice, took her hand, and in Armenian said, "*Geghetzik,*" addressing her by her name, which means beautiful, "thank you. I will speak to George about it."

Before leaving for Boston, I sent word to Geghetzik that George and I had decided against adopting the baby; it was too complicated a matter to consider at this time but we were both very grateful for their thoughtfulness. It was no surprise as we prepared to leave that I felt a sense of guilt; I would be returning home to comfort and safety, leaving people with whom I was beginning to feel a close bond. I could say good-bye only with the promise that I would return again very soon.

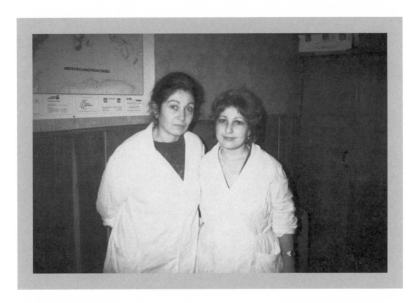

Dr. Lilit Boghosian, on the left, the day I met her. She is with the hospital's neonatologist. Maternity Hospital, Gyumri, 1989.

New mothers, all survivors of the earthquake, receiving gifts for their newborns.

CHAPTER 6

"Can We Trust You with Our Sorrow?"

During the summer of 1989 the political situation worsened. In retaliation for Armenia's support of Nagorno-Karabagh, the Azeris began to vandalize and block freight trains headed for the earthquake zone. Building materials, food, fuel, grain, and medical supplies were all targeted. By the end of the year, according to reports out of Moscow, thousands of freight cars destined for Armenia were stranded throughout the Soviet Union. Eighty-five percent of the trains that came to Armenia passed through Azerbaijan.

Earlier in the year, Gorbachev had placed Karabagh under the direct rule of Moscow, but in November the USSR Supreme Soviet voted to rescind his order, eliminating what was called Karabagh's "special status" and placing it back under Azerbaijani control. In Armenian SSR this action was seen as leaving the Karabagh Armenians without protection against the all-too-real threat of another genocide and took the following action reported on December 7, 1989, in the Armenian Reporter, an independent newspaper published in New York: "Armenia, in Provocative Challenge to Moscow, Annexes Karabagh—Moves to Delete 'Soviet Socialist' From Name of Country."

Nightly, thousands of people gathered in Yerevan's Opera Square and, as the newspaper went on to report, they "openly called for the secession of Armenia from the Soviet Union" to protest Gorbachev's and the Supreme Soviet's actions. In response, Soviet troops were dispatched to "keep the peace" in Armenia and in Karabagh.

By the end of the year, as a result of the Azeri blockade of landlocked Armenia, electricity blackouts were common throughout the country, food shortages began, the price of gasoline reached the equivalent of $3 per gallon, and reconstruction projects in the earthquake zone slowed. Turkey assisted the Azeris in the blockade by allowing only humanitarian aid (mostly that sent by the United States government) to pass through its territory en route to Armenia. Even those shipments were pilfered before reaching Armenia.

The relief effort expanded beyond the needs of the earthquake zone; diasporan Armenians began planning massive airlifts of food and other aid to assist the rest of Armenia and Karabagh.

I returned to Armenia in November 1989 to distribute the relief supplies we had collected under the banner of our newly formed nonprofit organization, the Armenian Health Alliance. Our supplies, along with those of countless other Armenian and non-Armenian organizations, had been sent on one of the first airlifts sponsored by another newly formed organization, the United Armenian Fund (UAF), a coalition of seven major Armenian organizations under the leadership of the Lincy Foundation and billionaire-benefactor Kirk Kerkorian. The establishment of these flights provided a way for Armenia to benefit from America's surplus.

Within the first few days of my arrival in Armenia I returned to Leninakan. Most of the traveling I did in Armenia in those early years after the earthquake was between the capital, Yerevan, and Leninakan, the city most devastated by the earthquake.

The two cities are separated by 110 kilometers (about 75 miles) of mountainous terrain. If all went well and one drove at reasonable speeds, the trip to Leninakan took less than two hours. I preferred to leave Yerevan early, before the morning rush hour, but despite my ardent attempts, I never seemed to be able to. No matter what arrangement might have been agreed to the night before, and no matter who my driver was that day, we never got on the road before 9 a.m. It was the rhythm of life in Armenia; everything started at 9:00 a.m.

By that hour in 1989 Yerevan's streets were congested with buses and trucks and the air was already heavy with black exhaust fumes coming from inefficient engines using leaded gasoline, the only kind of gasoline available. The city's workers were streaming out of their high rise apartment houses, forced to ignore the thick smoke, as they rushed to jobs that paid two or three dollars a month. But that was when gasoline, *benzene* as it is called in Armenia, was still plentiful. A few years later, when the Azeri-Turkish blockade of Armenia was preventing all but a trickle of gasoline from entering the country, prices rose beyond the reach of even government officials. In 1991 we could make our way across the city with hardly a stop. The traffic lights did not operate because there was no electricity, and there were no cars or buses in the streets. People who still had jobs were forced to walk many miles to work. There were secondary benefits, though not appreciated by anyone: the air was cleaner and people were getting exercise.

Even in the days of abundant gasoline, once out of Yerevan we had the road to ourselves except for an occasional truck or bus or government car. We would proceed northwest toward the small town of Ashtarak. Just beyond the vendors, who always line the main street with their flowers for sale, the road makes a right turn toward Leninakan. A mile or two outside Ashtarak, on the left side of the road, there are several large groves of apricot trees. When we make this trip in the early spring and the apricot trees are in blossom, my driver and I worry about the possibility of a late frost that could damage the blossoms and spoil Armenia's precious apricot crop. And in the fall, when the leaves turn to vibrant oranges and yellows, we talk about whether it has been a good season for apricots or not.

All along on our left, the volcanic Mount Ararat can be seen in the heart of ancient Armenia, beyond the Turkish border, now a backdrop for the apricot groves. The smaller Ararat stands next to it. A chain of mountains north of Ararat seems to rise up out of its great side. These mountains are referred to as "the dancing Armenians" because they resemble a line of traditional dancers linked arm in arm all along the horizon. Ararat never fails to take my breath away. It is always magnificent, whether the sun is glistening on the snow that covers its peak for most of the year or whether the clouds are covering it in part. The smaller Ararat, a beauty in its own right, looks like a child next to it. Armenians call these mountains Big *Massis* and Little *Massis*, not Ararat.

Aragatz, a massive four-peaked mountain in the heart of present day Armenia, soon appears on the right, facing *Massis*. According to Armenian folklore, the two great mountains were once together, but they argued and rebuffed the efforts of the surrounding mountains to reconcile them. Frustrated and angry, the other mountains placed a curse on them, causing them to remain forever separate, facing each other like great giants.

From a distance the foothills of Aragatz seem to be dotted with hundreds of rocks, not quite brown and not quite round. As the car gets closer, one sees that these shapes are hundreds of sheep and goats, their shepherds not far away, watching attentively as we pass by. Sometimes the road is blocked by herds of cows followed by the sheep and goats making their way across the road on their way home.

The road climbs and the vistas become grander. We often stop to breathe the clear air and to bathe in the beauty of these mountains. Climbing up to nearly 7,000 feet above sea level, the road continues through the mountains for over an hour before it begins to descend toward Leninakan. Slowly, the terrain changes from rock filled hillsides to large plateaus that fan out on both sides of the roadway. Women from the surrounding villages are in the fields, their dresses colorful, their heads wrapped in handwoven scarves for protection from the sun as they plant potatoes in the spring and "spring wheat" in the fall.

And then, with just a few more kilometers to go, we see the city Leninakan, spread out on the flat lands surrounded by these mountains. It is always a relief to see the city in the distance, to know that we have made the trip safely.

As beautiful as these roads are, they are also dangerous and must be approached with caution. The bright morning sun in Yerevan can deceive the traveler on any day of the year. The mountain passes are full of surprises, with flash rains that make the pavement slippery or, during the long winter months, sudden severe snowstorms that make the road impassable. When traveling in the winter it is wise to wait until late morning before setting out, and even wiser to find a traveler who has made it through and can report on road conditions. The vehicles we use have their own set of problems. Tires are worn thin by the rugged terrain, and unless meticulously maintained, motors break down due to the poor quality of gasoline and engine oil.

Halfway to Leninakan, on one of my trips during 1990, the car came to a sudden halt. When I asked Khachik, my driver, what happened, he simply said, "The motor died." Fortunately it was a warm sunny morning, unlike some of our breakdowns that have occurred late at night, or in the middle of a snowstorm. Khachik stayed with the car while I hiked up to the nearby village looking for help. Eventually he convinced a passing truck driver to tow the car back to Yerevan and I was taken in hand by the children I met playing by the first house I reached.

Their mother, a beautiful, rugged woman, with a deep voice, assured me that she would take care of everything, but first I had to eat some freshly baked bread and yogurt and of course drink a cup of coffee. While she fed me I learned that her husband had died three months ago of a massive heart attack while he was in Turkey visiting relatives; the children who helped me were all hers. She seemed happy to have someone to talk with, a woman, a sympathetic listener. I tried to appear relaxed about finding a way to get to Leninakan. An hour or so later, we set out on foot to her uncle's house.

The village, she told me, is named *Davtashen* named for David of Sasun, the hero of an Armenian legend; the villagers are from Sasun too, a town in Turkey (ancient Armenia). The village turned out to be much larger than it appeared from the road, winding around and behind the hills, one stone house after another, each with an adjacent yard surrounded by a matching stone wall. I could see the familiar fruit trees over the tops of the walls as we walked on. When we finally reached her uncle's house, her aunt informed us that he would be home soon and invited us in. They had a telephone but despite many attempts, she was unable to put a call through to Yerevan or to Leninakan. Finally, a small pickup truck was located along with a driver who took me the rest of the way to Leninakan. They accepted no money, not even to cover the cost of the gas.

❦

November 1989

By late 1989, one year after the earthquake, miles of the roadway on the approach to Leninakan were lined with debris removed from the central city: the twisted metal of buildings, broken beds and sinks, blocks and broken bits of cement that were once high rise apartments. The streets within the city, dusty and dirty in the summer, were now flowing with mud, ankle deep after the heavy rainfalls of early winter. The mud was everywhere, splashing on people as they tried to make their way through the narrow streets crowded with trucks and tractors, trailers and cars. The city was a maze of traffic amidst the destruction.

As much as had been removed, that much debris and destruction remained. Crumbled buildings, with their twisted steel frames, half-standing, half-leaning, revealed colorful papered walls of once-upon-a-time bedrooms and living rooms where families had lived. These images around every corner were (and still are) constant reminders of December 7, 1988, for the people of this city as they tried to go about the business of living.

There was no place for children to play except in these destroyed buildings yet to be demolished and on the mud-filled streets. Grade school classes were held in tents because most of the school buildings were destroyed; the few still standing were being used as hospitals. The tents, hot in the summer, were now in winter filled with smoke from wood-burning stoves placed in the middle of each tent. Classes were not held during the coldest months, a situation that would continue for years to come. Thus, the children remained at home, in domics perhaps colder than the school tents.

Telephone communications within Leninakan were nonexistent, and communication with Yerevan was possible only from government offices. Even then, it required a half-day's effort and luck to get a telephone call through to Yerevan.

None of the promised housing had been built and now, under gray skies and the first snow of winter, tens of thousands of men, women, and children, including the newborn, were still living in the inadequate shelters provided for them right after the earthquake one year ago: the same tin boxcars called *domics* that we had seen in Ashotsk. Domics were lined up one next to the other in any space available. Even these shelters were hard to obtain, requiring long days of waiting in line at government offices or under-the-table payments to those in charge of their distribution. Others, not fortunate enough to have a domic, had used tin and wood to make a shack or a place to sleep under a condemned building.

Every morning these survivors awoke to the problems of obtaining food, clean water, and fuel for cooking and staying warm. Power outages were common, sanitation was a problem, and indoor plumbing a rare luxury. Gyumri's underground water pipes as well as the sewerage systems had been damaged by the earthquake, leaving the city without natural gas and creating a critical clean water problem. Health officials told people to boil water before drinking it, but it was not always possible due to the power outages. The result was outbreaks of dysentery, pneumonia, hepatitis, and even botulism resulting from ingestion of bottled foods that had been inadequately boiled.

These were hard days filled with hopelessness, depression, and despair. But despair was not yet total; people believed that life could not get any harder than it was at that moment and that next year life would be better.

At the edge of the city our driver made a sharp right turn at the first major intersection to the temporary quarters of the Second Children's Hospital. The original hospital had been totally destroyed in the earthquake and was now housed in a series of buildings that were once a kindergarten. The small buildings, without any internal connections, each contained a different unit of the hospital, forcing the staff to go in and out of the cold to get from department to department. We pulled into a large courtyard that must have been the playground but was now filled with cars. People were going in and out of various doors, some carrying small children, while older children were held by hand and led into the hospital. I had come to donate medical supplies and to see if our small, new organization could help this hospital on a regular basis.

Two psychotherapists from the United States, Ida Karayan and Madeline Tashjian, were in Gyumri working as part of the project I had come with in April. It was a welcome surprise to find them in the office of the Chief Doctor, Robert Hamparian. They had been here for one week, and before they said a word, I knew from their expressions that the situation in Leninakan was grim.

The psychological state of Gyumri's inhabitants was much worse now than in April, they told me. As hope faded for the reconstruction of the city—and for that matter, individual lives—the population was increasingly depressed.

Dr. Hamparian listened, silent during our discussion. He too appeared depressed. His wife and daughter were killed in the earthquake. He managed to keep busy with his work, but there was no rest, no relief from the daily problems that confronted him at the hospital and at home trying to raise two teenage boys alone. Hamparian had just finished building a new home when the earthquake occurred. His wife had wanted to move into the new house weeks before the earthquake, but he had delayed the move, wanting to have everything in their new home completely finished. The only damage it sustained was a few cracks in some of the walls, but their old apartment building collapsed with his wife and daughter inside. His grief now was compounded by feelings of guilt.

Later I met with Ida and Madeline for a more private discussion. They told me about the many patients they had been seeing, people who had lost their entire families, parents who are haunted by the cries of children they could not reach, and on and on. With neither proper housing nor jobs, community life could not be restored. Grief could not be worked through. Every day they worked from early in the morning until late at night and everywhere they went people asked for psychiatric help. After only a week, they themselves were having difficulty coping with the profound sadness of the situation and their own sense of helplessness.

Back at the Children's Hospital the 30 cases of soy infant formula I had brought were stacked in the corner of Hamparian's office. Two people from the City Council arrived and asked Hamparian for two cases, which he gave them. I was upset: the infant formula was intended for sick hospitalized children only. Later, trying not to sound as though I was giving Hamparian orders, I emphasized that the infant formula must not be allowed to leave the hospital. He nodded that he understood and said no more.

It was years before I came to appreciate his position, a difficult one many doctors were forced into. In the Soviet system, at least in Armenia, in order to get anything done for yourself personally, in your workplace or for your children's education, a network of friendships was built: I scratch your back and you scratch mine. These networks depended most often on family

relationships through blood and marriage. Other strong alle-
giances were forged through childhood friendships, or through
the camaraderie of membership in the Communist Party. You
could count on these people when you needed almost any kind
of help. Through this network you could guarantee food and
clothing for your family, a decent place to live, and other essen-
tials such as the speedy repair of a malfunctioning telephone,
university admission for your children, and now, medicine or
infant formula.

Many of the doctors handling the relief aid that was coming
for the earthquake region were being called on to pay back their
friends. The two people who came from the City Council might
have smoothed Hamparian's path to his position as a chief doctor,
or maybe they helped him get the land on which he had built his
new home. I never asked. There was no way for him to refuse
their request, of that I was sure.

There were 20,000 children living in Leninakan at the end of
1989. Hamparian's make-shift hospital was filled to capacity with
95 patients, of whom 24 were less than one year old. The most
pressing problems facing the doctors were providing proper
nutrition for sick babies and children, obtaining a clean water
supply, and acquiring disposable syringes, since most medicine
was given by injection. Most of the children were either dehydrated or sick with infectious diseases: pneumonia, bronchitis,
dysentery, salmonella infections and hepatitis. Hepatitis A and B
were endemic, and Soviet health regulations required patients
diagnosed with hepatitis to be hospitalized, unlike practice in
the West.

The doctors saw 60 to 80 young children daily in the emergency room. Over the past 10 months, according to Hamparian's
records, there had been 8,225 cases of trauma involving children
up to age 14: injuries from playing among the destroyed buildings, motor vehicle accidents caused by the large trucks hauling
debris out of the city (often driven by half-drunk Soviets), and
burns from the kerosene and gas stoves used to heat tents and

domics. The children with traumatic injuries were hospitalized in a building separate from those with contagious diseases.

Hamparian took Ida, Madeline, and me to the intensive care areas where Médecins Sans Frontières (MSF) nurses and a doctor were working with the Armenian staff. Nurse Marie Jean had been in Armenia for five months and Dr. Nivet, the pediatrician, had spent all of his vacation time in Armenia and had made three trips to Leninakan since the earthquake. Nivet told me that the doctors in the ICU were not getting enough support from Hamparian. Part of the job of the Chief Doctor was to go to the local health officials and demand a fair share of supplies coming into the city. Hamparian was unable to do this; the MSF team agreed that he was a good man but too tired and depressed to be effective.

Nivet explained why so many babies were dying from dysentery. A vicious cycle had developed: they developed diarrhea from contaminated water supplies, were admitted to the hospital, recovered, then returned home to the same conditions that caused it initially. The illness made many infants unable to digest the lactose in milk, so they developed diarrhea again and became dangerously dehydrated. Lactose-free formula was desperately needed. The soy formula I brought was already being used. Could we bring more? When? Later, in Boston, the Armenian Children's Milk Fund was formed to meet this need.

Marie Jean showed us around the intensive care unit. There were eight incubators and within each was an infant with a different medical problem. In the first was a four-month old with pneumonia in both lungs. The baby was laboring to breathe and was not expected to live. Oxygen could not be monitored, therefore none was given, because too much might cause nerve damage. The electrical equipment on one side of the unit was connected to outlets on the other side by laying wires across the middle of the floor. Two electric hot plates supplied heat. Fluids and medications were being infused intravenously, but without the benefit of pumps that would allow for their more accurate measurement. Due to the low ambient temperature, the nurses had to keep the infusing fluids warm by periodically cradling the hanging bags in their hands. Marie Jean told me what I already suspected. The babies were often fluid overloaded, resulting in cardiac failure and pulmonary edema (fluid-filled lungs). There were no cardiac monitors; the sterilizers were inadequate. We took some pictures after asking permission. The infants looked so sick and vulnerable. Ida and Madeline exchange glances with me. They too were weeping silently, using the lens of their cameras to hide their tears. The struggle of these infants for life ripped at our emotions. Ida and Madeline excused themselves and left.

Just as I too was about to leave, the infant with pneumonia stopped breathing. The French team quickly resuscitated and intubated the infant, then hooked him up to a new respirator, but there is not enough electric current to operate the respirator. The Armenian doctors started running from one room to the other, searching for other outlets, plugs, anything that might provide more current. Everyone was yelling at each other. It was of no avail. The infant was ventilated manually for a long time, but the oxygen was not sufficient and the pneumonia too far advanced. The child's heart stopped. The family, anxious and crying, anticipating the worst, was huddled in the hallway, just outside the intensive care area. The temperature in the hallway was below freezing. None of the doctors wanted to give the family the bad news. This 4-month-old infant had survived the earthquake in his mother's belly. His birth must have brought great joy amidst the death and destruction of the earthquake. The family's loss was unfathomable.

On this trip I made my first visit to the Samaritar Hospital as well. Gulnara was with me. The hospital was located at the opposite end of the city, in a sturdy-looking two-story building made of gray tufa stone that had been the Communist Party headquarters before the earthquake. It had not been damaged by the earthquake. A German humanitarian organization had undertaken its renovation now nearly complete. German could be heard being spoken by the workers who added to the usual commotion in the lobby made by patients' families coming and going. Elderly women were mopping the floors in a fruitless effort to keep the lobby free of the mud flowing in the streets outside. We found a room where a number of people who looked like they might be nurses and doctors were sitting at small desks; the men were smoking. We asked where we could find Dr. Ruben Khatchatrian, the chief doctor. I quickly added, "America-*Hye* em." (I am an American-Armenian.) A flurry of activity ensued, as they welcomed us in, took our coats, offered coffee, and had their chief paged on the hospital's radio system. Word quickly spread through the hospital that an *America-Hye* was visiting. Heads poked through the narrow door into the room where we waited. The questions I had come to expect started: Who are you? Where do you come from? Why have you come?

We started to chat freely after the Armenian coffee was served. They talked first of hope. One nurse said she had no hope and wanted to leave Armenia. No one said she was wrong. Another said she could never leave, even though she has little hope for the future. They asked more questions, now about America. Were Armenians in America happy? Were they comfortable? I explained that the newcomers from Soviet Armenia had a difficult time, especially if they did not speak English. Family life and community life were very different. There was no time to visit with friends and relatives. Children were not as close to their parents as they were in Armenia. My message: we have problems too.

Finally, the door opened wide and a large, imposing figure filled the doorway. In an Armenian dialect that I understood with great difficulty I heard, "Where are our guests from America?" All eyes were on Ruben. His hand was offered to me in friendship. He smiled. This was our first face-to-face meeting, but not the first time I had seen him. Last April a member of our team, Herminé Mahseredjian, had met Ruben while his polyclinic and hospital were still functioning under tents, before the Germans renovated the building we were now in. She had videotaped him talking about his hospital's needs and sent a copy to me in Boston. In response, with funds raised for earthquake relief, the Cambridge-Yerevan Sister City Association purchased a Life-Line Mobile Clinic for Leninakan. Prior to shipping overseas, the clinic was brought to Cambridge and packed tight with medical supplies and equipment. The Soviet government agreed to ship the clinic on a soviet freighter to Leningrad. From Leningrad it was to be driven to Armenia. I was sure we would never see the clinic again, but, at the time, there was no other choice.

I had written Ruben a letter about the mobile clinic, explaining that he was to be the recipient of it. When he realized who I was, a smile covered his broad face and he started to recite parts of the letter: ". . . the clinic is filled with equipment and supplies. Under no circumstances is it to be opened until my arrival. I will bring the keys . . ." I reached into my bag, brought out the keys, and handed them to him! We were all laughing. It was a wonderful moment that was thoroughly enjoyed; laughter was so rare in Leninakan in those days.

In the midst of our laughter, a nurse came in to get one of the doctors. A woman had been brought in with "status asthmaticus," a serious asthma attack resistant to therapy. Several nurses and a doctor left the room. I wanted to follow, but had not been invited. "How will the patient be treated? Can you monitor the oxygen level and the carbon dioxide levels in her blood?" I asked. The others in the room laughed: "That is something we only read about. There is no such thing in all of Armenia nor anywhere else in the Soviet Union," came the replies from different corners of the small room. "How do you deliver oxygen to a patient like this?" I continued probing. One of the doctors went out and returned holding what looked like an inflated rubber pillow. They explained that the pillow was filled with oxygen and the patient breathed it through a tube attached on one side. There was no way to meter the amount of oxygen the patient received. I wondered how I could manage under these conditions. Not well, I suspected.

The following week, when I returned, Ruben informed me that one of his doctor's had offered to have me stay at her home so that I would not have to travel back and forth to Yerevan each day. Given the problems of finding cars and drivers and the problems associated with the trip itself, I happily accepted the invitation.

⚜

There were five people in the family that offered to host me: the mother, whose husband was killed in the earthquake, her son and his wife, her daughter, who is a doctor, and the daughter's husband. Their apartment was damaged in the earthquake, but the building itself remained structurally sound. They patched the cracks, found glass for the windows, and repaired the plumbing. During the four months it took to get all of the work done, they lived in a garage. Now they have moved back into their apartment house, one of the few families in Leninakan that have a place to live.

Even in these conditions and hard times, this family opened its door to me. In Armenia, homes are remarkable in that there is always room for one more person, and then one more, whether it means a place at the dinner table or a bed in which to spend the night. All Armenian homes have a supply of *doshags*, thick mats of lamb's wool, something like a sleeping bag except that one sleeps on a *doshag*, not in it. These are usually laid out for the guest on a couch or a wooden bench used for other purposes during the day. Every home also has an unlimited supply of *vermags* (quilts of lambs wool like the ones my family had), large pillows, and bed linens. What more is needed? A place to sleep can always be provided within minutes. In the morning the bedding is picked up, piled in an inconspicuous place and covered, preferably with a thin oriental carpet. Oriental carpets cover the walls too, providing beauty for otherwise barren walls, as well as helping to keep a house warm during the winter months.

Everyone in this family went to work early in the morning except the daughter-in-law, who stayed home to do the cooking and serving of all meals, the cleaning, and the laundry. She waited up until late at night for her husband to come home from work to feed and bathe him. (Years later I learned that she left him, taking their young child with her, unwilling to be the family's caretaker any longer.)

The cost of taking in their guest was borne by the mother, and the work fell to their daughter-in-law. The family was exceedingly gracious to me during those difficult days, willing to be my host for as long and as often as needed. The daughter and her husband gave up their bedroom, the only one in the small apartment. The very best of what the family had to offer—the best bed, the best food, and the best drinks—were provided for me, despite the hardship it might be causing.

My father had written about the same customs in his family. "Many provisions were stored away just for guests," he recalled in his memoir, "particularly when the honey was taken out of the hives. The lightest honey, considered to be the best, was stored in a separate jar and kept for guests. It was put out only for them. Sugar, which was very scarce, was also kept for the same purpose." My father would not have been surprised by how I was treated in Leninakan.

On the first night I was in their home, in the midst of the destruction and desolation of this city, they managed to set a traditional Armenian table, albeit on a small coffee table in the living room. An oriental rug hung on one wall. On the other was a large photograph of their deceased father. The coffee table was set with the dishes and drinking glasses they managed to salvage from their apartment after the earthquake. Six places were set, each with a small plate, a glass, and utensils. (Large dinner plates, the type used in the West, are never used by Armenians. Instead, small plates, the size of salad dishes, are used for all courses and changed periodically throughout the meal.) The first course was already on the table and consisted of various salads made from the foods that have been preserved for the winter: beets with walnuts and garlic, various types of red peppers with onions and other spices, beans of various kinds and my favorite, small tender sweet eggplants stuffed with tomatoes, onion, and garlic. Bread was arranged at the corners of the table, which seemed not to be able to hold any more food or drink. Boiled potatoes, sweet and bright yellow, were served later with some meat. At the end of the meal, tea was served with *mouraba*, a word borrowed from Persian and Arabic that refers to preserved fruits; tonight it will be small cherries and raspberries. Apricots, the fruit for which Armenia is most famous and which gives the apricot its genus, *Prunus armeniaca*, had also been preserved, but were saved for another day. It was here that I ate soft sweet walnuts for the first time, delighting in their delicacy, without knowing what I was eating. The women pick the walnuts when they are still soft and green and prepare the preserve through a tedious process that takes several weeks.

Family and friends gathered around and before we started to eat, a toast of thanksgiving was offered for life and for friendship. People came, joined in the eating and drinking for a while, exchanged stories and then took leave, then there would be another knock on the door, from another friend, another relative. All were welcomed. The small table, which was set for 6, seated 8, then 10, then 12 without difficulty.

There were many such dinners over the years in Leninakan, in Yerevan, and later in Karabagh. At first I tried to refuse dinner invitations, knowing that people would be using up their preserves for the winter, or selling a precious possession in order to buy what was considered proper to host the American doctor. But I came to understand that to refuse was to insult, and to refuse would deny them a few hours during which they could forget about the difficulty of their lives. The hours spent preparing for a dinner, then sitting around the table eating and drinking, were hours during which the past would be remembered, and the future, for which they so hoped, would be toasted.

All through this first evening one of the women guests sat quietly off to one side of the table, her hands folded and eyes lowered. She appeared to be about thirty-five years of age. I wrote in my diary, *"She had the flat affect of someone clinically depressed, nei-*

ther laughing nor weeping with the rest of us. She gave no indication that she heard what was being said." After she left I learned that her husband, children, brothers, and sisters, mother and father all died in the earthquake. Her home destroyed as well, she lived with relatives, the ones who brought her, probably forcing her to come, tonight. Her days were spent at the graveside, they told me, mourning and contemplating suicide.

Armenians have rarely turned to suicide as a solution to a problem. It is not part of the national consciousness as it is in certain cultures of the Far East. However, the earthquake and the dissolution of the Soviet Union combined to create a feeling that the very framework of the society was crumbling. Men and women who themselves had survived the earthquake, but who lost all or most of their family, were homeless and without daily work to occupy them and to help them feel useful. Social institutions, themselves in chaos, no longer provided support to sustain people until the crisis passed. Those considering suicide as a way to stop their pain were ordinary folks who until the earthquake led ordinary lives with the ordinary problems and ordinary amounts of sadness and happiness. Now they were clinically depressed, not just sad. For many, suicide seemed to be the only solution. The number of suicides rose after the earthquake from one or two a year to one or two a week. Many leaped from a bridge in the center of Leninakan. Others took poison.

How could this woman cope with her kind of loss? How could she face each day? Perhaps the only thing that kept her sane was the fact that she was not alone with her kind of grief and still had a few relatives to hold on to. The family asked me to arrange for one of the psychotherapists in Leninakan to see her.

As the evening continued, the daughter in my host family started to talk about the earthquake too. Her mother tried to stop her, but she could not. It poured out of the daughter for an hour, as she described in detail every moment from the time the earth started to shake. She did not know how it happened that she was saved. She had been on the top floor of the hospital when the earthquake started. She immediately started to run down the stairs, aware that the building was collapsing behind her. In a state of hysteria by the time she reached the ground level, seeing her hospital completely destroyed as she looked back at it over her shoulder, she began running through the city streets with hundreds of other people looking for survivors. Her father was found beneath the rubble at his workplace several days later and buried. Only after he was buried could the family tend to their own need to find a place to live.

Those who survived the earthquake needed someone to whom they could tell their stories of what happened to them the day of the earthquake and its aftermath. In the years that followed, many people also needed to talk about how they endured the worst years of the Azeri-Turkish blockade, when there was no electricity and no heat for days at a time. They would repeat the same stories over and over again, in the way that the other survivors I knew told their stories. I understood this need, but eventually it became difficult for me to listen. Each story stayed with me, and left me with feelings of helplessness, sorrow, and inevitable guilt. Sometimes I would have to stop someone and say, "I know, I was here afterward, I know how much you suffered. I know how hard it is to live in the cold, without electricity, without water, without a home." But, did I?

❦

In the soviet system of health care, and probably in many other parts of the world where sanitation is a problem, maternity wards are kept entirely apart from other medical facilities by making them separate hospitals. Thus, every city has a maternity hospital where babies are born and where women's gynecologic problems are treated. Leninakan's Maternity Hospital was totally destroyed by the earthquake, taking the lives of patients, babies, doctors, and nurses and had been set up temporarily in a school building.

The driver Ruben had provided maneuvered skillfully through broken streets and around crumbled buildings to a side street well behind the main thoroughfares before he was able to find the hospital. The building itself, a dark stone two-story structure, did not meet the standards of a hospital in any country, but at least it was structurally sound. It was easily identified by the crowd surrounding it of expectant fathers, anxiously waiting for news about their wives and newborn infants. Men were not allowed inside the hospital.

We entered the hospital through the front entrance, passing among the unshaven men, thin and worn like their clothes. Everyone was smoking. It was very cold, but no one was wearing an overcoat. There were no hats or gloves to be seen either. Samuel, my driver, spoke with the old woman who was guarding the front door to the hospital. She finally agreed to let us in after she noted that I was a foreigner and showed us the way to the chief doctor's office. At the top of the staircase that led from the narrow corridor to a second floor, women in white and others in colorful smocks were staring down at us. We had already attracted attention by our discussion with the doorkeeper. White sheets were hanging from wires attached to the walls on the landing above us, making a private space in the midst of all these people. A woman carrying a baby went behind the sheets with a nurse. It was later explained that this is the area from which mothers with their new infants were discharged from the hospital.

We found the Chief's small office at the end of a dark corridor. It was big enough for only a desk and several chairs lined up against the wall. After a few minutes, the Chief appeared, harried and preoccupied. His welcome was short. He told me that he must go into surgery and that Dr. Lilit Boghosian, the second in command, would be with me shortly. He apologized; I told him it was unnecessary. I waited patiently in the small room alone. Samuel, my driver, left for other duties but promised to come back for me in a few hours.

Before long Dr. Lilit Boghosian, a woman who appeared to be in her late forties, also harried with fresh blood spotting her white coat, entered the room. She must attend to a few administrative matters first, she explained, and proceeded to ask the first person waiting beyond the door to come in. Others followed. Permission was requested for this or that; workers needed time off or had already taken time and needed to be excused; forms had to be filled out; her stamp and signature were required. She handled each mater decisively but thoughtfully; her authority was not questioned.

None of the people who came into the small office looked directly at me, but I knew that each was aware that someone from another country, another world, was there listening. Each would go home to their families with a full description of what I looked like, what I was wearing, and whatever else they gleaned from those few moments of indirect observation.

When the last petitioner left, Dr. Boghosian told the nurse outside the door that we were not to be disturbed unless there was an emergency. She locked the door and took her seat again. We sat face to face in the very small room. Her hand extended across the desk that separated us, she introduced herself. "I am Lilit Boghosian." "I am Carolann Najarian." The moment would not be forgotten by either of us. Our eyes met and searched out the other's, conveying questions we could never voice. "Are you a good doctor?" mine asked. "Do you care about your patients?" And hers seemed to wonder, "Why have you waited so long to come? Will you come again or will you just make promises and never return? *Can we trust you with our sorrow?*"

There was a silent pause as we studied each other, an instant when questions and answers were not needed, when one knows the special friendship about to be formed will last for many years. Lilit's eyes were tired, sad eyes. The dignity that comes with aging and the stress of the past months had not completely covered the beauty she must have had when she was younger. Her auburn hair was pulled back loosely into a bun. She was not wearing any makeup and years later she told me that she would never wear makeup again.

Her attention was totally directed toward me.

It is impossible to convey all that Lilit told me over the next hour or the emotion with which she spoke, her eyes filling with tears from time to time. She poured out the pain that was in her heart, the pain for the lost city of Leninakan, for the dead, and for the living. It was nearly one year since the earthquake, and nothing much had changed in Leninakan. Only the cemeteries were new, she said, where people go every day to mourn the dead, whose portraits are etched on large granite headstones.

Suddenly she changed the subject and started talking about concrete facts, pulling us both out of the emotional pit we were sinking into. The Maternity Hospital opened in this building on February 16, 1989. The hospital has received little help from the central government.

Since February there had been 2335 births, including 17 still-births, 21 sets of twins, and 125 premature births. There had been no maternal deaths at delivery because of new surgical and birthing techniques introduced by MSF doctors and nurses. In addition, they had brought new ideas about post-partum care and the babies were now given to their mothers shortly after birth. The soviet system kept mother and infant apart for up to ten days—no wonder so many women were unable to breastfeed their infants!

"Yesterday I went to visit one of our new mothers," Lilit continued. "She has nothing, absolutely nothing for her baby or for herself. She has no breast milk to feed her baby. Her husband cannot find work. I went and cried with her. Today we will find some milk for the baby and take it to her. Do you have any milk with you?" I had given it all to the Children's Hospital, I explained, but maybe they would give us some to take to this new mother. Later I remembered that the milk I gave to them was soy milk, to be used for sick babies only.

There was a knock on the door. A young pregnant woman has been brought in bleeding and Lilit was needed. Together we went upstairs to a fairly large room with three examining tables that looked like delivery tables. There were no curtains for privacy, and from a distance we could see the patient lying on one of the tables, waiting for Lilit to examine her.

The room was very cold. As she approached, Lilit started talking to her patient in reassuring tones, "Everything will be all right. Don't worry. This will not hurt. You will be all right." She used the term *janig* to address the patient. Translated, *jan* (pronounced like the name "john")means "dear" and *janig* means "little dear." It is an endearing term and does not carry the condescending nuance to which American women object when they are called "dear," particularly by a doctor. I held the patient's hand, wanting to be useful in some way. She dug in her nails, I hoped more out of fear than pain. She was a very young girl. The procedure was over quickly, the bleeding stopped. Lilit shouted orders to the nurses.

After Lilit washed, we made rounds. From the long corridor I could see into most of the patient rooms. The rooms were cold and small, the floors and walls shabby. In each of the rooms were four beds, two on each side, foot to head lined against the walls. One large wood-burning stove in the corridor was meant to provide heat for all the rooms. A few patients were huddled around it. Several nurses were sitting close by, their hands folded in their laps, hoping that some warmth from the stove would reach them too. Most of the nurses appeared to be old, a striking contrast to the young patients.

A few women were pacing the corridor, holding their big bellies, in the early stages of labor. They tried to smile through their grimaces. Periodically a cry came from the end of the hallway where three women were in the more active stages of labor. Their beds, like all of the others, had old metal springs covered by a thin vinyl mat. The patients' discomfort was obvious.

Each woman had to bring her own bed sheets and towels, as all of the patients in Leninakan would do for years to come. The hospital did not have facilities for doing laundry; nor did it have enough hot water and detergent. In this way, it was hoped, infections would be minimized. Relatives, including the expectant fathers we had seen waiting in the cold, mud-filled streets, were also barred from the hospital for the same reason.

The first patient we spoke with was named Kohar, an 18-year-old who had been admitted to the hospital for a fertility workup: her menstrual periods had stopped after the earthquake and no one had been able to determine why. Kohar had other problems as well. She been trapped under the rubble of her apartment house for several days before a rescue team found and dug her out. Pinned with her arms over her head, she suffered what is described to me now as nerve damage, swelling in her arms and wound infections. Kohar also lost most of her hearing.

"Look at my hands. I can hardly use them, but it is better to have these hands than no hands at all." Her speech was pressured, reflecting her anxiety, and loud, due to her deafness. Her hands were badly deformed from scarring and muscle contractions. She continued. Although she was only 18 she felt very old. She talked about her mother, who died in the earthquake, and how she herself had been under the rubble. She felt fortunate to be alive, to have her hands, and to have a supportive husband. Now she wanted to have a baby. The loss of her periods upset her more than the condition of her hands, the loss of her hearing, and even her mother's death. Kohar started to cry. Lilit tried to console her.

Kohar probably had the most common type of injury caused by the earthquake: a "crush injury," the destruction of muscles and nerves due to pressure placed on them. As the muscles are crushed under pressure, a process called rhabdomyolysis takes place and causes substances toxic to the kidney to be released. If the process goes on for too long, damage to the kidneys occurs, resulting in kidney failure. The damage may be permanent. The doctors wanted to amputate Kohar's arms, the removal of damaged muscle the only method they had for preventing the further release of toxic substances into the bloodstream and possible kidney failure. Kohar refused, but other victims did have limbs amputated as they were pulled out of the rubble, or shortly thereafter. Many were left with severe kidney damage and required dialysis nonetheless.

Kohar avoided both amputation and kidney failure. Like many earthquake victims she was sent to Moscow for treatment of her injuries. Along with other medicines she received antibiotics. No one knew which ones. I suspected that her deafness was related to the antibiotics she received and not to the earthquake itself. Over the years I saw many patients, including children, who experienced hearing loss, usually after receiving the antibiotic streptomycin. It was frequently used in the Soviet Union, and for some diseases, such as tuberculosis, is still an important drug.

We talked about physical therapy and a neurology consultation for Kohar. I was not sure what was available in Leninakan or in Yerevan; several teams had come from the United States—I promised to try to get information for her.

It was clear, however, that the only thing that really concerned Kohar was the problem of getting pregnant. Evaluating her loss of menstruation would be very difficult without hormonal testing, which was simply not available in Leninakan. Lilit told me later that many women were in Kohar's situation. For some, their menstrual cycles start up again with rest and reassurance. Kohar would probably be treated with hormones, maybe even some thyroid medication along with herbs and vitamins. It might just work!

In the next room was a 25-year-old woman who had just given birth. Minutes before the earthquake, this young mother of two had gone to the local store to buy yogurt her son had asked for. Leaving her two children in the apartment alone for what was to be a few minutes, she ran down the stairs of their apartment to the store. The two little children were crushed to death as they sat waiting for their mother to return. Tears streamed down her face, covering her newborn son, as she told me her story. Fortunately, she still had a husband—many other women lost everyone they loved to the earthquake—and tomorrow he will come to take her back to the boxcar they now call home. Lilit asked if there was anything we could do for her and offered her a bar of soap. The young mother refused: "We can manage," she said, too proud to accept the small gift.

We saw several other patients before returning to the office. Mentally exhausted, my emotions drained, I asked Lilit how she managed to hold up? "I'm sure you have personal problems," I said, "yet you must perform your medical duties, cope with the shortage of supplies, and still have the energy needed to provide support for grieving patients who have insurmountable problems. How do you do this day after day?"

Lilit looked up to me, her eyes moist with tears, and simply said, "*Meradz enk.*" ("We are dead.") Her tone was matter-of-fact, but its impact was not. Feeling helpless and inadequate myself, hoping that in some way I could lighten her burden, I hugged her. I could find no words of consolation in the face of such profound sadness. Nothing in my training or in my life's experiences had prepared me for this; she felt the same way, I suspect, unprepared for what she was being asked to do.

She added, "Tell everyone in America that I light a candle for your health and well-being every day. Don't forget us. You see how we are living."

Before parting we gathered on the front steps of the hospital for a photo and said our good-byes as if we had known each other for a lifetime. My promise to return, I know, was not believed. Why would anyone come back to this forsaken, sad place. It would have been impossible to explain to them.

The survivors of the earthquake needed immediate progress toward rebuilding their communities with adequate housing and places to work. When solutions were not put in place within the first six months, they were unable to resume normal lives. It fostered dependence on handouts and impeded the grieving process; large numbers of people became chronically depressed. The scars left by these difficult days are deep and perhaps will never heal completely.

In 1997, years after these sorrowful days had passed, Stella Grigorian, my friend from Houston, invited me to go with her to see a play in Yerevan, written and performed by Leninakan's theatrical company. It was billed as a comedy about the earthquake. Many people, convinced that they had misunderstood the billing, did not go, fearing the play would be too sad to bear. But there was no mistake: true to their tradition, the players from Leninakan had us laughing so hard we could not laugh any more! It was a tribute to the courage of that city's people— only they could find a way to deal with their anguish through humor.

Refugees from Sumgait living somewhere in the outskirts of Yerevan in a temporary "domic" shaped like a water tank. 1990.

CHAPTER 7

Survivors and Refugees

The year 1990 was a turbulent one for the Armenians of the Soviet Union. The Supreme Soviet's return of Karabagh to Azeri control aroused fears of wholesale pogroms in Karabagh. In response, Armenia not only declared that Karabagh and Armenia were one, but also incorporated Karabagh's budget into its own. The Azeris retaliated by threatening a holy war against Armenians living in Azerbaijan and called for all of them to be driven out. After Sumgait most of the 300,000 Armenians who lived in Baku had left, but 30,000 still lived in there. In January rampaging mobs slaughtered more than 60 Armenians forcing the remainder to flee, among them Gary Kasparov, the World Chess Champion whose mother was Armenian. By the end of 1990 nearly 400,000 refugees had poured into Armenia. (Within the next several years, the number of Azeri refugees in Azerbaijan would approach 250,000.)

The unarmed civilian populations of Shahumian and Getashen, Armenian districts once part of Karabagh that had been incorporated into Azerbaijan in 1921, were now under periodic attack by the Azeris. There were reports that Soviet troops had assisted them in forcing residents from their homes; this caused confusion and rage in Armenia over Moscow's role in these atrocities.

In Yerevan, despite the ongoing ban on public gatherings, Armenians continued to attend nightly rallies in the Opera Square. By April the number of people gathering in the square each night reached 100,000 and more. In August the Supreme Soviet of Azerbaijan declared that Karabagh, as an autonomous district, was dissolved.

The blockade was tightened; food shortages and power outages began to worsen. Nearly all of the Soviet Union's planned reconstruction projects in the earthquake zone came to a stop by year's end. The few projects that did continue were those undertaken by European countries, bringing every last nut and bolt with them.

The Soviet Union was in a downward spiral. Its days were numbered. Latvia, Lithuania, and Estonia were flexing their nationalistic muscles, and in Armenia, the Armenian National Movement was formally organized in opposition to the ruling Communist Party.

Few dared to think of what the future might hold

I had just returned from my third trip when the director of the UAF called wanting to know if I wanted to accompany the next UAF cargo flight to Armenia. It meant returning to Armenia barely six weeks after my last trip, leaving little time to recover and to work on getting supplies together, but I decided to go. George agreed. It was my second flight aboard a cargo plane, and the first of several aboard the UAF sponsored flights.

The time was January 1990. Barely one month had passed since the Supreme Soviet of Armenia and the National Council of Karabagh had declared their unification *(Miatsum!)*. Given the political climate and the developing tensions between Moscow and Yerevan, it was remarkable that the Soviet government continued to allow the UAF to make these monthly humanitarian flights and to allow foreign relief workers access to the region. We worried that if the situation in Armenia or in Karabagh worsened, the flights would be stopped and the visas we needed, now processed through Moscow, would not be issued.

The departure day and time of a UAF flight could not be announced until rights for landing in Yerevan were granted by Moscow. Obtaining these landing rights was a tedious time consuming process. Often the flight would be delayed for days until the landing rights were granted. It was difficult for people like myself, who were going on the flight, but most of all for the UAF and the air-cargo carrier. There were times when the aircraft was loaded and ready to go, then had to be unloaded because the landing rights were delayed, only to be loaded onto another plane a few days later when the approval came through. It was a logistics juggling game that tested stamina and nerves.

This time we were lucky. There were no delays, and our January 27 departure date held firm. On the 26th, George and I drove to Newark from Boston in a friend's van packed tight with additional cargo. Many people had worked for days making the last of hundreds of first aid and personal care kits for the freedom fighters in Karabagh, layettes for the new mothers in Leninakan, and repackaging thousands of sample medicines into compact containers. Already in the plane's cargo were three new Air-Shield Vickers incubators for newborns, oxygen hoods, and a conglomeration of all kinds of medical supplies that I had promised the doctors in Leninakan. The rest of the cargo contained tens of thousands of dollars worth of relief supplies from other Armenian diaspora humanitarian organizations, churches, and individuals.

The next day and night meshed into one. I slept in a seated position in the small cabin between the cargo and the cockpit, eating and talking with the crew and my fellow passenger, a photographer from an Armenian newspaper in California. We landed first in Geland, Greenland, in a ferocious storm with high winds and heavy snows. Amsterdam was next, where the plane took on enough fuel to reach Yerevan and return to Europe. Due to the blockade, airplane fuel was in short supply in Yerevan.

(Within the next year even passenger planes were forced to refuel in cities in the south of Russia before landing in Armenia.)

It was January 28, at about 10 p.m., when we landed in Yerevan. For two hours we waited in the cold aircraft for the faculty members of the Yerevan Poly-Technique Institute who were responsible for the cargo. Their organization, called *Veradznount*, (Renaissance), had worked out an agreement with the UAF to meet the planes, warehouse, and distribute the cargo. Unable to get information on the plane's arrival, their members had been back and forth from the city to the airport all day, literally watching the skies for signs of our aircraft.

While we waited, Russian soldiers and KGB agents boarded the plane to check our passports and visas. (Unlike the days right after the earthquake, visas were now required and were granted by the Soviet Embassy in Washington only if one had an invitation from a government agency, a school, or a humanitarian group in Armenia.) The aircraft was surrounded by soldiers carrying machine guns, and by customs officials, airport workers, and an assortment of men standing on the perimeter, their hands in their pockets, just watching. It was never quite clear as to who the bystanders were, but they were always there.

Then, in the dark, on the cold black tarmac, under the watchful eyes of the Veradznount members who had arrived, the cargo was unloaded into waiting trucks by hand, since the airport still did not have a hydraulic lift. The trucks were sealed by the customs officials, who would be at the warehouse in the morning to supervise the unloading into the warehouse. Before the actual distribution of the cargo could get under way, the customs officials would check nearly every box: the donors, the recipients if there was a special group named, and the contents against the manifest that came with the aircraft. There were hundreds of boxes and crates, and the customs people will take nearly two days to complete their work.

When it was clear that there were no problems on the tarmac, I felt free to leave. My real work would start tomorrow. Dickran, a representative from the Ministry of Health, had come to escort me to the Hotel Armenia, but first I had to go through immigration and customs. The other passenger on the flight was cleared through quickly and I expected to follow right behind him. The Russian immigration officer checked my visa and waved me through, but when Dickran went to pick up my luggage, the customs officials standing watch told him that I had to wait for Sergei, the head of customs at the airport. This was highly unusual and came as a big surprise to both of us. What was going on? I had three pieces of luggage; two were mine and the third I had brought for the sister of a friend. We waited for Sergei in the customs area.

There were two possible explanations for this: either Sergei had it in for me because I had not given him any "gifts" or because on one of our previous trips we brought out a suitcase that belonged to a known Armenian dissident who was planning to leave Armenia. (At the time I had been annoyed with George for agreeing to do this. I was sure that the KGB was watching his apartment and following his family. They would have seen the dissident's daughter deliver the suitcase to our hotel room.) When we left Armenia, no one questioned us about our luggage, but curiously, none of our luggage arrived with us in Boston. All three suitcases were "lost." George believed that the luggage was really lost, but I, who tend more toward believing in conspiracy theories, believed that the KGB had kept the luggage to thoroughly inspect it. Two weeks later we were notified that our suitcases were at Logan airport. Delighted that nothing was missing, I had the feeling that someone had gone through them. Fortunately, there was nothing in the dissident's suitcases but clothing.

I was positive that the harassment to which I was now subjected was directly related to this incident. Sergei, stocky and quite gruff, finally came down from his upstairs office where he was known to spend his time drinking cognac with friends. He started asking me questions about my luggage. Pointing to the two suitcases that were actually mine, he asked about the contents and then asked me to open them. I did. One of them was filled with bottles of medicine. "Why aren't these medicines with the rest of the cargo? Why are you carrying them separately?" I explained that I bring these to use for the patients I will see during my trip. "Put it with the rest of the cargo," he ordered me. I refused! He took the medicine out of my suitcase. We argued. Then he asked me what was in the third suitcase. I kicked myself for not having asked my friend what was in the suitcase. I guessed: "Clothing." "Is this suitcase yours too?" he asked still pointing to my friend's suitcase. I lied. He ordered me to open it. Luck was with me. It contained women's clothing and a few pairs of shoes. He looked disappointed and returned to the issue of the medicine.

By now we both had our backs up, and having gotten through the problem of the third suitcase, I had gained confidence. Furious, I started talking in a very loud voice. "You know who I am and what I do; is this any way to treat me at two o'clock in the morning?" I turned to Dickran, who was by now at a complete loss as to what to do. "Dickran," I ordered, "put all of my things back on the plane. I AM LEAVING and I AM NEVER COMING BACK!" Everyone stared at me, not sure whether to believe what I was saying. I repeated it with some minor variation, wondering how I would carry out my threat after all it had taken to get here from Boston. Dickran pleaded, "Don't say that Dr. Najarian, we need you, Armenia needs you. Please don't go." "Unless my medicines are put back in my luggage right now, I am leaving Armenia. That is final!" I was yelling half in Armenian and half in English, carried by the momentum of what I had started. The customs chief showed signs of backing down. "We're only doing our job, don't get so excited," and after a few more exchanges proceeded to tell his men to put everything back into my suitcases and then told Dickran that we were free to leave. Then he assured me of my welcome in Armenia and that he was really happy to see me. We made a few jokes; I said something about inviting him to Boston, but I was not sure if he could get through customs. He thought that was funny. I suppose the Chief had made his point and I had made mine. Later Dickran asked me if I really would have gone back with the cargo plane. "I don't know Dickran, I don't know."

⁕⁘⁕

My friend Gulnara had made a reservation for me at the Hotel Armenia. It was the best of the three available hotels in Yerevan and most people stayed there. The accommodations were what I would call class C. This was a hotel for the people, not to be confused with the Communist Party hierarchy; theirs met a much higher standard.

The fact was that the Hotel Armenia got to look good to those of us who stayed there often. There was a certain familiar charm to its worn out look that we learned not to mind. The women who cleaned our rooms and those who sat at the desk that was on each floor became our friends and looked after us. Their job must have included "watching" the guests' activities and reporting back to the hotel's KGB agent, but we did not mind. They welcomed us as old friends, excited that we were back, and very helpful in making our stay comfortable. I never felt alone when I stayed at the Hotel Armenia. There was always someone to talk to, a fellow relief worker, a visitor from another country, one of the housekeepers, or the floor clerk. The French relief workers liked to get together in their rooms late at night; I always felt welcome. I met many Armenians from the United States as well as from other countries, people I never would have had the opportunity to meet and special friendships were formed.

The Hotel Armenia was "home" on these early trips, until it became so overcrowded with relief workers, Soviet soldiers, and at one low point, prostitutes, that staying there became impossible. Construction workers from places like Yugoslavia, Uzbekistan, and Russia proper, in Armenia to help rebuild the earthquake zone (until the blockade forced them to leave) would come to Yerevan for their R&R (rest and relaxation). They would party all night, drinking and singing, making it difficult for the rest of us to sleep. We looked to the floor clerks for help, but there was little they could do. (Later Gulnara was able to obtain approval for me to stay at the Hrazdan, the hotel complex reserved for special guests of the government. When that was no longer available, friends put me up in their homes until 1996 when I purchased an apartment.)

Finally, sometime after 3 a.m. I arrived on my floor. The woman who was on duty woke up as I came off the elevator and, knowing each other from past stays, we greeted each other warmly with a hug and the traditional Armenian greeting, *"Pari yegar,"* to which I responded, *"Pari desank."* ("It is good that you came," and "It is good that we see each other," the translation losing some of its warmth.)

She then helped me to settle in. What else would I like? Could she make some tea or coffee? Would I like a bucket of hot water? There was no running water at this hour so she offered to heat some that was stored in a tub. I gladly accepted both. In the morning I hoped for a real shower, but there was no guarantee that there would be one then either.

In the days ahead, when there was no electricity or heat in the hotel, these housekeepers helped out by finding extra blankets and candles for guests who were not prepared for these conditions. (Congressman Joe Kennedy had that experience in 1993 when he went to Armenia during one of the coldest winters on record.) The housekeepers earned extra rubles by washing and ironing clothes for guests too. They did the wash by hand and hung it on lines in the back corridors. The clothing would be returned a few days later, perfectly washed, perfectly ironed, and neatly folded.

It was still 1990 and on January 29 I wrote in my journal that I managed a few hours of sleep and a hot shower in the morning, had breakfast including a bowl of steaming *herisah* (a porridge made of whole wheat grain and chicken pieces that are slowly cooked for hours and topped with butter) and coffee.

I bundled up in my Eddie Bauer thermal coat (the one I had bought for my first trip after the earthquake), put on two pairs of mittens and socks, fur lined boots, pulled the coat's hood snug over my head, and started on the long walk to the warehouse. The Hotel Armenia is on Lenin Square (renamed Republic Square after independence), which is not a square at all but a huge traffic circle with six streets fanning out of it. Grand tall buildings made of hand-cut tufa stone line the square, their straight facades appearing curved, following the line of the traffic circle. Several of the buildings house government ministries. One is the central post office and the center for making local and international calls, another is a national art museum that I have not yet been in, and the Hotel Armenia.

Opposite the hotel on the other side of the square are a series of large fountains that spray up from pools of water where children play on hot summer days. And on summer nights, when the fountains are lit and dance, synchronized to music, they are a favorite place for people to gather. To the right of the hotel's entrance, opposite the water fountains, Lenin's gigantic statue dominated the square. Lenin's statue was the only ugly statue in this city whose parks and boulevards are filled with magnificent sculptures of important Armenian writers, musicians, poets, and heroes: Toumanian, Sayat Nova, Abovian, and David of Sasun to name a few. Overlooking the entire city, perched on top of one of Yerevan's hillsides, is a monumental statue depicting Mother Armenia in a majestic stance about to replace her sword in its sheath, but in clear readiness to defend her flock.

It was a brisk twenty minute walk from the hotel to the Poly-Technique Institute where the warehouse was located. By the time I arrived, the trucks that had been loaded at the airport during the night were lined up one behind the other along the broad avenue in front of the Institute. Starting from the first truck, the Institute's students had formed a relay line that went through the front doors, into the marble lobby, down the steep staircase, and into the basement where the warehouse was located.

Two boys were in the first truck, hurling the boxes down in rapid succession to the first boys in the relay. Some of the boxes are obviously very heavy, but the boys managed, shrugging off offers of help from those who stood around watching. (A two-wheeler would have been of great help here, but there were none in Armenia.) Hour after hour, in the cold, the boys passed the boxes, moving the cargo piece by piece from the trucks into the warehouse. Sometimes a new boy would come along and replace one who needed a break. None of them wore gloves or hats. They worked hard, competing with each other, showing how strong they were and how much they could carry, like young boys might anywhere.

Downstairs in the warehouse area several customs officials had already started to check the boxes as they were brought in by the last boys on the relay. After last night's experience with Sergei, none of these officials seemed quite as intimidating to me as they had in the past, and rather than trying to avoid them, I chatted with one or the other of them from time to time. When they realized that I understood what the medications in the warehouse were for, and that I was a good source of information and medical advice, they started to ask a lot of questions, including questions about their own health problems.

When the cargo was unloaded, the series of connecting rooms that was the warehouse became a maze of boxes on top of cartons and crates containing everything from baby clothes to hospital gowns, sewing needles to intravenous catheters, aspirin to sophisticated antibiotics, Band-Aids to sterile dressings, shoes and artificial limbs, children's toys, and farming tools. The professors tried hard to keep a semblance of organization in the warehouse, placing food on one side, clothing on another, medical supplies in yet another section, and so on. But, once distribution started, it was impossible to maintain order.

Medical supplies and medicine had come from many countries and were labeled in their respective languages, some in sample boxes as well as in bulk packaging. A Western medical background was needed to be able to sort through it to determine which were useful and which should be disposed of. It was similar to the problems faced in Etchmiadzin on that first trip. Over the next weeks, as I sorted through these donations I tried to organize medicines into logical groupings and put together groups of supplies appropriate for Karabagh and border villages, especially the border with Azerbaijan. Specifically, I included products for wound care like betadine ointment, suturing material, and silvadine ointment, in addition to sterile gloves, syringes, gauze, tape, alcohol, and suturing material.

The warehouse was in the usual state of confusion on the first working day. Part of the cargo had been cleared by customs. Scores of doctors and hospital chiefs came searching for medical supplies for their hospitals. Others who had been notified to come to the warehouse to pick up their shipment came from schools, various institutes, the University, libraries, hospitals, and a myriad of governmental agencies. Still others came poking and pushing through the boxes, on one or another pretext, looking to see what there was in this new shipment. The warehouse area was so large it was hard to keep control. Once we tried locking the doors, letting in only people we knew and those who had been called to pick up their shipments. Complaints were voiced, accusing us of favoritism. The process of distributing the cargo was stressful.

In the summer the coolness of the basement where the warehouse was located was welcome, but in the winter, it was hard to bear the cold. By 4 p.m. everyone agreed it was impossible to continue working. The lights were turned off and the huge glass doors leading into the warehouse were pulled closed. Iron bars were placed through the handles of the doors and large chains secured them. A customs official hung his seal across the place where the two doors came together, a warning to anyone who might think of entering without permission.

The next morning, when I arrived at the warehouse at 10 a.m., the lobby of the Institute was empty, the corridors were dark, and the warehouse doors were still chained, the customs seal intact. The old watchman, who was checking around the downstairs hallways, told me that the professors would probably not open the warehouse because it was too cold. It was a relief to know that I did not have to spend the day in that cold place. Instead, I headed back to the hotel for more sleep and then to Gulnara's apartment where a hot cup of tea could be shared over some good conversation.

On January 30, 1990, I wrote in my journal: *Tonight at Gulnara's everyone eagerly awaited the evening news from Moscow, but when it came on there was not a single word about Armenia or Karabagh. Nothing! However, news has spread throughout the city that something bad was happening in the regions of Shahumian and Getashen (two regions northwest of Karabagh and east of Armenia that are entirely populated by Armenians). Helicopters have been bringing the inhabitants out of there, town by town, but for three days there have been no helicopters. We know that there is very little food in the region. Everyone is concerned about what this means. Why aren't there any helicopters bringing out the inhabitants of that region? No news is bad news.*

Yerevan has changed. It is not simply that it is cold and the middle of winter. The people here now seem as depressed as the people in the earthquake zone. Throughout Armenia schools are closed because there is no fuel for heat. There are fewer cars in the streets. It is difficult to find transportation to get anywhere. Although I have just arrived, I feel that time is running short already. There is so much to do but I will not be able to work efficiently. Too much time will be spent trying to find transportation and coping with communication problems."

On January 31 I wrote: *We continued sorting through the boxes and the supplies at the warehouse in the afternoon. Opening the boxes was like opening Christmas presents! Some of the doctors who came today had never seen packets of alcohol wipes before. Three physicians came from the First Children's Hospital. We gave them antibiotics but they refused to take vitamins that were in the warehouse because the expiration date had passed a few months before. Tomorrow I am going to Leninakan.*

⁂

In the two months since I was last in Leninakan not much had changed; I had not expected it to. It was becoming clear to everyone that conditions would not improve soon. Yet people still had hope that life would get better, if not this year, certainly next year, and if not next year, then the year after that. Perhaps this ability to be patient came from the constraints imposed by life in the Soviet Union.

There was a popular joke about waiting that gives a hint at the kinds of delays the Soviet people routinely endured. The joke is about a man who saves enough money over many years to buy a car. He orders the car, and some months later is called to the car bureau. The clerk informs him that in five years, on June 2 at 10 a.m., his car will be delivered. Distraught by the news, the man pleads with the clerk to change the day. The clerk asks why—to which the man replies, "Because I have my dentist's appointment that day!" Americans hardly chuckle at the exaggerated point made by the joke; it is too remote from anything we have experienced. Not so for the average Soviet citizen. Now, they were forced to wait for the barest of necessities, showing a remarkable propensity for patience.

My first stop in Leninakan was at the Second Children's Hospital to talk with Raffi Manjikian, a young psychologist from Boston who was working there. I have a surprise for him: mops and brooms. He had requested these for the hospital workers since, in Armenia, the only type available were short handled ones, back-breakers to use. (Years later, I discovered that these brooms made of straw by village women actually worked quite well and were not as difficult to use as we thought.)

After expressing his delight over the brooms, we got right into a conversation about conditions. Raffi told me that the children coming to the hospital were showing a high level of anxiety and depression. They talked about living "minute by minute." Apparently the children were quoting things they had heard from the adults, in particular from a speech made by the secretary of the Communist Party for this region. Death was constantly on their minds. If they made it through the week, they felt they would be lucky. There was also a growing fear among the children of being kidnapped by Turks and murdered. One child was telling everyone that he saw two men in black in the shed behind his house. The men tried to grab him, but he managed to escape. He has told this story to all of the children in his school; the story spread rapidly through the city.

Later I asked several people whether Turks could actually come across the border. Quite possible, was the answer. In fact, people in this city were sure that carloads of Turks came across the border, spoke and looked Armenian, and therefore could not be identified easily. Some people were sure that these marauding Turks killed people at random. Another rumor was that six Turks were actually discovered and arrested in a local restaurant, but that the authorities were keeping it quiet to prevent panic.

The people of this region were obviously feeling vulnerable. There were many Armenian refugees from Azerbaijan who had come here and were living in villages close to the Turkish border. The border with Turkey, just a few miles away, was guarded (and still is) by Soviet soldiers. More soldiers had been placed along the border and in the surrounding mountains to help keep the area secure.

Under enormous mental strain, people were looking for ways to cope with and find relief from their worries; the Armenian Church was not able to help everyone. Proselytizers from various religious sects and cults began to move into Armenia, Hari Krishnas, Jehovah's Witnesses, and those preaching transcendental meditation (TM). Large numbers of people started to attend their meetings—at least initially.

Raffi's impression about medicine was that some was still coming in from Russia but that the amount reaching Armenia had decreased. We speculated as to why. Was it that the Armenian government could not afford to buy the medicine? Was Russia withholding the medicine? Was it being pilfered on route to Armenia? All of Armenia had become dependent on relief shipments of medicines and medical supplies, not just in the earthquake zone. Even aspirin was becoming a hard commodity to find.

Doctors complained, he added, about the lack of disposable syringes. Every day, three hundred syringes were needed by this hospital and polyclinic alone. The number startled me. Unlike the West, nearly all medicine in the Soviet Union was given in the form of injections. Patients expected injections and did not believe that tablets were as effective. I brought what I thought was a one month supply of syringes, only to find out it would not even be enough for one week! More infant formula was needed for the many sick infants that were being admitted with dysentery.

The picture was clear: living conditions were getting worse. Water and electricity shortages were becoming more critical. The Children's Hospital had no water most days, resulting in poor sanitary conditions. Without electricity there was no heat in the hospital. The hospital's chief, Dr. Hamparian, had obtained two generators from French relief workers. These were now being installed in the intensive care area and in the surgical unit, but who would pay for the diesel required to run them?

We talked until midnight, sitting in a corner of Hamparian's home. The exchange was important for both of us. For Raffi, I was the first American he has seen in a month. He said it was a relief to be able to speak in English for a few hours, even though he could speak Armenian without any effort, unlike me. And Raffi gave me valuable information I had no other way of obtaining.

We talked too about Dr. Hamparian, with whom Raffi was staying. As Chief Doctor, Hamparian had full responsibility for every aspect of running the hospital, both clinical and non-clinical. He hired and fired all personnel from the doctors who ran the intensive care unit to the janitors. He was the one who decided if someone's pay would be docked for a day out of work, or whether someone else could take a day off. The patients' families brought their complaints to him too. He was responsible for keeping the hospital in good repair as well as providing an adequate supply of medicines and supplies. He also had to answer to the higher authorities for the quality of the care his doctors delivered.

By 1990, the Azeri-Turkish blockade and the beginning of the break-up of the Soviet Union had made running hospitals very difficult all over Armenia, but in places like Leninakan it was more difficult.

Again and again we asked the question: how could Dr. Hamparian pay attention to medical problems of the patients when so much of his time was consumed with providing water, heat, and electricity. To add to his problems, Hamparian was coping with his own grief over their death of his wife and daughter while trying to raise his two sons and carry on with their daily lives. My friend, Dr. Ruben Khatchatrian, was in the same predicament; he and his wife Louisa had lost their only children, two daughters and a grandchild in the earthquake. Raffi's presence was, we were sure, helping Hamparian. Khatchatrian, we knew, was trying to work himself to death. (In all the years I have known him, he has never touched any alcohol; he will tell you, "If I start, I will never stop.") Hamparian and Khatchatrian were not the only ones faced with this problem.

In the morning I went to see Lilit. She had not expected to see me back so soon. I explained that the UAF had made it possible. Her doctors were thrilled to receive the supplies and equipment they had asked for: infant incubators, oxygen hoods, oximeters, syringes, needles, and suturing material. I had layettes too, for the newborn, a project organized by two of our members and carried out by the women of various Armenian organizations.

Lilit asked me to distribute the layettes with her. I agreed, understanding her reluctance to handle "relief aid" herself. Together we went room by room, giving each of the new mothers, and those about to deliver, a layette. Tucked into some were letters written by the women who prepared them. Many of the new mothers wept when they found the letters, touched by the personal connection someone from America had made with them. The nurses hovered around us during the distribution. I knew what they were thinking: "We are poor too—we have needs—isn't there anything for us?" I was prepared: each would receive a bar of soap, in those days a very special gift.

After we finished, coffee was served. The nurses had prepared "the table," grateful for the soap. It was set for one person: one cup of coffee and one dish, some bread, some cheese. When I asked those standing around to join me, they refused. This is for you, I was told. The Armenian word for hospitality is *hiurasiratiun*, literally translated, "loving the guest." I could not refuse their offer.

Before I left Lilit asked me to do one more thing: examine one of the young obstetricians. He has a heart problem she told me, and is very sick. The young doctor had just finished with a delivery. His name was Gagik Altunian.

A tall, lanky young man with a musty appearance to his skin, sweating profusely, and still in his surgical scrubs, came in. He was breathing as if he had just run up several flights of stairs. Lilit introduced us and left the room. We chatted for a minute and after taking a brief history, I asked to examine him. He took his shirt off and through the thin wall of his chest his heart's beating could be seen, and when I placed my hand over it, the murmurs could be felt. My stethoscope did not add much to what I already knew: Gagik had had rheumatic fever as a child, a consequence of not receiving penicillin for a streptococcal infection. As a result, he now had a malfunctioning mitral heart valve and signs of heart failure.

What I did not understand was how he was managing to deliver babies in this condition. He tried to explain, "I have two small children and a wife—I have to work." Lilit came back in. I did not tell either of them my prognosis; in his present condition, Gagik had only six months to live. "Please," she pleaded, "help him." Gagik was embarrassed. I suggested that he use a diuretic to help alleviate some of his symptoms. He put his shirt on, sensing my gravity, and in a cavalier manner said, "Don't worry, I'll be all right. Nothing is going to happen to me," and left the room as he lit a cigarette. I tried to explain to Lilit the difficulties of finding a hospital that would provide free surgical care for an adult. But I would try.

Feeling overwhelmed by the responsibility she had put on me, I made my way to the Samaritar Hospital where Ruben and Armen were waiting for me. This was the city's medical center and where, as an internist, I felt most at home. It had taken several trips, bringing supplies, textbooks, medicines, talking with the doctors, listening to their medical problems and even to their personal problems, to gain their confidence. I was asked to make patient rounds with them. Finally, I could be trusted to see the real state of the medicine they are forced to practice, for lack of supplies and medicine, and for lack of up-to-date medical information and proper training. The younger doctors had many questions about how things were done in American hospitals and were eager to learn; the older doctors, understandably, were defensive and not interested.

I had been away from Yerevan for only two days but could sense an increase in tension within the city. The crisis with the Azeri's over Karabagh had raised the fear of new repression (like tightening the curfew already in place, increasing the presence of the military) on the part of the central government. No one knew what to expect. Gasoline was in very short supply. People waited in line for up to 10 hours to purchase 5 gallons. Few vehicles were in the streets. Every night on television the news broadcast included a report on the number of railroad cars that arrived safely in Armenia with grain and flour and on the number of cars that were vandalized while passing through other republics on their way to Armenia.

On the second of February I noted in my journal that Gulnara and I planned to find the center for refugees tomorrow if transportation could be found.

Thanks to Gulnara's ingenuity we had a car, a driver, and gasoline enough for the day. In between stops at various government agencies in our effort to locate the refugee center, our driver told us about his life. His sister and niece miraculously escaped from Sumgait at the time of the pogroms there. Relatives who lived in Leninakan took them in and there, at the time of the earthquake, they all perished. (They were not the only refugees who died in the earthquake, compounding the problem of determining how many people died in the quake because no one knew the number of refugees in the region.)

Our driver was working in Siberia as a laborer at the time because he could earn higher wages there and had also been promised an apartment upon his return to Armenia. At that time he had been on a waiting list for eight years; that was seven years ago. Now with the refugees coming into Armenia and the thousands of families made homeless by the earthquake, he knew he would never be given an apartment. His family, 12 people in all, were living in two rooms in a town on the outskirts of Yerevan. With the extra money he had earned in Siberia, he put a down payment on an apartment being built by a newly formed cooperative, a peculiar mixture of private and government ownership. He was afraid the builders would not complete the project and may have already absconded with his money. The story sounded too awful to be believable, but Gulnara assured me that it was most likely true.

We finally found the refugee center tucked behind a row of large buildings on a back street in a part of Yerevan I had not been to. People who looked like refugees, scruffy, unkempt and tired, were standing outside the storefront office. The office itself was a simple large room with a desk, a telephone, and a few old wooden chairs scattered around. Boxes of used clothes were piled up on one side and a large map of Armenia covered the wall. More people were inside, sitting or standing, looking distraught, as though waiting for something they knew would not happen. The frazzled man behind the desk was very busy on the telephone. He gave no indication of having seen us, or anyone else for that matter, but when he finished with his calls, nearly a half hour after our arrival, he looked directly at us, said his name was Garnik, and asked how he could be of help. Gulnara introduced us and asked about the refugees.

He explained that the major problem was the resettling of refugees in villages. The refugees are city people, do not speak much Armenian, and do not want to live in villages far from the cities, but there is no other housing available. All of the places in and close to Yerevan, hotel rooms, *pensions*, rest homes, and boarding schools are filled with people from the earthquake zone and with refugees who came in the earlier waves of exodus from Azerbaijan. Now, the refugees were met at the airport, given between 100 and 200 rubles, some clothing, and taken directly to a village. But many were refusing to go.

A refugee came in, interrupted Garnik, and gave the following account: he was driving a truck of supplies into one of the villages being resettled only to be turned back by *fedayeen* (freedom fighters) who were active in the area. They had taken over some houses that refugees were living in and forced the refugees out. Garnik shook his head in frustration.

One of the other refugees who was sitting on the side said that the houses the government is offering are ones the Azeris abandoned when fleeing Armenia. These houses, he added, were in a terrible state, dirty and foul-smelling. Another man added that when he flicked on the light in his house, the bed exploded. The

Azeri owner had wired a homemade bomb to the light switch before fleeing.

Garnik told us that there were 150,000 refugees in Armenia now; ten thousand had arrived in the past week. How could Armenia provide housing for all of these people? Garnik complained too about the clothing his group was receiving, pointing to the piles of boxes in the corner. These were leftovers—rags— and he showed me the dirty, torn clothing in the boxes. I had seen the good clothes being separated out in the warehouse, but I did not tell him that. His complaint was justified. Before leaving, Garnik invited us to a special meeting of refugees with members of the Karabagh Committee tonight. We told him we would try to be there.

It was 4 p.m. on Sunday afternoon when Gulnara and I found the old theater where the special meeting of refugees was being held. As we entered through the lobby we could see that the theater was jammed with people, with standing room only. Making our way through the crowd, we stood near the front rows, off to the side of the theater. Over the heads in front of us, we could see representatives from the Karabagh Committee and other officials from the government seated on the stage behind a long table. Garnik was there too with two empty seats next to him. To our great surprise, someone we did not know came down from the stage and made his way through the crowd in our direction. He opened a path through the people in front of us and stretched out his hand to us. Gulnara whispered, "Do you want to go? Those seats are for us!" Not sure of what to do, but not wanting to disappoint Garnik, I agreed.

Garnik interrupted the refugee who was speaking from the floor to introduce us. He told the gathering that the presence of a Westerner indicated that there was concern with the situation regarding the refugees. The meeting continued with the refugees voicing their complaints and describing their problems. Gulnara interpreted for me, since almost all speakers spoke in Russian. Several people complained that they were being discriminated against because they could not speak Armenian. One man said, "My wife and son speak only Russian, what are we to do? No one will speak to us." He was agitated, almost out of control. One woman said that her children were still in Baku. How could she get them out?

Others continued: Who will compensate us for the apartments vacated in Azerbaijan? Would we get work permits in Armenia? Many people were on pensions in Azerbaijan and have not received their pensions since they arrived in Armenia. Who is going to pay these? There was no special status for "internal" refugees in the Soviet Union. After all, how could a person be a refugee in their own country? A new law is needed.

The restrictive laws of the Soviet Union caused the problem. Movement of Soviet citizens was severely restricted. Under normal circumstances permission was needed to travel from city to city and sometimes proof of residence was needed to buy food in a local government shop (especially during hard times). The law needed to be changed so that hundreds of thousands of people living in a part of the Soviet Union where they were not legal residents could be accommodated. That was the problem these refugees were facing.

Many of the refugees were wearing fur coats and fur hats, a sign of the affluence they once enjoyed. Adjusting to their substandard living conditions was extremely difficult for them, most of whom were urban professionals or merchants. Khachik Stamboltzian, a much revered member of the Karabagh Committee at that time, who fell into disrepute later, spoke now: "Armenians are coming back to their homeland. We must try to overcome the difficulties. One year living in a village is not too much to ask for under these difficult circumstances. You must try to understand. Please consider going to a village now. Then, you can come to Yerevan, or Spitak, or Leninakan. The refugees who have gone to the villages have something, but those who stay here now have nothing. We need a good leader who will struggle against Moscow for your rights. You need courage."

Referring to the Catholicos, the Supreme Patriarch of the Armenian Apostolic Church, one woman yelled out, "Vasken I has given money to the refugees. Where is this money?" Khachik replied, "I don't know." Another man lamented that the Armenians in Yerevan were not accepting them. Another man stood and threw papers into the air, "These are the unanswered telegrams we have sent to the government. Gorbachev thinks that we are going back to Baku. He wants to force us back, that is why he is not creating a special status for refugees. Mr. Stamboltzian, please tell Gorbachev that I will never go back to Baku." A general roar of agreement rose up through the auditorium.

Garnik spoke next: "We are not here just for show. We must make some decisions. We must elect a committee of well known people." Then looking at me he said, "Our guest from the West can help us. Please tell us how this is done in the United States." To my surprise, all eyes turned toward me and I was, for a moment, not clear as to why. Gulnara whispered, "They want you to discuss how, in the United States, you would obtain a protocol for the special status of refugees." I hesitated, not at all sure how to answer, then took the easy way out. I ask her to tell the gathering that in the United States we have not had to cope with a similar problem, but I would be happy to see what I could find out on the subject. Garnik continued on another strain: "The government will never be able to feed you. If you go to the villages we will give you land for free. The land will feed you. I have sent 52 families to villages and they are doing well."

The crowd was becoming agitated. More people were speaking and were very angry. A journalist sitting next to me showed me three Communist Party cards with letters of resignation, "I have no need for these now. I have no land, no home, no money, and have had to flee to save my life. We have heard that Prime Minister Markaryantz has gone to see Gorbachev to ask 'when will you end the blockade.' Gorbachev said, 'It is not your day. Go out and work.'"

Then the journalist stood and announced he was tearing up his Communist Party card. Others came to the front of the room and did the same. Gulnara and I were now extremely uncomfortable. There must be government observers here: the KGB must be watching. Gulnara had a government job and could find herself in big trouble for being at this meeting. I asked her if she thought the KGB was here. "Yes, of course they are, but don't worry. As long as you don't say anything now we will be OK." I wondered if her assurances were made despite her own concern about the situation.

My journal does not have any notes as to how or why the meeting finished, but within a few minutes, it was clear that the meeting was over.

Garnik invited us to go with him to visit the town of Biureghavan, 18 kilometers outside Yerevan, a place where a city for refugees was started by a man referred to simply as Tartarian. Tartarian was the Chief of Gas in Armenia and a very wealthy but apparently benevolent man. He planned to have 1,200 families resettled in this area within the next year. Financing it initially himself, he had hopes of collecting seven million rubles for the remainder. To do all of this, Tartarian had started an organization called, "Repatriation."

Two hundred and fifty refugees had been settled so far. Each refugee received a temporary home in exchange for working on his permanent house and the overall building of the town. For starters, Tartarian provided a food store, a restaurant, a library, a medical post, a shoe repair shop and a clothing store. The surrounding fields would eventually be farmed, he hoped; he also had plans to build a crystal manufacturing factory, to be owned and operated by the refugees, a cinema, and a cultural center. The town was to be self-sufficient.

We visited several of the refugees in their temporary domics. In each the refugees point to their beds, their children's cribs, their TV sets, and told me that whatever they have, Tartarian has given them. They were very thankful to him. There was no running water yet and the electricity came on sporadically. But, they were hopeful for the future.

But Tartarian was never able to carry through on his plans. He was only 63 years old and had throat cancer and a bad heart. He died not long after our visit.

All this was happening while the Soviet Union was still intact and the Communist Party a very real part of people's lives.

⚜

My journal entries in early February show the crisis was worsening.

February 4, 1990. *George called Gulnara from Boston this morning at 4:30 a.m. He said that the next UAF plane has been canceled. The UAF is being denied landing rights for Yerevan. Could Carolann try to find out what is going on. I found Vahe Khatchadurian in his room, a few doors down from mine. (Vahe is directing the Armenian Relief Society's housing project in the earthquake zone) We discussed how to approach the problem. First we tried unsuccessfully to find the leaders of Veradznount. We went to the warehouse but it was locked. Next we went to see Bishop Karekin. The Bishop told us not to be too alarmed yet. Tomorrow he will try to find out from some of his friends in the government what is going on. There is nothing more we can do today. We have to wait.*

Tonight at Gulnara's house we saw Zori Balayan, the representative of Karabagh to the Soviet Parliament, on television interviewing a Russian army general about events transpiring in the regions of Getashen and Shahumian. Zori read a telegram that the people of Getashen have sent saying that they are being forced from their homes by Soviet soldiers. The General denied the allegations. There was also a report that four people have been kidnapped in the Shahumian region. People believe the telegram, not the General's denials.

Later that night we met in Vahe's room with a few of the Veradznount professors we had located. One of them said, "It is our end." This was the general attitude among most people I knew— one of great fear for what the future held. The cancellation of the UAF plane was interpreted as Moscow's support for the Azeri blockade of Armenia. Land routes were blockaded, now Moscow was showing that it could block air routes. The message was "Armenians beware!" A delegation had gone to Moscow to talk about Karabagh, the blockade, and Moscow's position. No one was hopeful; they felt betrayed.

Rumors were spreading through the city. One rumor was that the UAF plane was not coming simply because it was not ready to come. But another rumor was that the decision to stop the plane was the Armenian government's. Was it true? Or, did Moscow force Armenia to stop the plane? Moscow still rules its republics. There was no way to know exactly what is going on.

I tried to send a fax to George that morning asking that he speak with the UAF to send food if possible, if a cargo plane is allowed in: grains, canned sausage, hams, and other sources of protein, but not TUNA— no one here likes tuna!

February 5. *Despite our best attempts it is impossible to call the States. Gulnara tried using lines at the City Hall; the operators say the same thing over and over, "No lines to the United States." Matthew Der Manuelian offered use of the Armenian Assembly's satellite dish. The dish has been moved to Bishop Karekin's offices located on a hill without any tall buildings around it. Together we went to see the Bishop, but when we arrived there was no electricity and despite everyone's best efforts, their generator could not provide enough power to operate the satellite.*

News today that the talks being held in Riga, Latvia, regarding the status of Karabagh have broken off. This is indeed bad news. Rumor is spreading now that four people have been burned alive in Getashen.

Everyone I speak with is worried that some kind of action will be taken to provoke Armenians into an aggressive act that can then be used as an excuse to take repressive measures against Armenia and Karabagh.

February 6. *I worked in the warehouse today hoping that the drudgery of the work will give me some emotional relief from the mounting tension over the UAF plane. At midday I walked around the city with Isabelle, the French dialysis nurse who has been working here for several months. We chatted about absolutely nothing. What a relief for both of us.*

This afternoon we went back to the Bishop's. He successfully got a call through to George over the regular telephone lines! It was so good to hear George's voice. I told him that we do not have any reliable information to pass on and gave him a quick version of the various rumors circulating. Our recommendation is that the UAF send a telegram to the Armenian government saying, "PLANES ARE READY. WE DO NOT HAVE LANDING RIGHTS," followed by the contents of cargo.

The confusion persisted for a few more days and then, without any clear explanation, landing rights were forwarded from Moscow for the next plane and on February 12 the UAF plane arrived! That is how it is here. One never knows how or why things happen or don't happen. Everyone is relieved that the crisis has been resolved, but no one is happy about the situation. There is a new level of anxiety in the atmosphere. No one knows what is going on.

Our relief activities started because of the earthquake, but the needs of Karabagh were more and more on our minds.

A friend from the States, Lucik, had a cousin who was the chief doctor of one of the regional hospitals in Karabagh. His name was Jora. She had word through her relatives that he had absolutely nothing with which to treat his patients. She had given me his name and telephone number before I left the States. If possible, she had asked, try to get supplies to him. The opportunity presented itself while I was in Leninakan, early in February. It was when the Cambridge-Yerevan Sister City Association's mobile clinic finally arrived in Leninakan, four months after it had left Cambridge. Unfortunately, the fuel tanks and the generator had been stolen, I was told, on the wharf in Leningrad. In addition, someone had broken the locks and had gotten into the clinic itself, pilfering the medical supplies. Fortunately, not too much was missing.

The key that I had presented to Ruben at our first meeting was therefore not needed. It was a thrill to see this enormous clinic in the Health Ministry's parking lot, the words we had carefully decided on, in red letters, "A gift to the people of Leninakan from the people of the city of Cambridge. . . ." Ruben and I entered the dark inside of the clinic together to examine the boxes that had been packed that warm summer day in Cambridge, one on top of the other into the vehicle. We were in the middle of this formidable task, trying to decide what should go where, etc. when he asked, "Don't you want to send some of this to Karabagh?" I was astonished and delighted. A doctor in charge of a large medical hospital with enormous needs was offering to send his supplies to Karabagh. I asked him how?

Later that day he introduced me to three men who were flying into Karabagh from Leninakan regularly via helicopter. One of the men had a big hat, the other a big mustache, and the third a big mustache and a beard. They were unforgettable characters. Together we went back to the mobile clinic so that they could see how much in supplies we would be sending with them and arranged to make the transfer the next day at noon.

My journal notes that day was February 9, 1990, a day none of us can ever forget. It was freezing cold, the ground was covered with snow and ice, and a fierce wind was blowing in our faces. I sorted the boxes in the clinic while the men packed the truck. There was no way to escape the bitter cold, but we worked until they had enough supplies for two flights. When we were finished my toes were like blocks of ice, nearly frostbitten. In my journal I listed what we sent that day: antibiotics, gauze sponges, tens of thousands of syringes and needles of different sizes, catheters, dressings, several back braces, and even some shoes and clothing that we had stuffed into the mobile clinic before we locked the doors.

Then the men made a tempting offer: come to Karabagh with us. But I had promised George that I would not go to Karabagh—at least, not yet. Jora made the overland trip to Yerevan from Chanaghgee in June when I was again in Armenia, just to say "Thank you." He had been greatly touched by the receipt of the supplies in boxes with his name on them that came from the United States all the way to Chanaghgee in Karabagh. (Unfortunately, years later, Jora's son along with two friends wandered into a restricted zone between Karabagh and Azerbaijan. They were intercepted by Azeris. The two friends were found by Armenian border guards, dead; Jora's son was taken prisoner and is still in captivity.)

One of my goals on this trip was to find an easy, consistently reliable way to send supplies to Karabagh, directly from Yerevan. (Unfortunately, the men from Leninakan did not work out of Yerevan.) A reliable contact with whom I could establish a working relationship was needed, just one person who could be trusted. Day after day people came to the warehouse saying that they were taking supplies to Karabagh, but there was no way of knowing who they were or how reliable they were. I asked a young Armenian-American, Robert Krikorian, who was living in Armenia, if he had any suggestions. He was volunteering at the warehouse between classes at Yerevan State University where he was studying Armenian. Robert would also disappear for long periods of time without saying where he had gone. We suspected that he was with a company of freedom fighters in Karabagh; we were right.

He wrote down a name and telephone number in the back of my journal. "This is the number of the man you want to know. He is one of the best contacts you could have for working in Karabagh. You can rely on him fully. If he can't get through, no one can. His name is Gourgen Melikian, he is a professor at the University and, by the way," he added with a smile, "he has a big mustache." I thanked him for the recommendation and wondered why he had made the point about the mustache.

One morning before going to the warehouse I dialed the number. It was my luck that the telephones were working and that Gourgen was home. After explaining who I was, and how I got his name, we made an appointment to meet at the warehouse later in the day. He arrived more than two hours late. It was not a good way to start off our relationship and had it not been for the unequivocal recommendation my friend had given him, I would have dismissed the possibility of working with him even before taking the time to say "Hello."

I was on top of one of the many piles of boxes that filled the warehouse when I noticed a man standing at the entrance, between the big glass doors, calmly surveying the activity in the warehouse. He stood with his hands in the pockets of his raincoat, the collar still turned up for protection against the cold wind. He wore a golfer's cap, though I am sure he has never been on a golf course. Even at a distance it was impressive. Now I understood why my friend had noted the mustache. I remember thinking that Gourgen looked like a character out of a John leCarré mystery novel appearing through the fog on a deserted wharf.

When he approached I could see that he had a kind, warm expression and that his eyes were compassionate. My anger was dispelled. Up close he looked more like William Saroyan, for whom he has been mistaken more than once, rather than a leCarré character. He made no apologies for being late, and using the formal form of the Armenian language, without any extraneous conversation, he simply asked as he did on all subsequent meetings, "What do you have for Karabagh?" Then he would add before I could answer, "They have nothing. Everything is needed. Please give as much as you can." I would explain each time that most of the supplies we had brought were for the earthquake zone and that I was obliged to send them there, but some of the supplies were specifically for Karabagh.

Gourgen was not happy with my explanations, but he did not argue. A few days later he returned with a truck and we loaded the boxes of medical supplies for Karabagh, each with the contents listed on the outside. After the truck was loaded, he asked one more time, "And what else do you have for Karabagh?" It was hard to refuse, knowing how great the need was in Karabagh. I went back into the warehouse and filled another box. Then he disappeared until the next time. We had found our route to Karabagh! It would be years before I would learn how a professor of Persian studies got involved in smuggling supplies into Karabagh.

On February 15 the then Executive Director of the United Armenian Fund, Mike Mahdesian, and an Armenian woman from England, Frieda Jordan, returned to Leninakan with me. I wanted as many people as possible to see firsthand what conditions were like in the hospitals; telling them about it wasn't the same.

Our first stop was at the intensive care unit at Hamparian's hospital. All of the incubators, lined up on both sides of the square room, had babies in them. The doctor in charge told us that there was a big increase in the number of infants and young children with pneumonia and bronchitis. The weather was very cold and the domics that they lived in were not heated sufficiently. We made our way through the cold corridors to the hospital's wards. Here too, every bed was filled with sick children, their mothers standing close by, there to prepare meals and perform much of the care that nurses in the West would normally do. Seeing these primitive conditions for the first time, my guests were visibly shaken.

Frieda and Mike had brought candy and soap to distribute to the children. Word spread rapidly through the hospital that soap and candy were being distributed. People ran from all over, possibly even from the streets, gathering and pushing in on us, in the large ward-like room where Mike and Frieda had started the distribution. Using the sternest voice I had, I ordered everyone out of the room except for the patients and families assigned to this room. I gave assurances that there was enough candy and soap for everyone. *Please*, don't be afraid—everyone will receive theirs in turn. Calm was restored and we were able to proceed. We talked later about how great their needs were that a bar of candy and of soap could generate so much excitement.

Our next stop was the Maternity Hospital. Lilit told us about a 43-year-old woman whose 22-year-old son died in the earthquake and who had just given birth again. The woman had a potentially serious heart condition called aortic stenosis and was warned against becoming pregnant, especially given her age. Moments before our arrival, she had delivered a boy. Both mother and baby appeared to be well. The baby was named after her dead son.

Lilit gave Frieda a short tour of the hospital and then we distributed soap to everyone, including all of the nurses and other workers. This time, the process went smoothly.

Before returning to Yerevan we found where my friend's sister, Rosa, was living, the one for whom I had brought the extra suitcase. Rosa's son and his wife lived with her in the center of the city, in the ruins of a building. The steel frame of the building was still erect, twisted and exposed, the outer walls lying in piles of rock here and there. Using scraps of metal and wood Rosa and her son had enclosed an area under the first floor of the building somehow securing a tiny space in which to live. A piece of wood with crudely made hinges covered the front entrance. Inside, a partition divided the space. On one side, a cabinet retrieved from a destroyed building and a hot plate defined the kitchen, and on the other side, mattresses created a place for them to sleep. Somehow they were living here.

Our arrival was unexpected. Rosa was grieving for four friends who had died in a motor vehicle accident the previous week, including a newly engaged couple. She was distraught. Her mood changed when I walked in with Frieda and Mike. After introductions, she insisted on making coffee and serving us *mandarins*. "My dream," she said, "is that Armenia will once again grow fruit and flowers and all will be beautiful again." We tried unsuccessfully to refuse the coffee and the fruit saying that we could not stay long. I promised to come for a longer visit with George, who was expected to arrive in Armenia next week. She brightened up. "You and George must stay here with us!" "Rosa, please don't count on it." Then I asked futilely, "Where will we sleep?"

"On my head if necessary, we'll make room!" She added, "What gift can I give to you. I'll cut out my heart and give it to you. *Mehrnem kez!*" (I'll die for you.) Her black eyes flashed as she spoke and her face radiated passion as she hugged and kissed me! I wondered how long she could carry on with such hope for the future?

❦

One day the doorman at the Hotel Armenia pulled me aside to ask a favor in private. First he inquired as to whether I had any pills that he could take for his diabetes. I tried to explain that pills for his diabetes should be taken only under a doctor's supervision. In Armenia it was common practice for people to take medicine for diabetes and hypertension, even antibiotics for infections, without a doctor's prescription, which was not needed for their purchase. People regularly passed medication around to each other—if it worked for me, it might work for you. As drugs became more expensive and often impossible to find, these practices increased.

I hoped that the doorman did not think my response was just an excuse to not provide him with the medication. The issue was not resolved when he asked another favor: his son, a *fedayee* had been wounded in skirmishes in the mountains—would I examine him? Definitely yes! I asked him to have his son come to my room in the evening.

After 10 p.m. that night the wounded *fedayee* came accompanied by a few of his friends, *fedayeen* also. The young man told me that four months ago he sustained a bullet shot to his right leg. Then two months ago he fell and since then had pain in both knees when he walked. Pain was his only complaint—he had no redness or swelling. Doctors at the Orthopedic Hospital had told him he needed surgery but he refused it. It would mean that he could not return to the mountains for a long time.

I examined his legs. Except for pain that he experienced when I put his knees in a fully flexed (bent) position, the exam was normal. I explained that he had probably injured some tendons or a ligament. It might heal with rest—but there was no way I could know for sure. Continuing to walk on mountain terrain would worsen his condition. I advised rest, the use of an ACE bandage for support, heat, and the use of aspirin or ibuprofen. I would see him back in a week.

Before leaving, he asked me if I would come to the Physio-Therapy Hospital to see some of his friends who were hospitalized there. I was free the next day and arranged to meet him in the morning.

It was my first visit to this hospital in the center of Yerevan, where many earthquake victims as well as injured *fedayeen* were hospitalized. The doorman's son took me to see several of his friends and a 17-year-old boy injured in the earthquake. The boy had been trapped under the rubble of his house, in the city of Nalband, the epicenter of the December 7 earthquake. He suffered a spinal injury resulting in paralysis from the waist down. His right foot had been amputated during one of his ten operations, and a large open wound over his right hip appeared infected. His mother had not left his side since the earthquake, caring for his every need, cooking his meals, cleaning his bed, and washing his body. Every day, his father went into the streets and marketplaces looking for the bandages, medicines, and other medical supplies that the doctors had prescribed. In addition to all of these problems, since their home was more than one hour away by car they lived with relatives in Yerevan. The boy had had several unsuccessful operations in Moscow. (How did they get him there, I wondered, without a wheelchair or special transport?)

His parents hoped that I would say, "Your son will be cured in America. The doctors there will make him walk again." Unfortunately, this was the expectation that most people had about America; in America everything was possible. Trying to convince them otherwise was difficult. Sometimes they thought we simply did not want to help.

After examining the young boy who could not feel anything in his lifeless legs, I could only offer some suggestions for the care of his infected wound and strengthening his arm muscles. I doubted that he would ever get the use of his legs back, but knew that his parents were not ready to hear that—maybe there would be a miracle. The family continued to have hope and I had no right to destroy that. After all, I had nothing else to offer them.

⚜

On February 24 George arrived in Yerevan to spend the last ten days of my trip with me. His arrival was not only eagerly awaited by me, but by our friends too, even the women who worked on my floor at the Hotel Armenia. George had a kind of energy about him that made everyone feel good; his arrival lifted people's spirits, even if for only a few days. The pretzels and bananas we knew he would bring would also cheer us up!

That night at Gulnara's house we watched the nightly news again. Moscow reported that the Leningrad National Front was threatening to kill Armenians and Jews on the 25th of this month, tomorrow. Gulnara was clearly concerned. She told us that only one flight had come from Moscow today, instead of the usual three or four. No one knew why. Was there a connection between the number of flights and tonight's news report? Is the news report true?

February 25. *There were no reports of killings in Leningrad today. Everyone was relieved.*

March 1. *At 8 a.m. today we were awakened by helicopters flying low over the city. George counted at least 25 of them from the balcony of our hotel room as they passed overhead. Later we learned that they were headed to Getashen and Shahumian. The villagers have been forced out and are fleeing into the woods. There are reports that tanks came in and bulldozed the villages. (Whose tanks? Russians?) Many people are said to have died.*

There was only one flight a day going to Moscow and it is impossible to know when it would actually depart. We heard that people were waiting at the airport for 24 to 36 hours with hopes of getting on the flight, only to be turned away from the boarding gate. Fights were breaking out over who will get on the plane. We heard that the same thing was happening in Moscow with the incoming flights to Armenia. Traveling between Moscow and Yerevan was a problem we would face many times in the years ahead, but this time we were spared. The UAF had a flight scheduled to arrive on March 4, and gave us permission to return to the States aboard it.

A few days before our planned departure, Anahid Tevosian, a self-taught psychologist working with refugees, took George and me to see a group who had arrived from Baku in January. They were living in a school building in Avan, outside of Yerevan. Three women were sitting on the front steps of the desolate structure. One of them was knitting with colorful yarn. Anahid knew them and explained why we had come. One of the women told Anahid that a boy known to her, who had witnessed his father's murder in Baku, had been taken to the hospital a few days ago. Anahid was distressed by the news. Which hospital? They did not know.

The three women followed behind us as we went through the building knocking on doors and looking for people with whom we could speak. We found them sitting in their small rooms, fitted with a bed or two, a small electric cook plate, a few pots and pans, and whatever other worldly belonging they had. We heard from them firsthand what had happened during those awful days in Baku.

I wrote the following about one woman's account in my journal: *She attempted to reach the train station where Russian soldiers were getting Armenians out of the city, but her group was surrounded by "Turks," referring to the Azeris. They asked to see their documents. "They started to beat me, then asked me for my money and belongings.*

I gave them whatever I had. They threw it all in a fire they had made, and then one of the Turks threw me in too, yelling at me, 'You are Armenian. I will cut you into pieces with a knife.' I was terrified, but I knew that if I could just get to the train station, I might be saved. I had on a heavy fur coat that did not burn, and I managed to get out of the fire thanks to another Azeri standing close by who helped me. But others died there. We saw them chop a man to death and throw his body parts on the fire. Later the Russians put us on boats leaving the city. Three people died on the boat because they had been so badly beaten."

And so the stories went. We left small gifts and some money with each family. There was nothing more we could do. Back in the hotel when George and I wept over what we had heard, we kept saying to each other, "It was as if we were sitting with Mama and Papa—your father—my grandmother. It is the same thing all over again."

March 4, our last day, was difficult. The phone in our room did not stop ringing and people came by all day. It was a panorama of Armenian life—city officials, doctors, scientists, activists, ordinary citizens, Armenian students, Armenian-American students, relief workers, and people who were ill.

Most had requests of some kind. Someone asked us to take a package back to the States, but we had learned from our past experience to ask about the contents. It turned out to be an antique Armenian carpet that was illegal to take from the country: the answer was, "No." Others brought videos and photos, but we had to refuse those too since they might be considered politically sensitive and be confiscated at the airport.

Stella, our friend from Houston, who was in Armenia supervising the building of a rehabilitation center in Leninakan, came to talk about another project: the proposal by Watertown, Massachusetts, to become a sister city with *Djrashen*, which means "water-town." (She also gave us her telephone number in Houston and asked that we call her husband, "Please tell him that you have actually seen me and I really am OK!"

A group of young people who worked for Armenian television came to discuss a nonprofit organization they have set up and outlined the help they needed. Could we find a group in the States that might help them?

The head of the Foreign Relations Department in the Ministry of Health, Dr. Sevak Avakian, with whom we worked closely over those first years, came to introduce doctors who had set up an organization called *Noyan Tapan* (Noah's Ark). Under its umbrella they had a sports training program for disabled children called *Pyunik* (Phoenix). The video they brought demonstrated how they were teaching amputees to ski and swim. They needed special skis and poles, ski clothes, hats, and mittens. Could we help?

Gourgen came too. He had a list of medical supplies needed in Karabagh: scalpels and other types of surgical instruments, more first aid kits (don't forget matches), and antibiotics. I asked him to write in my journal the names of the villages in Karabagh that he was helping: using Armenian letters he wrote *Matchkalashen, Hér-Hér, and Sos*. Next to it in English, I wrote his parting words: "*If we lose Karabagh, we lose Armenia.*"

A man we had never seen had been sitting at the desk with the floor clerk all day and through the evening. We wondered if he was KGB?

At 3:30 a.m. Gulnara and her husband, Samuel, arrived to take us to the airport. The plane was loaded and ready for us. Our luggage, the customs officer informed us, did not need to be checked! The Russian immigration officers stamped our passports and we were free to board the aircraft.

Just as the door to the main cabin was about to be closed, the hatch leading to the cargo area opened and Raffi Hovannisian, a lawyer from California working for the Armenian Assembly, poked his head in to say good-bye to us. His mustache appeared first and then his big smile. What a nice surprise! Jokingly we asked, "Who else is back there?" In a scene reminiscent of the little car in the circus, one-by-one, our friends started poking their heads through the hatch: Vahe, who worked with Raffi; Robert from the warehouse; and several of the professors. Each squeezed his head through the hatch, kissed us, and wished us a safe journey. They were at the airport to receive the cargo that this plane had brought—the cycle, unloading, loading, customs checks, and distribution to start all over again.

Our trip home was uneventful. During a one-hour stopover in Stockholm, we placed a call to the United States. After six weeks in Armenia, it was a shock to be able to make a telephone call without any difficulty. The man placing our call asked where we had come from. Armenia? For some reason he placed the call for free.

Back up in the air the pilot pointed out the great icebergs and the vast ice shelves north of Greenland as we passed over the glaciers of the northeast, the vast barren lands of ice. I looked out of the cockpit window and let my mind retreat into the nothingness. I let it rest for a while, trying not to think about anything. Nothing at all.

But only for a while. There will be a lot to do as soon as we arrive home. I had to write an article for the Armenian newspapers, give some interviews, a talk in Boston for the community, raise money for the work of the Armenian Health Alliance, and collect medicines and medical supplies. There were the promises I made to people in Armenia that had to be fulfilled, especially to Gagik Altunian, who needed surgery. I could not forget Gagik. Nor could I forget Gourgen's parting words: "If we lose Karabagh, we lose Armenia."

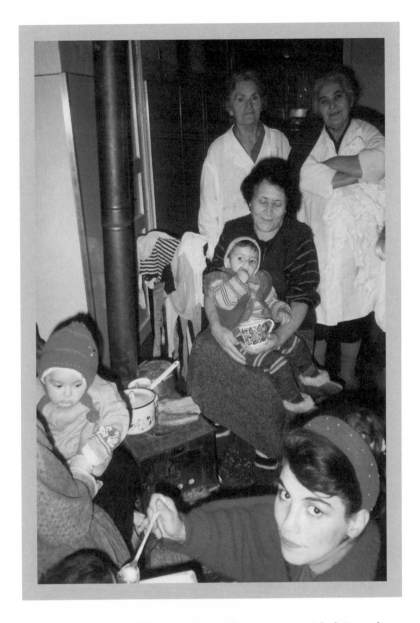

Pediatric patients huddled around wood-burning stove with their mothers or grandmothers. Pediatric Infectious Disease Hospital, Yerevan, 1991.

CHAPTER 8

Independence 1991

In 1991 events in Armenia as
well as in the rest of the Soviet
Union were unfolding at a
pace that we of the West, with our stable democracies, rarely
experience. Moves and countermoves kept the people and the
leadership in a constant state of uncertainty about what was coming next. The dramatic metamorphosis the Soviet Union was
undergoing held center stage, as one by one, the 15 republics
voted for independence. In a stunning series of moves, an end
was brought to their union.

On September 21, 1991, Armenians voted nearly unanimously
for independence, despite the economic consequences separation from the Soviet Union would bring. Already faced with a
long list of problems imposed by the earthquake, the blockade,
and the fighting in Karabagh, independence meant cutting the
economic and political ties that had sustained it for 70 years
before new ones could be formed.

In the midst of this turmoil, the Azeris tightened their grip
around Karabagh by turning the Lachin Corridor into a military
zone, effectively closing the only road from Armenia. And the
city of Shushi, high up on the mountains overlooking
Stepanakert, became one of their launching pads for Grad missile
attacks on Stepanakert. The conflict escalated. The Azeri offensives were met by bands of freedom fighters, *fedayeen*, loosely

organized into militia units that would eventually be merged to form a regular army.

Few Armenians were optimistic about anything during these years, least of all the success of Karabagh's struggle for independence. Men were dying and the ground was giving way.

After independence was declared and the Soviet Union ceased to exist, many cities and regions were renamed. For example, in Russia, *Lenin*grad was renamed St. Petersburg; in Armenia, *Leni*nakan, once known as Alexandropol, now reverted to one of its former Armenian names, Gyumri. Nagorno-Karabagh adopted its ancient Armenian name of *Artsakh* though the former name continues in use internationally.

I arrived in Yerevan on October 25, the day AT&T inaugurated its direct telephone lines to Armenia. The capital seemed almost upbeat in the aftermath of the vote for independence. It was as if a small giant had just discovered his strength, after waking from a long sleep, moving one leg and then the other, next stretching his arms, now standing, looking around, and discovering that he was free. Just a few days before my arrival, nearly 100 percent of the eligible voters had taken part in Armenia's first free presidential elections. Levon Ter-Petrossian won by an overwhelming majority, receiving nearly 95 percent of the votes.

The days were warm and the leaves were still full on the trees. Yerevan's streets bustled with people and traffic. That week gasoline could be found and purchased at reasonable prices, and although food was not plentiful, there seemed to be an adequate supply. The nightly news continued to report the number of freight trains getting through to Armenia. The numbers were not high.

In Yerevan the new American University of Armenia (AUA) had opened it doors with Dr. Mihran Aghbabian of California, a known educator, engineer, and humanitarian in his own right, as its first president. The university was funded by USAID and the

Armenian General Benevolent Union, one of the oldest Armenian diasporan organizations.

In Ashotsk the 12 million dollar hospital built by the Caritas Christi of Italy under the Pope's direct orders was ready to admit its first patients, and in Gyumri, formerly Leninakan, several European countries had undertaken the construction of outpatient clinics and a children's hospital. Dr. Hamparian had showed me the land in the center of the city on which the Austrians proposed to build a pediatric hospital. It was the site of a multistory apartment house complex that had been completely destroyed by the earthquake. After the rubble was removed, survivors had brought their small domics there and lined them up one next to the other. The day Hamparian showed me the site, children ran all around the small temporary homes, hiding behind the sheets and towels that had been hung out to dry on the clotheslines that flanked each domic, playing games about earthquakes and war. The chosen site was excellent. "But look," he said, his face lean and his eyes sadder than when I last saw him, "there is no place for these people to go. Over one hundred families are living here. Where can I tell them to take their domics? How can I force them to leave? It is a terrible problem." Today, when I passed the site, there were no domics and the clotheslines were gone, replaced by huge machinery preparing the ground for the new hospital's foundation. I was happy to see that the hospital was finally going to be built, but what had happened to the domics and the families—I did not ask.

At the Samaritar Hospital a small dialysis unit had been established through the efforts of the Ministry of Health. It meant that Gyumri's dialysis patients would not have to travel to Yerevan for their treatment three times a week, a terrible burden for patients and their families. When I visited the unit located next to Armen's intensive care department, I was appalled by the conditions, but awestruck by the ingenuity and dedication of the doctors and nurses who kept the unit operational. There were no ready-made dialysis solutions; the team had to mix these by hand, often using salts that were impure. The dialysis machines needed constant repair not only because they were old, but because the electrical current would surge, then go off and come back on again, playing havoc with the fragile equipment (not to mention the patients). The patients suffered quietly, happy to be alive and grateful that they did not have to make the trip to Yerevan.

A few months later arrangements were made to have the electricity turned on at midnight for several hours so that the dialysis could continue without interruption. The patients would come at about 11:30 p.m. with their needles, alcohol, and bandages in hand, having made their way through the dark streets of Gyumri, into the dark halls of the hospital and up to the second floor where they would receive their lifesaving treatment. The nurses, who had been in the unit for several hours preparing the patients' beds and working with the doctors to mix the necessary solutions, would greet patients when they arrived, document their weight, then escort them to beds spread with clean white sheets, next to dialysis machines. As the midnight hour approached, quiet fell over the unit. Everyone was in place, the only movement that of the flickering flame of a candle, back and forth, reflecting off the eyes peering toward it from all around the room. It was what I imagine a movie set to be like in the moments before a director yells, "Lights, camera, action!"

This was no movie, though, and the director was the invisible man who pulled the switches at the power station, controlling the flow of current as it came through the grids. He decided who would get electricity and who would not, and he held the fate of these patients in his hands. Until the light actually filled the room, there was always a nagging uncertainty: would tonight be different? Would he fail to provide the electricity? What if he had no electricity to give? If so, how could the dialysis schedule be adjusted to fit these patients in with the others who would be coming for their turn tomorrow night?

When the electricity did come on, everyone burst into action; not a second could be wasted. The needles were placed into the patients' arms, and the hum of the dialysis machines took over under the watchful eyes of the staff, who hoped that there would be no breakdowns and that they had mixed the solutions properly. It was a scene that would be repeated night after night and year after year.

Changes had taken place at the Maternity Hospital as well. It had moved to a newly constructed single-story building, with larger rooms and wide corridors and finished with tile that would be easier to keep clean. When I arrived, Gagik Altunian was just coming out of the operating room behind Lilit. They greeted me with the usual bear hugs and kisses. Gagik's color had vastly improved since his surgery last year. We sat in Lilit's office and rehashed the events that had saved his life, savoring every minute of the remarkable story:

After I had returned to Boston, I had been unable to find a hospital willing to underwrite the cost of the surgery Gagik needed and had, in fact, given up on being able to help him. One day, while sitting in my office, I got a telephone call from an orthopedic surgeon, Harry Sirounian, in Portland, Oregon. Harry and I had never met, but right after the earthquake we had spoken by phone several times. He was one of the few Armenian doctors who had gone to Armenia with a surgical team after the earthquake. Now he was calling to ask my advice about how to help an Armenian pediatrician, who had relocated to Portland from Armenia, find a residency program. During the course of our conversation I remember saying to him, "Harry, at least this woman has her health. I have a doctor in Leninakan..." and proceeded to tell him about Gagik, adding at the end, "I think he has less than six months to live."

To my total amazement, Harry said, "I have a friend out here who might do the surgery. His name is Hrair Hovaguimian. He is a cardiac surgeon who works with Dr. Starr." "You mean THE Dr. Starr as in the Starr-Edwards heart valve?" I asked, not able to believe what I was hearing. "Yes," he said and promised to call back in a few days after talking with Hrair. When he called back he gave me a list of telephone numbers for Hrair, including his pager number. Hrair was waiting to hear from me he said. I reached Hrair at home late that same night. I described Gagik's case to him, his clinical picture and my assessment. Hrair told me that they would be happy to do the case and that the hospital will cover the expenses. He added that he was hoping to go to Armenia as well to become involved with cardiac surgery there.

As quickly as I could, I prepared an official invitation for Gagik to come to the United States for medical treatment, and sent it, accompanied by an airline ticket, with a friend who was going to Armenia. As soon as Gagik received the invitation, he called me from Gyumri. Very excited and yelling over the static-filled lines, he wanted to know if it was really true. He had looked for Portland on a map of the United States. Was it above Boston? I tried to explain that he had found the wrong Portland—he seemed disappointed that he would be so far from us. Then he told me that he would go immediately to the Ministry of Health to start the process for obtaining an exit visa. I implored him to stop smoking just before we were disconnected.

The next time I saw Gagik was when George and I picked him up at New York's Kennedy airport. His skin color was more sallow now and each breath was labored, but he still denied any discomfort just as he had in Gyumri. We drove him to our home in Boston for a few days of rest before putting him on a flight to Portland.

On May 9, 1991, the day of Gagik's surgery, I nervously paced the floor of our home in Boston. What had I done? Why? What if he does die? What would I say to his wife? How could I forgive myself? I would forever be responsible for Gagik's two sons I promised myself. After the surgery, Hrair confessed that he had had his own dark thoughts. He chided himself for accepting a patient he had never seen from a doctor he had never met. What if there were complications during the surgery and Gagik died? Hrair knew that Gagik had a young wife and two young sons; he would have to go to Armenia to find them. Gagik, after all, had traveled over 10,000 miles for this operation, putting his fate in the hands of a surgeon he did not know without asking any questions.

"My insides shook as I made the incision opening his chest, the responsibility I felt was so great." As soon as Hrair saw the diseased valve, however, he knew that we had all done the right thing. The valve was badly thickened and calcified, barely moving under the changing pressures of the heart. The nonfunctioning valve allowed blood to flow in the wrong direction and pool in the chambers on the left side of the heart. No wonder Gagik could not even walk across a room without becoming severely short of breath. Gagik's condition, he told me, was worse than the examinations had led him to believe. Without surgery, he would have died within three months, not the six that I had estimated.

Thanks to Hrair's expertise, modern surgical technique, and Gagik's youthful resilience, he was back in Gyumri after one month, and soon back to work.

Gagik wanted me to listen to his heart. A stethoscope was not needed. Just placing my ear against his chest enabled me to hear the opening and closing of the artificial valve Hrair had inserted. I asked if the noise bothered him. He laughed at the thought. "This is the kind of noise that could never bother anyone. Sometimes my wife lies awake next to me, just listening to it." Gagik told me something else that was interesting. He had become so used to his breathlessness and lack of energy that only now, when he looked back, did he realize how sick he had been.

The pleasant fall days, the euphoria over independence, the feeling that things were changing, all dampened the impact of the continued Azeri attacks on Armenia's borders. People seemed hopeful that conditions would improve, though no one really knew how or why. If AT&T had come to Armenia, how bad could things be?

In Yerevan, I stayed with Stepan Zakarian and his wife, Gariné. Stepan was a professor at the Poly-Technique Institute where the Veradznount warehouse was located and would often come down to see me when I worked there. When they invited me to stay with them, I accepted without hesitation. Their apartment was large and comfortable; having me as a guest, I thought, would not be an imposition.

One morning, during the second week after my arrival, I got up at around 8 a.m. and went into the kitchen expecting to find Gariné and Stepan having coffee with their son Rubic. They were all there, but there was no coffee. Instead they were huddled over their gas stove, opening and closing the jets. Stepan looked up at me as I walked in on them and gave me the bad news. "I think the gas supply has been cut off." Gariné went to the sink and opened the faucet, "Look, there is no water either." I already knew that there was no electricity since the light in the bathroom did not come on a few minutes ago when I turned the switch.

We stood in the cold kitchen looking at each other, not quite believing that there was no gas, no water, and no electricity. We were sure the problem was temporary—or were we? The radio—a single station line connected in most of Armenia's homes, not requiring electricity to operate—was on, but there was no news about the gas supply.

Armenia was dependent on natural gas for most of its energy needs. Without it, buildings could not be heated, factories would shut down, electricity could not be produced, water could not be pumped, and the large bakeries that supplied the nation's bread would have to reduce their production. There were no alternative sources of energy. The kerosene heaters and wood-burning stoves that would become necessities within a few months for heating homes were not yet widely available.

In Yerevan major problems were occurring with the water supply because the underground infrastructure had deteriorated so much. The problems would now be made worse because of the cuts in the supply of electricity caused by the blockade. Electricity was needed to run the pumping stations. When these pumps were run intermittently, damage occurred to their mechanisms and the changing water pressures caused breaks in the underground water system. The combination of breaks and changing pressures also contributed to occasional problems with sewerage mingling with the clean water system.

In most areas tap water ran for only a few hours a day. Sometimes there was not enough pressure to get water to the second or third floor of apartment buildings; and many families who lived on the higher floors routinely had to go to the first floor for water. Year after year they carried pails of water up twelve and thirteen flights while their elevators sat paralyzed for lack of electricity. I learned that one can live without electricity, but not without water.

This time the disruption of all utilities lasted four days. Stepan and Gariné started to make preparations for what was coming. Stepan found and installed a wood-burning stove in the kitchen, and Gariné stockpiled food for the winter. Their days, like that of everyone else we knew, were consumed with finding basic necessities they needed to live. It meant networking with friends and family to learn where to go for a particular food item, to figure out who sold the best candles, to decide who could wait in the long lines that formed for all necessary purchases.

No matter how many layers of clothing I wore, the damp cold penetrated my bones and I came down with the flu-like illness making its rounds through the population. On the fifth day the gas, the electricity, and the water came back on. Gariné lit the oven, leaving the door open so that the kitchen could warm up and we were able to take hot baths again. But no one had any illusions about what lay ahead. Independence was not going to be easy. Over Stepan's and Garine's strenuous objections, I knew it was time to move to the Hotel Armenia. Life was getting too difficult.

Over the next two weeks I traveled to the earthquake zone several times. The mood had darkened. People in the earthquake zone had been living in hope that each new year would bring some improvement in their living conditions, that they might slowly begin to rebuild their lives and their communities. The worsening energy crisis caused by the blockade of natural gas had weakened that hope and unmasked their anxiety. If Yerevan, the "mother city," the ancient capital, the cultural and academic center of Armenia's life, could be plunged into darkness and cold, what hope could there be for those in the earthquake zone?

The government tried to maintain the supply of electricity to hospitals, but there were times when there was no electricity to give. Both in the earthquake zone and in Yerevan, people who lived close to hospitals learned how to tap into the hospital's power lines by pulling what were called "left lines" from the hospital's electric supply line to their domic. Chief doctors spent considerable time pulling down these illegal lines, which usually reappeared the next morning. Some collected a tariff for the "left line," while others gave up the struggle. It was hard to deny energy to the poor families living in cold domics who could not afford wood or kerosene and might otherwise freeze to death. Over the years, many men were electrocuted while working on these wires that often carried currents that exceeded 240 volts.

At the Samaritar Hospital I met with Dr. Armen Pirouzyan, the head of the intensive care unit, who had caught my eye on my first visit: young and intent, he had said little, but listened closely while everyone else scrambled to make comments and ask questions. Since that time, two years ago, we had developed a close relationship. Armen was eager to learn and remembered everything he read. At our first meeting he told me, "We have no current medical literature, journals or textbooks. We need information on how to treat the patients we are seeing and about the medicines being brought here from the West." I asked, "If I bring English textbooks and journals, will you be able to read them?" He assured me that they would; the doctors in his department were learning to read English. I brought books and journals and Armen learned English!

Now he told me that the number of heart attack and stroke patients he was admitting to his unit had increased by 50 percent and that alcoholism and suicides were on the rise as well. Armen and the chief of the dialysis unit were very concerned about the effect of the decreasing supply of energy on their hospital over the winter. Patients would not come unless they were very ill.

Some hospitals had generators to provide light and heat for their surgical and intensive care units, but this was too costly for Armen's group. Would the government pay for the diesel fuel to run a generator 24 hours a day? Would diesel fuel be available?

At the Maternity Hospital, Lilit and the chief doctor asked if I would purchase a small generator for the operating room. Unlike the situation in Armen's unit, they would not have to run the generator more than an hour or two a day. Although the city officials had promised not to turn their electricity off, it had already gone off several times while they were performing surgery; with a gasoline generator they could have emergency lighting within half a minute of a power outage. Small generators cost about $600 and could be purchased locally. I agreed to help, and before I left Armenia, they had purchased and installed it.

In Yerevan, Dr. Ara Asoian, chief of the Pediatric Infectious Diseases Hospital, had already installed wood-burning stoves in several of the patient care areas. He was able to bring wood in from mountainous regions, but he needed a gas-driven saw. Manually cutting the wood, as his workers were doing, was too difficult and time consuming. Could I send him one? He did not allow his staff or the patient's families to use the *pleetas*, Russian for small hot plates made of electric coils, used for cooking and warming a room. "It takes too much energy." He would lecture, as he went around turning off unnecessary lights left on around the hospital. "We do not have energy to waste."

Regarding infectious diseases, Ara confirmed that what I had heard in Gyumri was true for the entire republic: the rates of dysentery, tuberculosis, hepatitis, and even polio were increasing. Botulism was also on the rise. Every week several families were brought to his hospital sick with the disease contracted by eating improperly bottled food. Other diseases that I had only read about—brucellosis, yersiniosis, salmonella meningitis—were now occurring; he had several cases of each in the hospital. (These diseases were on the rise as a result of the breakdown in livestock inspection and unsanitary food handling due to the shortages of water and electricity.)

Ara asked if I could help him procure medical glucose for preparing intravenous infusions. The hospital had its own equipment to make the solutions, but since the break-up of the Soviet Union it had no way of obtaining glucose.

On a subsequent visit Ara showed me a number of very young children who were suffering from protein-calorie malnutrition. He explained how the condition developed. First a baby or young child got diarrhea. Following local folk medicine practice, some mothers gave the child only rice water, often for weeks at a time. The child, without any nutrient reserves, would become even sicker and develop the characteristic swollen body and skin sores.

The first of these young children, very sick on admission, had died. As more and more were brought to his hospital, Ara and his staff began to learn how to slowly hydrate and refeed them. Ara wanted to know if we could find intravenous albumin for him for the worst cases. I promised to try.

By the time I left Armenia, electricity outages were occurring daily—in fact, it was more usual not to have electricity than to have it. Most families lived in one room of their apartment—usually the kitchen—where their wood-burning stove or kerosene heater could provide at least a few hours of heat. Wood and kerosene were expensive, and therefore most people could not afford to burn them for more than a few hours each day. Those who were poor, disabled, or elderly, living on fixed pensions or alone, could not afford to at all.

Winter was in full swing. Would people survive? Leaving was getting harder and harder, but I knew that staying on would be of no help to anyone and would serve no purpose. There was work to do in Boston. I had also gone back into clinical practice, and so I now had commitments to patients that I had to keep. It was one way of drawing limits on how much time I could spend in Armenia. It worked, but only for a while!

· PART III ·

CHANGING THE COURSE
1992-1994

Map showing our journey from Armenia to Karabagh, 1992.

Stepanakert is seen from the road to Shushi.
Karabagh, May 1992.

CHAPTER 9

Smiles Amid the Rubble

By the beginning of 1992 the blockade of Armenia by Azerbaijan and Turkey had so hampered daily existence that the term "living conditions" was a grim joke more than a description. A report by the United States Department of Public Health Centers for Disease Control (CDC) later confirmed what I had heard from doctors in Gyumri and Yerevan: the incidence of infectious diseases like measles, viral hepatitis, tuberculosis, and diarrheal illnesses had increased dramatically. The report noted, "As of December 1992, no fuel oil had been received in Armenia for three months, and the fuel supply for the power system was adequate for only eight days. The shortage of fuel also prevents distribution of commodities and cooking. Power blackouts of 12 hours or more per day throughout the country have reduced availability of running water and, by compromising sanitation, increased the risk of certain infectious diseases (e.g., hepatitis A, enterovirus, giardiasis, and shigellosis). These conditions also may result in adverse health effects related to nutritional deficiencies, cold exposure, inadequate vaccination levels, and inadequate drinking water supplies."

Many international relief organizations and foreign governments sent humanitarian aid, but it was not enough to prevent people from starving to death and dying of cold. Armenia faced tough decisions and, seeing no other way out of its energy crisis, announced plans to reopen its nuclear power plant: Medzamor. Unfortunately, the plant was in such a state of disrepair that it would take two years before it could help alleviate the energy crisis. (Ironically, Turkey vehemently objected to the reopening of the nuclear power plant.)

Grain and flour supplies reached critically low levels; often reserves were enough for only one or two days of the country's needs. In order to avoid panic, the government rationed bread, the main staple of the Armenian diet. Lines formed outside the bread stores starting at 3 a.m. even in the winter, just so people could be sure of getting their small daily ration.

It seemed cruel to me that in the midst of this hardship, the World Bank required Armenia to triple and quadruple the price of bread, even the rationed bread. I could never understand how a move that caused such hardship for so many people could make Armenia financially sound and improve the country's economic picture.

Gasoline and heating fuel, as the CDC report noted, were not available. Even government offices were cold, and meetings were held with everyone wearing overcoats. Student's fingers froze as they tried to take notes and write exams, so the schools were forced to close down during the winter's coldest months, causing major disruption in the education of Armenia's younger generation. Factories had long since been closed down, incomes and self-esteem lost. The gears of the country were grinding to a halt.

The exodus of teachers, artists, writers, and doctors, as well as skilled and unskilled workers, quickened in pace. Some left with no plans ever to return, others intended to find work and send money home, still hoping the future would brighten.

In May 1992 the first good news in a long time came from the frontlines in Karabagh: Shushi and the Lachin Corridor were captured by Armenian forces, bringing to a temporary halt the missile attacks on Stepanakert and breaking the Azeri blockade of Karabagh. The overland route to Karabagh was opened by the taking of the Lachin Corridor. It meant that the connection between Armenia and Karabagh was reestablished, although the two countries remained blockaded by their neighbors.

I had been wanting to go to Karabagh for years. It had become the symbol of survival for the Armenian nation, and the spirit of the Armenians of Karabagh had dazzled us all. They were facing another genocide—ethnic-cleansing if you will—and the refugees I had seen in Moscow and in Yerevan were closely associated in my mind with those who survived 1915, especially those of my family from Shek Hadji and Arapkir. I was extremely impatient to go. On my next trip to Armenia, at the end of May 1992, the opportunity presented itself, and I grabbed it. The head of the new Karabagh Committee, the official representative of the government of Karabagh, was going there by helicopter, and I was invited to join him.

My journal: May 29, 1992

Promptly at 10 a.m. Gourgen picked me up at the Hotel Armenia and we drove to Yerevan's municipal airport. The other passengers headed for Karabagh had already begun to assemble around the helicopter at the far end of the airfield.

Our pilot, a tall, confident, handsome young man with a rifle at his side, is busy with preparations for the flight. I am told Raffi has been in many battles, including the fight for Shushi. A machine gun is on board, and the other two crew members also have rifles slung over their shoulders. These are precautionary measures, I am told; they do not expect to draw sniper fire in the area over which we will fly.

I am the only passenger making the trip for the first time. It is, however, everyone's first trip to Karabagh after the victories at Shushi and Lachin. There is great excitement and anticipation among all of us as the helicopter lifts off. It moves through the narrow canyons and the green mountains of eastern Armenia, so different from the barren brown mountains of the north. We pass over one village after another, some clustered closely together, some isolated and remote. From the helicopter the mountains look like huge waves, the villages hugging their slopes like rafts riding their crests. From above it is a beautiful scene, the difficulties of village life obscured by the distance.

Our helicopter follows the path of a narrow road we see winding through the mountains below us. We will take this road many times in the years ahead; it is the only one from Armenia to Karabagh. We fly over a region called Yeghegnadzor and then onto Sisian, high on a mountain plateau. The open fields and pastures, green with spring grasses and grazing sheep, give no hint of the icy rain, drifting snow, cold winds, and fog that make traveling through here extremely dangerous.

A small aircraft is visible alongside the road below. It has a big hole through its top: the first sign of the war. Shouting over the noise of the engine, Gourgen tells me that the plane was en route from Karabagh to Armenia when it was hit by an Azeri fighter jet. The pilot crash landed the plane, and before it exploded the few men aboard escaped. A Russian journalist on board tells me that the pilot was badly injured and is now in a Yerevan hospital.

Gourgen points out Goris, the last city in Armenia before we approach the border. Within a few minutes we are out of Armenia and passing over the Lachin Corridor, the narrow strip of land formerly under Azeri control through which the road to Karabagh passes. Caravans of trucks and some smaller vehicles can be seen making their way to Karabagh now that the blockade has been broken.

Everyone is very excited, shouting to each other above the noise of the whirling helicopter blades, moving from window to window, pointing to this and that on the ground, poking our heads into the cockpit, congratulating the crew, hugging each other. Some weep from the joy of seeing the road below, the road to Karabagh, filled with trucks: the impossible has been done.

We see smoke rising from Lachin as we get closer. Slowly the white stone houses, scores of them dotting the mountainside, become clearer. They were deserted long ago; knowing that the war would reach here, the civilian population abandoned the city. During the last months it was an Azeri military base from which the road to Karabagh was controlled. The victorious Armenians burned the city so that Azeris could never return. My joy over the opening of the road is mixed with sadness at the sight of the destruction. I know that innocent people have suffered. Azeri mothers have also lost sons and lost their homes; they too are victims of a war Gorbachev could have prevented.

The road appears and then disappears from our view as it continues to wind around the magnificent mountains. In the years to come, making the journey by car, we get to know every kilometer of this serpentine track—the dangerous curves, the falling rocks, the potholes where our tires blow out; the pockets of fog that sometimes make passage almost impossible. The road itself becomes part of our story, a never ending series of adventures.

Gourgen yells over the noise of the helicopter, "You are now in the Autonomous Region of Nagorno-Karabagh, the Black Garden," and then even louder, "YOU-ARE-IN-*ARTSAKH!*" His eyes are filled with tears, overflowing with happiness; he uses the ancient Armenian name for Karabagh—Artsakh.

We pass over a village built on the edge of a mountaintop cliff. "It is Bertadzor," Gourgen yells again. We had just visited the wounded in Yerevan's orthopedic hospital, and several young men in one room were from Bertadzor. They stood out because they were so jovial and friendly despite their injuries. They were among the luckier ones, for many men died in that place that looks so peaceful and quiet from the air.

Raffi sends word that Shushi is in sight and invites me to join the crew for the last part of the trip. Holding onto the sides of the helicopter for balance, I move into the front of the cockpit. The crew makes a place for me between the pilot and co-pilot. Gourgen is leaning over my shoulder; this is the first time he has seen Shushi from the air. The shadow of the helicopter with its whirling blades is clearly visible on the ground below.

Shushi slowly comes into view. It is built on a massive mountain with cliffs of solid rock. Raffi explains that in order to take the city, Karabagh forces had to scale these cliffs. "*Shu-shi! Shu-shi!*" everyone yells, their fists held up in a victory sign. The crew, which took part in that successful mission, is beaming with pride.

We pass over the magnificent Armenian cathedral made of white marble. Later we will see what toll the war has taken on this beautiful city, in centuries past the capital of Armenian cultural life.

The rocky summit falls away below us, and the city of Stepanakert appears, filling the valley below like a sacrificial lamb laid out at Shushi's feet. What a sight! The city fills the valley; its vulnerability and lack of any possible defense become painfully clear. The strategic importance of Shushi now is evident. Month after month, the Azeris used Shushi as a launching point for missile attacks on Stepanakert. The helicopter moves in low over the rooftops now. House after house shows the destruction wreaked by the missiles as they came whirling through the sky from Shushi. Very few structures seem to have escaped the fireballs.

But there is peace for the moment, and we can see people and vehicles moving about the city. We even spot a group of children, no longer confined to their basement sanctuaries, playing in what must be a school yard.

On the far side of Stepanakert, our helicopter sets down in an open field next to the symbol of Karabagh: a monument of orange tufa stone depicting a *dadik* and a *babik*, a grandmother and a grandfather ten times life size. Our excitement grows. In the single hour since we left Yerevan we have seen so much. Even before the helicopter blades come to a full stop, children are running across the field to greet us, cars and vans pull up, and soldiers come over the mound facing the road. As we emerge from the aircraft, some of the children gather around, smiling and laughing, while others observe us from a distance, their big eyes just staring. We sense sadness emanating from all of the children, even those who are laughing. They are not really children any longer, despite their small bodies and playful ways; they have lived through war.

Gourgen and I bid our traveling companions good-bye, hugging and kissing each, still sharing the excitement of the trip. The Karabagh official who organized the flight instructs us to be back at this site at exactly 4 p.m. The helicopter must leave then in order to make it safely back to Yerevan. Air currents through the mountain passes change dramatically from moment to moment, especially as the sun is setting, making the trip dangerous. I nod vigorously, indicating that we will be back on the spot without any question. It is now 12 noon.

Just as I begin to wonder how we are going to get into the city and up to Shushi, a van pulls up and a stocky, jovial man who knows Gourgen gets out. He has been sent to be with us for the day, he informs us. His name is Hamo, short for Hamlet. The obvious questions go unasked and unanswered: who knew we were coming and who sent him? In Armenia, when good things happen, I have learned not to ask any questions. The van, though, is not good news. It is in terrible condition: the front windshield is shattered (how it remained in place over the bumpy roads defies logic); the side windows are broken; the seats are coming apart; the upholstery is torn; and the metal interior is rusted. But the motor starts, and when the crew, along with a few other stranded strangers, all pile in with us, the van holds up under the weight.

After we are all in, Hamo tells Gourgen that he has only enough gasoline to get to the area's sole filling station, and there might not be any gasoline even then. (I thought that it might be time now to ask a few questions, but I held back.)

Gasoline was a big problem for Karabagh during those years, when every available drop had to be reserved for the army. When we traveled into Karabagh, we filled our tank in Goris. A few times when we ran out of gasoline the army gave us some, but we always felt very guilty. Many people carried extra gasoline in canisters they kept in their cars, a practice I always thought risky.

Our immediate need is to find some gasoline to get us through the day. We are fortunate. Although the station appears to be closed, there is a young man there who appears to be in charge. No gasoline, he claims, but Gourgen is not about to accept that. Using all of the charm he possessed, half-singing and half-talking, describing how important the people in the van are, he talks the boy into selling us a few liters. Hamo turns the gasoline pump by hand until the young man motions that it is all he can spare. He is paid, and we are on our way up the road into Stepanakert.

Despite the destruction, Stepanakert's beauty remains. The city has a light, airy quality; its streets are wide, and its buildings, made of various shades of pink tufa stone, are no more than four stories tall. Many buildings are decorated with reliefs, and the remnants of planted gardens are evident everywhere.

All of the windows in the city are shattered, and the rooms beyond them are empty and exposed where missiles have hit. The people who survived the missile attacks are in the streets reclaiming their city—cleaning, shoveling the debris, surveying the damage, planning their lives again. These are the people Gourgen has been talking about for years, people who lived in basements with candles their only light, who had their babies, and taught their children to read and write as they crouched under the Azeri attacks, terrified and hungry but resolute. Despite all of the sadness they have endured they seem cheerful; willing to make eye contact with a stranger and smiling first when they do.

During the next few hours we visit two hospital units set up in the basements of large, abandoned buildings. Our first stop is an emergency treatment center for soldiers and civilians wounded during the war. The wounded from the front lines are treated first in field hospitals, then they may come here; now, they might even be flown to Yerevan for further treatment.

The Chief Doctor comes out to greet us. It is Dr. Valerie Marutian, whose truck we had surreptitiously filled in Etchmi-adzin more than three years ago with supplies for Karabagh. We have been sending supplies to his military hospital since then, but he had not made the connection with me and that night. We are delighted to meet again.

He takes me through the facilities for a preliminary view before we settle down to discuss specific problems. The unit is made up of several adjoining rooms, each used for a different purpose. Marutian shows me the storage area first where, among many other boxes, I spot several with the orange dots George puts on our medical supplies for easy identification.

Next, we go into the patient care area where a young man is lying unconscious, injured by a land mine. My emotions suddenly get the better of me and, unable to speak, I turn my back on the scene and leave the unit, heading for the stairs and the light outside.

Gourgen comes after me, "What happened? Are you all right?"

"Yes, I'm OK." I lie, "Nothing happened. I just needed some air."

I do not want my tears seen or mistaken for tears of pity. It is the crispness of the doctor's coats, the white sheets on the patient's bed, the way the single intravenous line is attached to his arm without the benefit of even a bandage, the eagerness on the faces that came out of the darkness to greet me that makes me cry. It is the dignity that I see, the obvious dignity with which they bear their plight and face death every minute of the day, determined to survive, that causes my emotions to well up. After a few minutes I am able to return, feigning an excuse for my behavior, which they accept, happy to see that there was nothing seriously wrong that might cut my visit short.

They have enough antibiotics now, the doctors tell me, but they need sterile bandages, tape, gauze, and dressing materials for wounds. I ask about the oximeter I had sent to them one month ago. This machine measures the saturation of oxygen in the blood through a sensor placed on the patient's finger. It has not been put into use because the plug does not fit their electrical outlet. I sent the right plug with the oximeter but apparently it was lost. How frustrating it is to get a machine all the way to Stepanakert, but lose the adapter on the plug! I promise to send the right plug as soon as I get back to Yerevan. (I know I have another one in my Franzus kit of travel adaptors!)

Our next visit is to the Maternity Hospital, which has been set up in the basement of one of the government's administrative buildings on the city's central square. The square is filled with trucks loaded with foodstuffs and supplies waiting to be distributed. Before going into the hospital, Gourgen takes me to the end of a corridor on the ground floor where the building simply is no more: the site of a missile hit.

The five rooms of the maternity unit are filled with women, some newly delivered, some in active labor. One doctor and several nurses are in attendance. All appear sad and look exhausted, like the children at the landing field. Bullet holes pock the walls opposite the windows. Their surgical instruments are being sterilized on a wood-burning stove in the middle of the main room, causing soot and smoke to fill the air. Some patients offer welcoming looks; others turn and cover their faces. The newborns are here too. Another room, dark and filled with a musty odor, contains four women with pregnancy complications. There is nothing much that can be done except keep them on bed rest, I am told. I look from bed to bed, avoiding their eyes, wishing for a moment that I had not seen them.

My dilemma now will confront me many times: As a doctor, I would like to know more about these women's complications but what would be the point, except perhaps a kind of medical voyeurism? Since I cannot help them, what right do I have to invade their privacy? None!

The hours pass quickly, and I remind Gourgen of our 4 p.m. rendezvous with the helicopter. He tells me there has been a change in plans: the helicopter will leave from Shushi, not the field where we landed. I had been with him the whole time, how and when were these plans changed?

Our next stop is the home of Bishop Barkev Mardirossian, the Primate of Karabagh. The house has no windows, and part of the structure is totally demolished. Miraculously, the young Bishop had just awakened and gone into the adjoining room to say his prayers when the missile hit. His bedroom was destroyed.

Stepanakert was torn apart by missiles, Gyumri by an earthquake, but the cities look much the same. We have just as much trouble negotiating Stepanakert's rubble-strewn streets as

Gyumri's, and everywhere we see the same destroyed, crumbling, half-standing structures, their insides exposed and uninhabitable.

Before going up to Shushi, we must find a woman whose husband was killed in the war one week ago. Gourgen has brought money for her, part of a program sponsored by a few California Armenians to support the widows and children of the men dying in this war. We find the family in a small dark apartment off one of Stepanakert's side streets. An old woman, dressed in black with a scarf wrapped around her head, lets us in after Gourgen explains the purpose of the visit.

"Ah," she says, looking at his mustache, "I have heard of you. You are the man with the mustache who comes to Karabagh even when the missiles are flying. The people talk about you. Come in, come in," she says without a smile. The young widow appears behind her. She too is dressed all in black; her eyes are swollen and red from crying. Her children peek at us from behind the heavy curtain that hangs around the doorway. Gourgen introduces me. We are invited to sit in the living room. The widow's oldest boy, about 10 years old, sits next to his mother as Gourgen starts to talk with her. He holds a book stiffly and pretends to read, never looking up and never showing any sign of hearing the conversation. She is a doctor the widow tells us, and so was her husband. She has three children. Together with her mother-in-law they had been living in the basement of this building until Shushi was freed.

Her voice is soft and gentle. She makes no complaints, does not wail or weep. I can only imagine how hard life is for her now. How will she manage in the war zone, with an old mother-in-law and three young children? How will she feed and clothe them? Who will bring them fire wood? How will her children be educated? She took care of her family's everyday needs while her husband was fighting, but now the total responsibility is hers; now she must be the fighter.

Her husband died for his homeland and his people, Gourgen tells her. The entire nation of Armenia and all of Karabagh honor her sacrifice and her courage. Her husband is a hero; she is a heroine. She must be strong. His words touch her, and she smiles. He has managed to elevate her from a simple widow to an honored woman. At least for these moments, he has given her new pride and relieved her agony. A master at reaching out to people in their darkest moments of suffering and pain, Gourgen is not afraid of exposing himself to other people's pain, and they respond.

He goes on to tell the widow that every month she will receive 1500 rubles from this private charity's sponsors. He explains how and from whom she will receive the money. She signs a receipt for the first month's payment, and I sign as a witness, happy to do something to lessen the feeling of again being simply a voyeur. I had not said a single word through it all. I simply sat and watched Gourgen, wishing that I too had a book to put between myself and the family's pain.

After we leave I tell Gourgen how uncomfortable I was sitting there, with no help to offer, nothing to add to his eloquent words. We still have two more homes to visit; maybe I will not go in with him. "What are you saying? Do you understand how wrong you are? How can you say such a thing?" he almost yells, clearly annoyed. "First, you can't really help improve conditions you have not observed. Now that you are finally seeing and feeling Karabagh, you will do much more. And secondly," he continues, "your presence was very meaningful for that family. Those children will never forget that an Armenian from America came to their home, and the young widow will never forget that you extended your hand to her in friendship and in condolence. What more do you want to do now?" I nod my head, but I still do not fully understand.

We make the other visits and finally start up the mountainside toward Shushi. It is now 3 p.m. We pass an Armenian tank that was destroyed in the battle for Shushi. It is now a shrine, draped in lilacs by the people living here. We too pause for a few moments to pay our respects to the two young soldiers who died in the tank: Shahen and Ashod.

Shushi's battered beauty recalls another unfortunate city, Dubrovnik, in the former Yugoslavia. Shushi was once an architectural gem, carefully planned and executed with its Moslem and Christian sections. It is made even more wonderful by the idyllic setting up on the cliffs. The Azeri section of the city is distinguished by its arches and turrets and a delicate Persian mosque decorated with blue mosaics. "A mosque is a house of God," Gourgen says "and must be preserved."

The Armenian section, whose last inhabitants were removed four years earlier in the aftermath of the Sumgait pogroms, is now a series of charred buildings with few of their walls intact. The city has a surreal quality. Smiling women walk in the streets carrying bouquets of wild flowers, their children tagging along, unmindful of the destruction around them. It does not seem to matter to them where they are coming from or where they are going. It only matters that they are here at this very moment. The same seems true of us.

A few more turns and we reach the imposing 18th century Armenian cathedral made of white marble that we had seen from the air. Hundreds of narrow, long green boxes are piled one on top of the other outside the church. Each contains a missile. The Azeris kept the missiles in the cathedral, knowing that if the Armenians struck by air they would not fire on the church. People meander around the church, grouped here and there, chatting; all appear very happy. Several soldiers recognize Gourgen and run to him; they hug and kiss, congratulating each other on their victory. Overwhelming joy wells up in these men as they talk about the recent victories. No small part of their elation comes from the fact that they accomplished something everyone said could not be done. They hold no illusions about the future. No one thinks that the days ahead will be easy.

It is now 4 p.m. Over an hour ago I decided to try to stop worrying about how we were going to get back to Yerevan. The frustration I so often feel over not being able to control how things happen around me is counterproductive I know; I must learn to just "go with the flow." But the warning we were given earlier, ". . . air currents change . . . it is not safe" echoes in my ears. I am very happy to see our helicopter crew among the soldiers at the cathedral.

Raffi tells me the helicopter is on a plateau not far from here. We will be leaving soon, but first the men want to go up to the city's highest point, where the view of the cliffs and the canyon below is most dramatic.

After admiring the great cathedral and examining the damage to the church—birds fly through holes and leaks, in the high vaulted ceiling, and glassless windows admit snow and rain—we each say a prayer for peace before leaving.

The helicopter, surrounded by other travelers, waits for us on a large open field filled with red poppies on the mountaintop overlooking a massive canyon. Several people offer cognac for toasts, Gourgen starts to sing, the men pose for pictures—there is a party atmosphere that no one wants to end. But shortly after 5 p.m. Raffi announces that we must be airborne within a few minutes. There are twenty-three people on board, including several freedom fighters. The aircraft puts down twice in nearby villages to let out some fighters going home for a few days of rest.

With the final lift-off, we all relax and start chatting, viewing from time to time the sights below us and noting that the sun is rapidly getting lower in the sky. No more than 15 minutes into the flight, our helicopter lands unexpectedly in the town of Goris. Another helicopter alights just after we do, coming from the opposite direction. It turns out that Yerevan is experiencing one of the strongest windstorms in recent memory. The second helicopter, 5 minutes ahead of us, met with heavy winds as it entered the next mountain pass. The pilot, knowing that we were behind him, radioed Raffi to land as fast as possible. The pilot tells us that the winds were so turbulent their helicopter was nearly hurled into the mountain.

After waiting for two hours in lightning, thunder, and heavy rains, we realize that there will be no change in the weather and that we must spend the night in Goris. Raffi observes that if we had left at 4 p.m. as planned, we would have been caught in the storm as we approached Yerevan.

Several hours later, ten of us are packed into a small car headed for Goris. On the way, I see flashing lights streaking into the sky and ask Gourgen, in English, what these were. I am not too happy about his answer: Grad missiles. Goris is being hit nightly! Last night, 17 missiles were fired at the city. "Why," I ask this time in Armenian, "are we going toward the city?" "What else can we do?" came the response. I said nothing more!

When we arrive in the downtown area, I see sandbags piled high around the ground floor windows of every house. At night, people retreat to their basements for protection, I am told. Some have left the city for villages farther from the border. Most of the children have been evacuated. The other women in the group do not seem concerned, and Gourgen is calm. I try to emulate them.

Our car pulls up to a house made of stone on a street of similar buildings all very close to one another. They are quite lovely, and I can see why Goris is one of Armenia's resort towns. The front door opens to reveal—of all people—our pilot Raffi, who somehow managed to get here before us. This was a restaurant and the table has already been set for 18 people.

Again, I have trouble understanding what is going on. Isn't anyone else worried about where we are going to spend the night amid Grad missile attacks? "First things first. Now we must eat!" Gourgen tries to reassure me. Dinner takes several hours—not that there's much food, but there are a lot of speeches and toasts made. Most of the soldiers at the table are returning from a mission in the mountains. This dinner offers a chance for them to honor the valor of their comrades who died in the fighting. Emotions are highly charged, and the vodka does its job; I'm not thinking about the missiles any more! Gourgen makes a speech; even I make a speech. At midnight, all 18 of us walk through the city, singing all the way to the hotel!

That night, unable to sleep, I decide to take my chances with the missiles and sit on the front steps of the hotel. The air smells sweet and is much more pleasing than my musty room. At about

2 a.m., half asleep, I hear a voice saying in Armenian, "Doctor-jan, is that you?" I am startled to see my friends from Gyumri, the men who flew our supplies to Karabagh three years ago walking toward me in army fatigues, their rifles slung over their shoulders and big smiles on their faces. "What are you doing here?" they ask incredulously as the rest of the soldiers, all from Gyumri, gather around us. I explain. They tell me they are on their way back to Karabagh. Everyone in the troop is a volunteer from Gyumri. Despite all their city's problems, Karabagh is still more important to them.

As we sit there, another company of soldiers arrives, also on the way to Karabagh. Their commander approaches and asks if any of us know where the hospital is; they have a sick soldier with them. The men from Gyumri look at me; I volunteer my services. The commander is delighted and as soon as the soldier is settled in a room, I go up to examine him.

He is 52 years old and is having abdominal pain. Based on the history he gives me, it sounds like an ulcer. Fortunately, I have Tagamet with me, give him a supply sufficient for two weeks, and instruct him not to drink any alcohol. The soldier pleads with me, "Please tell the commander that I am well enough to fight. I don't want to be sent home." I wonder: at age 52, with a family in Armenia, why are you going to fight in Karabagh? I simply reply that I cannot say anything to the commander, it is a matter between the two of them.

In the morning I tease Gourgen that he had missed a very exciting night on the hotel steps. Why did he go to sleep?

As soon as everyone is up and assembled we head back to last night's restaurant, where, unknown to me, Gourgen has asked the owners, a refugee family from Baku, to bake a special bread for our breakfast. It is a delicacy made by Karabagh's Armenians that most other Armenians have never eaten, called *jengalov hatz*. It is made by rolling out a bread dough, spreading 10 or 15 types of greens picked fresh from the open fields on it, folding the dough back over itself, and baking it over a hot wood fire. The moment is captured on video to bring back to George.

"Mmmm" I am saying while I stand next to the fire, "George, we are drinking to your health and wishing you were here! This is dee-lish-ous!!"

Packed into the same small cars, we make the trip back to the airport and finally, at about 10 a.m., head for Yerevan under blue, calm skies. Raffi flew back on a different route that took us over some of Armenia's most beautiful monasteries, including the famous ones at Datev and Geghart.

Gourgen says to me later, "You know, Raffi did that just for you. Can you understand what your being with us meant to these soldiers?" Slowly, very slowly, maybe. I wonder, could they understand what being with them on this trip has meant to me? It was reliving the past with a different ending. We have been victims for centuries, and now these young men from Karabagh and the volunteers from Armenia are changing the course of our 3000 year history. It is unbelievable!

Lenin Square, now called Republic Square. This photo was taken from Hotel Armenia before the blockade. Yerevan, 1990.

CHAPTER 10

From Bad to Worse

The war in Karabagh raged on. The Azeris began aerial bombings of Karabagh's civilian population, concentrating on the city of Stepanakert while they continued to fire missiles from nearby locations. It was all-out-war with hand-to-hand battles taking place in many regions as the Azeris made significant gains deep within Karabagh. Gourgen Melikian still accompanied caravans of medical supplies, including ours, through the Lachin Corridor to Shushi and Stepanakert, but it was too dangerous for me to venture another trip. It was the fall of 1992.

The blockade of Armenia tightened. By November, Turkey was no longer allowing humanitarian aid (even that from the United States) to pass through its territory en route to Armenia. It also stopped the sale of electricity to Armenia that had begun when Armenia's nuclear plant was shut down. (Previously, Armenia sold electricity to Turkey) By the end of the year, the natural gas pipelines that passed through Azerbaijan to Armenia, from Russia and Turkmenistan, were totally blocked by the Azeris.

In mid October I arrived in Yerevan for a one month stay. My stepdaughter, Nancy, had recently taken a job teaching English at the newly established Haigazian College and was among the small group of Armenian-Americans living there at the time. We shared an apartment a few blocks from Republic Square. Nancy had acclimated quite well to conditions and took most of the hardships of daily living in stride.

Each morning, before I was up, Nancy heated two buckets of water on the gas stove (while we still had gas) for what we affectionately and accurately referred to as our "bucket baths." A few weeks later, when the gas was permanently turned off, and the electricity was cut to only a few hours a day, we looked back on these baths as a luxury.

Nancy's apartment was on the fourth floor, and although the building had an elevator, she warned me never to use it. She had been trapped several times between floors when the electricity was shut off unexpectedly. Her warnings were sufficient for me!

We carried flashlights with us at all times and had learned to keep a lookout in the markets for the good candles that burned slowly. Like everyone else, we kept buckets and pitchers filled with water in the kitchen and in the bathroom. Often, while sitting and chatting in the late afternoon, or in the morning over coffee, Nancy's expression would change suddenly. "Nancy, what's the matter?" I asked every time. Her reply was always the same, "I think we're getting water." "How do you know?" I would ask, incredulously. "Can't you hear it in the pipes?" she'd say.

I never could, not until 1996 when George and I were in our own apartment in Yerevan. Then, at 6 a.m., the first sounds made by the water as it trickled into the pipes on the first floor would wake me immediately no matter how sound my sleep. I too became completely attuned to the tap water's comings and goings!

Nancy and I began to understand why extended families lived together and how work was shared among the women of the household. When the water came on, there was always someone at home who could fill the buckets, do the laundry, and clean the house. With water fresh from the tap they could wash the greens for the evening meal—the tarragon, parsley, mint, and cilantro that were sold in bunches by venders on the streets. When the electricity came on, they were home to cook, using small electric burners that had replaced gas stoves.

We experienced how difficult it was to run a household without vacuum cleaners, washing machines and dryers, dishwashers, electric mixers, and food processors. We marveled at how these women accomplished all of this in addition to getting their children off to school, clean and neat in their freshly ironed clothes.

When we shopped, the paucity of food for sale made us hesitant to buy, feeling guilty that we were taking food from the people we had come to help. This was especially true when it came to buying bread, because it was so scarce due to the shortage of flour. Fortunately, we had a supply of canned tuna, packaged dry soups, and cereals from the States that helped us get by.

During this trip I visited 17 hospitals, more than on any other trip. In Gyumri, Armen brought me up to date on his intensive care unit. The most alarming news he gave me was that the death rate had increased by 50 percent. People delayed coming to the hospital until they had no choice, often when it was too late to do anything for them. They knew their families could afford neither the transportation costs to visit them, nor the quality and kind of food it was customary to bring to someone hospitalized. Therefore, hoping to avoid hospitalization, they remained at home as long as possible.

The incidence of strokes, heart attacks, and severe hypertension had all increased. The suicide rate was up 15 to 20 percent, and Armen was seeing many more patients with acute problems related to drinking contaminated alcohol. All of the doctors I talked with noted the sharp rise of insulin-dependent diabetes, especially among young people. Many were convinced it was due to the extreme stress they now lived under. (At the time, I discounted these observations, but more recently, there has been a growing consensus among some researchers in the West that illnesses such as insulin-dependent diabetes could be brought on by extreme stress.)

At the Maternity Hospital, Lilit told me the hospital had recorded 2000 births thus far in 1992, compared to 4000 at the same time last year. The newborns had a lower average birth weight and lower APGAR scores. (This universally used scoring system for newborns reflects health at birth; it was developed by Dr. Virginia Apgarian, an Armenian-American anesthesiologist.) The rate of premature births was increasing, and there was a rise in spontaneous abortions. Only about 20 percent of the new mothers were able to breast feed, compared to 50 percent in 1991.

These were not official statistics, but I knew that the trends the doctors observed were real. This was occurring in a setting of diminishing medical supplies and medicines. Due to the blockade and the financial crisis it caused for the central government, the healthcare system was almost entirely dependent on humanitarian aid—though significant, hardly enough to supply the needs of the country.

Other worrisome health problems alarmed officials at the Ministry of Health, among them the resurgence of tuberculosis. It was hardly surprising. More than 400,000 refugees had poured into Armenia, and the vast majority were crammed into tiny living quarters—six to ten people in a single room or domic, struggling to survive. The non-refugee population's lifestyle was not much better. Under these conditions, coupled with poor nutrition, tuberculosis was sure to spread.

Gyumri's Tuberculosis Hospital had been completely destroyed by the earthquake and now operated out of a few boxcars set up under a tent. When I visited, there was just one in-patient. Chief Doctor Irina Mkurdumian, a young, intense woman, sat me down in her office and went over her statistics. "The problem," she explained, "is that we do not have the Mantoux tests for screening the population. In 1985 we screened 40,000 people for tuberculosis; in 1991, only 2,800. We are not picking up the new cases of tuberculosis." She was afraid that there would be an explosion of new cases, dangerously advanced by the time they were detected.

A week later I visited Armenia's main facility for treating tuberculosis located about 20 minutes outside Yerevan, in the city of Abovian. The day I visited, it held 375 patients, including 35 children, with active and chronic TB. Most of them were refugees, many hospitalized with other members of their family. Room after room was filled with ailing children and mothers. The chief doctor introduced me to one woman tending her sick child, then after we left the room told me that two of her children had already died of tuberculous meningitis. My notes do not tell me anything else about this woman or her child. What did I say to them? Did I offer them anything? Why didn't I provide help? I don't remember anything except that I was overwhelmed with sadness.

The hospital was in extremely poor physical condition. However, the patients received three hot meals a day—thanks to the United States government's donation of rations left over from the Gulf War!

⁂

Wherever we looked during these darkest of days, there were compelling needs. How could we help? Would anything we did make a difference in the face of so much deprivation?

Relief work in Armenia was not easy for anyone, but it was especially difficult for those of Armenian heritage. People held us to a standard much more exacting than the one for non-Armenian relief workers. They assumed we could do anything we wanted; we simply had to want to do it. This put excessive pressure on me and on others like me. When we said that we could not help with something, it was sometimes interpreted as not caring. Many of the people who came to me for evaluation of medical problems hoped to find a way to obtain treatment abroad.

Often there was nothing I could do to help. Sometimes I could refer the person to others who might help, sometimes things just fell into place, as they did with a 4-month-old infant who had lost one eye to glaucoma shortly after birth. The family was concerned about the other eye. By luck Frieda Jordan, the Armenian woman who had traveled to Gyumri with me, was able to arrange for the baby to be treated in London.

Organizations like AmeriCares, Medical Outreach For Armenians, and the Armenian General Benevolent Union enabled hundreds of earthquake victims to go abroad for treatment of their injuries. Special documents had to be prepared by the Ministry of Health and submitted to the respective embassies of countries to which the patients were going. In the early days, these documents had to be sent to Moscow for approval, a time-consuming and difficult task in itself. Hospitals across America, Canada, and Europe donated use of their facilities, and doctors donated their services to treat earthquake victims. Airlines even donated trans-Atlantic transportation.

Despite these massive efforts, the great need for special medical care that surfaced in Armenia could not be met. The organizations taking patients abroad were forced to set limits on whom they would take, based on the patient's age, type of injury, and expected outcome. One young boy, taken to California for treatment of what was supposed to be an earthquake related injury, turned out to have metastatic bone cancer. The former qualified him for being taken abroad; the latter disease did not. Who could blame the desperate parents for working the deception?

Taking care of patients abroad was not an easy task. Children usually had to be accompanied by a parent, and diasporan Armenians were called upon to house, feed, and chauffeur the visitors, sometimes for months at a time. They needed translators, and the expenses they incurred had to be covered. It was all done willingly and with great concern for those who came to be healed.

In Armenia I found it emotionally difficult to see the needs people had, to want to help, but know that it was not always possible; I was often left with a sense of helplessness. For my own sanity, and for the sake of our small group of volunteers back in Boston, I decided to confine our activities to the kind of things we were already involved with by 1992: providing supplies and assistance to three hospitals in Gyumri and for Yerevan's Pediatric Infectious Disease Hospital; aid to Karabagh; and running a project called Adopt-A-Sister for the refugees of Getashen. Those were to be our limits.

I made the following journal entry on October 26, 1992:

"This was my second day in Gyumri. I arrived back to Lilit's house after dinner at Ruben's. By candlelight I looked at the gifts people gave me today: a carved box, a bottle of cognac, a pin of amber and silver. Why do people spend money on gifts for me when they have so little? As I write this my tears are flowing.

Armenia today is like biblical Egypt and the story of the seven years of plagues sent by God. First there was the earthquake, death and homelessness, then the blockade, and the war, with each winter getting worse than the last. Last winter there was no gas and no heat anywhere. And now, as if all of this was not enough, there is no bread.

I saw the bread today in Gyumri, the bread people wait in line for. It is black. It is hard. It is not edible. Without bread Armenians will die. The saddest part of this is that the light has gone out, the little light of hope that was left has completely gone out. The twinkle in the eyes of my friends, the twinkle that remained even during the worst of last year's winter, the twinkle of hope is gone.

Can anything I write change this? If not, there is no reason to write anymore. Is there any hope that someone in power will do something or can do something to end the terrible blockade of this country? People will die of starvation and from the cold, but many are already dead from hopelessness. Children will die of malnutrition. I see it on their faces already. The children are thinner now, and pale.

How will they survive in their cold domics? What can we do? Again, I am keenly aware that I will go home in a few weeks. No matter how bad I feel, I am not the one suffering. For the first time I sense that the people around me are aware of this as well.

Congressman Joseph P. Kennedy welcomed by Armenians
of Greater Boston upon his return from Armenia in
mid-winter. Logan Airport, Boston, 1993.

CHAPTER 11

"Better Days Will Come"

M arch 1993
I am back in Gyumri.
When I entered the city
after an absence of four months, an eerie feeling came over me.
There were people everywhere, but there was no life. Hunched
over, wrapped in dark shawls or coats, their arms pressed tight
against their bodies, and their faces not visible, they seemed
to me to be shadows of themselves, not the real people that
they were.

The winter of 1991–1992 had been hard, but people still
hoped things would be getting better. This past winter proved
them wrong; daily existence became a seemingly never-ending
hell. The United States government shipped kerosene to Armenia for use with small kerosene stoves. These helped keep many
people alive, but not everyone.

In Gyumri's Maternity Hospital eight babies died during the
winter due to the cold and the lack of electricity to run the incubators. The staff tried to warm the incubators by placing bottles
of hot water inside them, but this was insufficient to maintain
the temperature of a sick baby. The ambient temperature in the
hospital was often between 0 and 5 degrees centigrade (32–40
degrees Fahrenheit). The generator, I was told, had worked very
well in the surgical unit, but would have been too costly to run
incubators around the clock.

On my first day at the Samaritar Hospital an 18-year-old young man was admitted to the intensive care unit, comatose and with dangerously low blood pressure. His parents told us he had not been feeling well for several days and had been drinking large amounts of water (a sign of diabetes). His condition deteriorated rapidly during the previous night. They had taken him to two other hospitals where doctors would not admit him because his illness was not within their specialty. Then, they brought him to the Samaritar.

Armen's diagnosis of diabetic ketoacidosis—a condition that develops when blood sugar rises to very high levels—was quickly confirmed by the patient's blood sugar (measured on the glucometer we had given Armen two years ago): over 500, as high as the glucometer went. Now we had to come up with a course of treatment. Since blood test results would not come back from the lab in less than 24 hours, we decided against giving him insulin (insulin could cause his potassium level to drop dangerously low). Therefore, we started with administering fluids and antibiotics.

This critical care was being given in a hospital unit whose room temperature was about 40 degrees Fahrenheit. We worked with our coats on, our fingers frozen. The patient was under several *vermags* and a wool hat was pulled over his head and ears. One of the doctors wiggled the cardiac monitor wires under the vermags and made the connections, while the nurses discussed how they would try to keep the intravenous fluids warm. I was fixed on the waves of the patient's electrocardiogram as they started to move across the monitor when suddenly the room was thrown into darkness. I was the only one to let out a loud gasp of horror. The others hardly noticed. The nurses lit a few candles and everyone continued working. After the first liter of fluid was administered, the patient stirred and was able to respond to simple commands. We decided to give him very small doses of insulin, adding some potassium to the intravenous fluid. It was frightening to have to work without the benefit of a laboratory or monitoring equipment.

Ten members of the boy's family waited outside for news. Fortunately, Armen was able to reassure them; the young man would live.

The following morning I had time to chat with the staff in the ICU. I had brought them buttons and bumper stickers used in the grassroots campaign my family had started, called the Committee to Lift the Blockade of Armenia. Kathryn Manuelian of New York had come up with the slogan and Carol Der Boghosian of Connecticut had the buttons made. Nancy Najarian organized the sending of thousands of letters to the White House, to Congress, and to newspapers, pleading for some action to help stop the blockade. Armenians wrote, of course, but the idea was to get our non-Armenian friends involved as well.

I hoped to encourage these young doctors by showing them that people outside their borders were working hard to let the world know what was going on in Armenia. I pulled out the buttons and banners saying, "NO HEAT, NO WATER, NO LIGHT: Help lift the energy blockade of Armenia." They laughed and said that we had forgotten a few things: "NO FOOD, NO FUTURE, NO HOPE." It was not the time, I realized, to try to convince them otherwise.

Before leaving Gyumri I met with Dr. Khatchatrian, who was now health director for the city. He poignantly summed up their frustration and the extent of the suffering: "If we survived the winter, we must conclude that we are not human. If we get through the spring and summer without major epidemics, we will have to rewrite the textbooks of medicine because we will know they are wrong."

I left Gyumri, frustrated and distraught. I too was beginning to wonder if anything would ever change; if, as the young doctors believed, Armenia was destined for extinction. The blockade by the Azeris, now fully supported by Turkey, was in fact seen by people like Armen as another attempt at genocide, this time slowly choking the life out of a people.

❧

Back in Yerevan I was staying with Lena Gazazian, the daughter of good friends who had moved to Moscow to work. Lena, a student at the Institute of Theater and Drama, was living in their apartment with her grandfather. One morning Lena noted that although I had slept under a heavy vermag, I had also worn several layers of clothing as well as my socks. "It is warm now," she said laughing. "If you had been here during the winter, you would have turned into ice cream!"

Lena lost 15 kilos (over 30 lbs) this winter, but managed to remain cheerful. After her joke about ice cream, the electricity came on, filling the room with light and us with elation. "Where else could I go to have such happiness when the electricity comes on and we can heat the water for a bath?" she asked. Then, her eyes bright with a bit of mischief in them, she added, "Do you ever get this happy in America?" *Touché Lena*!

I asked Armen to write a letter to his fellow doctors in America explaining a little about his life. After outlining the desperate conditions I have already described, Armen closed on a note of optimism:

"Now, when I am writing these lines (even writing was hard then because ink was freezing and my fingers were not functioning) the winter is left behind. I have in my memory an image of dark and cold night shifts, standing in my winter coat next to the stove that could hardly warm us. But I want to say that there were also days full of hope and images of light. If not for the humanitarian aid of the United States and other countries, many children, elderly people, and patients would have died in Gyumri. Without the financial and moral support of our countrymen in the diaspora, it would have been hard for our nation to survive the difficulties. I know that internationally there is also an informational blockade; many things that are now happening in Armenia are not known to the people of other countries. I am giving this letter to our good friend, Carolann Najarian, in order for her to bring it to American and Armenian doctors and to other people of good will.

The energy blockade of Armenia organized by the Azeris and Turks is not a form of politics; it is a crime against a nation and human beings. I am not saying this only as an Armenian, but as a human being and a physician. I call on the international community to continue to help Armenia under these difficult conditions. Now it is spring in Gyumri, life is going on. New trees are being planted. The severe traces of winter are being smoothed over, and our nation that has seen the earthquake and is living under the conditions of a blockade still has faith that better days will come for Armenia."

In the Fall of 1993 a campaign to provide heating fuel (called mazout) for apartments, schools, and hospitals with intact central heating systems, was organized by the United Armenian Fund under the direction of its Executive Director Harut Sassounian. Kirk Kerkorian's Lincy Foundation gave 14 million dollars matching 2:1 the seven million dollars raised in the diaspora. Thousands of people were warm through the winter of 1993–1994 because of this massive project. It also gave people hope that things might be getting better.

The kindergarten's director stood next to me as we prepared to distribute gifts to the children. It was then that she told me her story. Matchkalashen, 1994.

CHAPTER 12

Beyond Grief

April 1, 1994
We had arrived in Karabagh one week ago after the 10-hour journey from Yerevan to Goris, through the Lachin Corridor, and finally to Stepanakert. There was no question that we had entered a war zone. Along the way there were three army posts where we were stopped and questioned by the soldiers. Five of us were traveling together. Since Gourgen Melikian was well-known by the soldiers we were allowed to continue on after exchanging greetings. The soldiers radioed to the next post and ahead to Stepanakert's government offices that we were en route.

When we passed the last post close to Shushi, and were no farther than 10 miles from Stepanakert, we saw the most amazing thing—an Armenian city at night! We could see the city in the distance! It was midnight and we could see Stepanakert! Stepanakert had electricity. Lights were burning in the city! We had just come from Armenia where there was no electricity and where the cities were in total darkness. What a shock to see an Armenian city with electricity. We stopped the car and we lined up alongside the road, gasping with amazement. Gourgen pointed out that several of the neighboring villages had electricity too! (Karabagh's electricity was coming from the hydroelectric power plant it had recaptured and from Armenia. Armenia was sharing its electricity with Karabagh.)

It was past midnight when we arrived but Robert Kocharian, the Chairman of the Defense Committee of Karabagh, was still in his office working. After a brief stop at the government's head-quarters located in the main square, we settled into the government hotel located on the edge of the city. The hotel was in disrepair, the walls full of holes that appeared to have been made from machine guns and the windows shattered. As expected, there was no running water, but we had electricity. And thanks to Julia, the dear woman who looked after the hotel's guests, we were reasonably comfortable.

The next morning, at about 8 a.m., I was awakened by sirens that sounded for several minutes. The hotel's windows and walls shook. The muffled sound of shooting could be heard in the distance. The sun shone and the sky was blue; a great day for an Azeri offensive. I grabbed my robe and ran out into the hallway. Dr. Mihran Aghbabian from California, the president of the new American University of Armenia, was on his way down to breakfast, appearing quite calm. He informed me that according to plan the others in my group had just left for a neighboring village to inspect a cow that one of the men owned.

Seeing the unsettled look on my face he added that the others had said not to worry about the fighting, which was about 20 miles away. Mihran did not appear concerned either. I decided to ignore it too and go about getting ready for the day. Life had to go on even if men were dying just a few miles away from us. All of the people who were here were here for much more serious reasons than to look at a cow. The cow, however, was important too. It was part of a humanitarian program one of the men had started. Cows were purchased and given to the local farmers. The farmers in return had to give the owners of the cows some cheese and yogurt whenever he was in Karabagh. The rest of the time, the cow's milk was the farmer's to do with as he pleased.

Later that morning, with the sound of fighting still in the distance, children, perfectly groomed and carrying their school bags, were making their way to school. If they were not afraid, how could I be? These children had spent the winter and the months before living in basements, without water, without electricity, and with very little to keep them warm. That was when the city was being hit by Grad missiles on a daily basis. I suppose now that the missiles have been stopped, the sound of fighting in the distance did not frighten them.

The next day we went to Matchkalashen, a village in the south of Karabagh, in the region called Marduni, just a few miles from the fifth century Armenian monastery and school, *Amaras*. By the time we arrived at the medical post, a line of patients had already formed outside the front door. The *feldsher* who worked here, a rather elderly man, was there too. Before seeing any patients we talked about the medications that I had brought last November. He told me that the aspirin I had brought had been very helpful during the winter. I checked the supply of medicine that he had in the back room. He still had many of the antibiotics and heart medication I had brought to him last fall. I wondered why? Was it because he did not know how to use them or had not had the need for them. It was something I had to figure out.

The patients came with all kinds of ailments, from minor skin rashes to deeply penetrating infections of osteomyelitis. Everyone went to work in the fields or to war despite their ailments, ignoring their pain and disabilities for as long as they could. I tried to give helpful suggestions, practical things that might help. For some, I had nothing to offer. For others there was medicine, and some of it was in the medical post already. Now I knew that the feldsher had not dispensed the medications because he did not know *how* to use them, despite the instructions he had written down and which were on his desk. I could only try again and explain their use in the hope that he would make better use of the drugs. Perhaps I was expecting too much of him.

The next afternoon we distributed gifts we had brought for the kindergarten children. Children in Karabagh started kindergarten at age 4 and continued through age 7. The night before, at Vera and Armik's house, where we usually stay, we had separated the gifts by these ages. Each was put in a colorful box the shape of a doctor's bag that had been donated to us by the Kendall Company. (They had been helping with lots of medical supplies as well.) A long table was carried out by some of the older children from inside the small school house and placed in the courtyard next to our car.

I took my place behind the table where the colorful boxes had been lined up. The director of the kindergarten came and stood firmly at my side, without saying a word. Her head, which barely came to my shoulders, was wrapped in a scarf despite the midday heat. Her face neither smiled nor wept. Her very dark eyes were devoid of expression. This was a new expression I had begun to see on many of the women I was meeting. I soon realized that it was the appearance of profound grief; it was, in fact, beyond grief.

At first I was not sure who the woman standing by me was. There were a few toys among the gifts. These, she said, would be better left to the school for all of the children to play with. I agreed. Some moments passed as we waited for the children and their parents to gather in the school yard. She spoke again. "Seven teachers who work in this kindergarten are widowed. They have many children among them. Help is needed for them to survive," she said in a flat tone of voice and without any facial expression.

Then she told me her story there, under the heat of the day, in that courtyard beginning to fill with noisy children excited about the prospect of receiving a gift, a rare and wonderful occasion in their young lives. For the next few moments I was aware of nothing else except her words as they came out of her lips, barely moving, hypnotizing me by the intensity of her presence. Three weeks ago her husband, who was a fighter along with many others, was reported missing by the army. The Azeris listed him as having been taken alive to Baku. She was filled with hope that he would survive. Then, one week ago, in a body exchange with the Azeris, ten bodies were returned to this region. She was asked to look at the corpses and identified her husband by a tattoo he had on his foot; his corpse was headless. Her five children, all under the age of ten, were now fatherless. Her expression was no longer a puzzle to me. I forced my tears to wait until she would not see them.

Before the day was over, I learned that the village had no soap and that clothing and shoes were desperately needed for the children. Although each of the gift boxes we gave the children that day contained a sweater or some other item of clothing, more was needed especially for the winter. We promised to help the village with more soap for all of the families, stipends for the widows, food for the kindergarten, clothes for the children, and paper for the grade school. In the meantime we were also providing first-aid kits for the soldiers stationed on the frontlines here and would continue bringing medicine to the medical post.

Late in the afternoon, before leaving the village I stopped in to say good-bye to the feldsher and to review the medications and my recommendations for some of the sicker patients we had seen together. We had a light dinner of fresh bread and newly made cheese and headed back to Stepanakert. Gourgen and the rest of the group would be leaving for Yerevan in the morning. I stayed in Karabagh for another week. I needed time to walk the streets, talk to people, visit with the doctors, to just be there. I needed time to think about what I was seeing and experiencing.

⚜

The day after our group left, Dr. Marutian invited me to a nearby village to have dinner with a family there. The village had been subjected to heavy bombing and shelling by missiles. Its position, on the mountain exactly opposite Shushi, where the Azeris had their stronghold, had made it a convenient target.

When we arrived the women were in the yard baking bread in a *tonir*. A tonir is an oven of sorts, made by digging a hole in the ground and lining the sides with big flat rocks. (The tonir these women were using was built above the ground.) A wood fire made on the bottom of the hole heats the rocks. When the flames quiet down and the rocks are very hot, thin rounds of dough are slapped onto the rocks and baked into a tasty bread. The men in the meantime were preparing another fire for the *khorovatz*, the pig already slaughtered and butchered, that would now be barbecued. Other women, daughters and daughters-in-law, were busy in the house putting finishing touches on the long table that filled an entire room and would accommodate as many guests as may arrive. There were more than twenty of us when we finally sat down to dinner; aside from the family whose home this was, the others were all young doctors at the military hospital. But before we sat down at the table, the most delicious parts of the *khorovatz* were passed around for everyone to enjoy, hot off the fire. We stood around the fire, drinking vodka, toasting our heroes, gazing from time to time at Shushi on the hill beyond, under a cool drizzle that everyone ignored.

The thin breads were piled high all around the table after we were seated. The table was set in typical Armenian fashion, two small plates, one on top of the other, and multiples of the same salads placed everywhere so that no one had to reach or ask for something to be passed. The salads were mostly of potatoes and herbs and various preserved pickled vegetables. The lack of fresh foods was evident. The soldier sitting next to me assumed the responsibility for being sure my plate and glass were always full. Marutian periodically looked over my way to be sure that the soldier was performing his duty as was expected.

I recognized most of the faces as I looked around the table. They have seen more death in the past two years than most of us see in a lifetime. The worst injuries, they have told me, are incurred when a tank goes over a landmine. The men inside the tank are burned, legs are blown off, and most have no chance of surviving. Today they have already performed seven operations. One of the doctors, an anesthesiologist, says that sometimes he must handle three operations in the field at the same time. They are learning a lot about trauma. Marutian estimated that he has performed 5,000 operations in the field. But enough, someone started to sing and the others join in. The next three hours were spent singing and telling funny stories. No one seemed in a hurry to have the afternoon end.

⚜

It was Easter Sunday, April 3, 1994. I left Julia's apartment and headed for the Military Hospital. As I walked through the streets and watched people going about their daily routines, I was filled with thoughts about the Easters of my childhood. The preparations would start weeks before, planning at whose house Easter dinner would be, and who would make which of the special dishes that would be eaten that day. There might be a new coat or a new dress for me. There would be a new hat for sure, or maybe my sister's from last year. The day started early at 7 a.m. with a special Easter service at Radio City Music Hall in Manhattan. Then, holding my father's hand, Mom and Rose alongside, we would walk down Fifth Avenue heading for our own church on East 34th Street where we would attend services again. Later at home, before dinner, we would play the traditional Armenian game of cracking each other's eggs.

Today though, there were no outward signs of Easter. There was work to do which would not wait for a holiday. When I reached the hospital I was therefore surprised to hear two nurses exchanging the traditional Armenian Easter greeting based on the biblical account of the morning. The one said, *"Krisdos haryav ee merelotz"* (Christ is risen from the dead), but neither was able to remember the full response. I completed it saying, *"Orhnyal eh haroutiun e Krisdosi,"* (Blessed is the resurrection of Christ). Together we practiced the greeting over and over again. Since Karabagh Armenians were not allowed to learn Armenian under Azeris rule, pronouncing the words was as difficult for them as it was for me.

There were 75 wounded men in the hospital that day. The intensive care unit was filled with those who were critically ill, some of whom were waiting to be transferred to Yerevan. Marutian was there too. He was checking up on a child who had been brought in last night with a gunshot wound that had torn through his abdomen. The surgeons at the Children's Hospital had refused to operate on him, saying that the surgeons at the military hospital would be much better qualified to perform the needed surgery. Marutian had hopefully done just that.

There was another child, I was told, who was less fortunate at the Children's Hospital. He is the sole survivor of his family after a cassette bomb exploded in his house. (Cassette bombs were dropped by the Azeris on Stepanakert. These bombs, outlawed by the international community, do not fully explode on impact but scatter hundreds of colorful balls that children find and play with, even years later. These cassette, anti-personnel bombs, are continuing to explode in Karabagh.)

Marutian moved from bed to bed examining his patients and changing their dressings; he explained the wounds that each soldier had sustained. Just as one might expect, nothing was simple; the wounds were multiple and the surgery complicated. Postoperative care, here as in Armenia, was a major problem. Medical doctors were not trained well enough to care for these complicated cases; neither were the nurses. Whatever they did for these patients had been learned through the experiences of the past years, just as the surgeons had learned. Doctors like myself, who are not surgeons, could only consult on some patients and review the use of antibiotics and other drugs that had been sent to them. Communication was a problem too. Most of the Karabagh doctors had been trained in Baku or in Russia and spoke very little Armenian. No one spoke English and finding someone to translate in those days was not always possible.

I had been unable to find a car to take me back to Yerevan; fuel was scarce and only military vehicles and transport trucks were making the trip. Anticipating the problem, Gourgen had instructed me to see Robert Kocharian when I was ready to return. He would arrange for my transportation back to Yerevan. I thought that Mr. Kocharian had more important things to worry about than how I was to return to Yerevan. Somehow I would get back, I was sure. Marutian informed me that on Easter Sunday an oil truck was going to Yerevan that night and there was room in it for me. I was delighted!

Julia was not happy to learn how I would be making the trip back to Yerevan. "An oil truck? Are they crazy sending you to Yerevan in an oil truck?" Julia, the woman who took care of the guests at the government hotel, had refused to let me stay there alone after the others had left and invited me to her apartment to live with her family for the rest of my time in Karabagh.

Julia was always pleased when our group, Gourgen, George, and I along with any number of other travelers, arrived at the hotel. If she was alerted to our arrival, she saved the suite for me. It had two big beds and an adjoining living room and a large balcony accessed through French doors. Since there was rarely running water at the hotel, Julia saved water in the bathtub for general use and in the morning would place a kettle of hot water at my door for washing up.

Julia told me that when she first met me she could not understand one word of my Armenian. Now she could understand me easily. She was happy to learn that I now understood her too. We always found time to sit over a cup of tea in the late afternoon and chat about life. Julia had remained in Stepanakert during the Soviet occupation, during the worst days of the war that followed, the bombing and the missile attacks. The problems of her life would be too much for any one of us to handle. She worried most about her son Albert, who was wounded and was now in the Rehabilitation Hospital in Yerevan.

In her apartment our conversations continued. She started to teach me the language that Karabaghtsis speak amongst themselves, a mixture of Armenian, Turkish, Russian, Persian, Sanskrit, and even English! For example, the word for bottle is *bottle*, who is *who*, and rock is *rock*. My attempts at imitating Julia's sing-song intonations of this language that has no written form left us both laughing. In the midst of this, a few of her neighbors came in to say good-bye to me. The word had quickly spread that I was leaving that night. Several of the neighbors had come on other evenings during the week seeking advice about their medical ailments. Their problems were simple enough to diagnose, like bronchitis and arthritis, but providing treatment was another problem. Again, I gave them whatever medication I had with me, but could not make any promises for the future.

Julia had prepared a lunch that we sat down to eat with her husband and daughter. The table was set on their porch next to the wood-burning stove. The table was covered with a white cloth and pushed up against the inner wall, opposite the windows. She insisted that I sit at the table while they finished getting the food ready. Julia was handing her husband a kettle to put on the stove, and while passing it over to him, pointed out where the shrapnel had pierced the walls, narrowly missing her husband as he sat in this very spot.

Bread, honey, boiled potatoes, and eggs colored with the dye of red onion skins were placed on the table. We cracked the eggs in the traditional Armenian way, each of us selecting an egg by tapping the shell on our front teeth to determine its strength, then cupping it in one hand with just the tip showing—the place where the challenger would hit it just once, with his egg, hoping to crack the shell. "Your egg cracked, now turn the other side over," the winner said, and so on, until both sides of all the eggs were cracked, save one. They were amazed that I knew the game, and I, that they knew it.

We ate the eggs with the bread and honey that Julia had set out, laughing and joking, trying not to think about the moment we would have to say good-bye. Julia rose from the table and started to put some of the food left over in a plastic wrap, meant for my trip. I objected. "It would be a shame on us and on every Karabaghtsi to send you without food. What will the people you are traveling with think of me? What will Gourgen think of us?" I assured her that I would not tell Gourgen, but I knew that to refuse her offer would inflict a wound greater than any bullet could. I accepted the food. I would never really understand the spirit of a person who gives you food when she barely has enough for herself and her family. It was indeed a special Easter.

And now a delicate moment. I wanted to leave money with Julia, but knew that if I were not careful, I could inflict yet another kind of wound. I invited her into my room. "Julia," as I gently pressed the money into her hand, her eyes opening wide almost in horror, "this is not for you, but for your grandchildren." She relaxed and said," I did not bring you here for this." I repeated, "Julia, this is not for you, but for your grandchildren. I would have bought them gifts, but you know much better than I what they need. Please, take this for them." She smiled and we both felt much better.

At 5 p.m., after saying our good-byes, I was taken to the appointed place where I was to meet the oil truck. Before leaving, however, I managed to call Gourgen in Yerevan to let him know that I was leaving and how I was traveling. He was not happy about the oil truck either but there was nothing much he could do about it; I was all set to leave Stepanakert.

There were two drivers and, I was happy to see, another woman traveling with us. We sat four across on the seat of the truck that was so high I needed help to hoist myself up to it.

The trip progressed without any problems until midnight when the drivers announced they were getting sleepy and that we would be stopping in Yeghegnadzor, about two hours outside of Yerevan. They planned to sleep for several hours before continuing on in the morning. That meant we would not arrive in Yerevan until 8 or 9 a.m. in the morning. The Melikians would be worried, but there was nothing I could do about it now; there was no way of calling them to let them know about the delay and that I was safe.

By the time I walked into the Melikian's apartment the following morning, Laura, who had stayed home from work, said that Gourgen had been up most of the night, and had finally gone to the University to make arrangements for starting a search. They were sure that I was lying dead or injured somewhere on the road from Karabagh.

A lot of sparks flew over this incident, in Karabagh and Boston, too. I promised never to travel on an oil truck again.

But that morning, as the oil truck came over the mountains from Yeghegnadzor, through the pass, over the last hill, looking to the Ararat valley, looking straight out at Big and Little Massis, the sun sparkling off the snow on their summits, I managed to capture it in one of the most beautiful photos of Ararat that I have ever taken!

The doctors and nurses who staff the Primary Care Center. Dr. Ruben Khatchatrian is seated next to me. Gyumri, 1996.

CHAPTER 13

The Primary Care Center, Gyumri

B y 1994 it had become obvious to me that I needed to undertake a project that would make a more lasting contribution to health care in Armenia. Although I had been seeing patients and working with doctors all along, the bulk of my work in Armenia was focused on the distribution of medical supplies and other relief aid. I felt that my clinical skills were underutilized. For some time I had been thinking about starting a small clinic for adults that would not only treat patients but also serve as a training center for local doctors.

Outpatient health care under the soviet system was provided through a centrally planned and funded network of regional polyclinics. Polyclinics for adults were staffed by both general medical doctors, called *therapefts*, and various medical and surgical specialists. About 80 percent of outpatient care was delivered by these specialists, while the therapeft, the least prestigious of all physicians, delivered the remaining 20 percent.

A patient with a sore throat or swollen tonsils might consult his or her therapeft first, but would usually be referred to an ear, nose, and throat specialist for treatment. Similarly, someone with a headache or a backache would be referred to a neurologist. Many patients simply went directly to a specialist rather than consulting their therapeft first.

It seemed to me, and others, that it would be a big step toward developing a more efficient and cost-effective health care system if therapefts, like primary care physicians in the West, could treat most of their patients' medical problems, referring only complicated cases to specialists. In February 1994, to discuss the problem I met with Dr. Krikor Soghikian, a primary care physician from California who had been chairing a committee of professionals studying Armenia's primary health care system. We began plans for a small primary care training center and clinic to be established in Gyumri. When I returned to Gyumri in April, I presented the plan to Ruben, who was now head of the Department of Health for the entire region of Shirak. He was intrigued by the concept.

At the end of our meeting Ruben repeated the words "primary care" in English, very slowly, with a heavy accent. Then he said in Armenian, "This is very important for Gyumri and for Armenia." The long-term effects of the earthquake, the breakup of the Soviet Union, the blockade, and the war were forcing major cuts in every area of the nation's federal budget, including health care. Regional administrators like Ruben had to fire hundreds of healthcare workers, eliminate hospitals beds, and reduce the amount of money spent on patient care. Ruben quickly grasped the benefits of the primary care system. His doctors would be better utilized and patients would receive better care for less money. He wanted to know how soon we could get started!

In the fall we opened the Primary Care Center of Gyumri in six rooms located on the first floor of a polyclinic. Donated furniture and equipment, medications for the patients, and a small library of journals and textbooks were sent from Boston by sea container to Georgia and then by rail to Armenia, a route that bypassed the blockade.

Our trainees were three therapefts and nurses from the polyclinic. Several doctors, including Dr. Soghikian, volunteered to spend time teaching at the clinic. Fortunately, Armen, who had come to Boston for training in 1993, had developed into an outstanding internist; he provided the oversight needed in our absence.

Before the project got under way, I had understood that major differences existed between the Soviet system and the West, but had not appreciated the magnitude of those differences. The iron curtain had effectively isolated Soviet medical practice from many of the advances of Western medicine. New textbooks and journals were not available, and professors who did not keep up to date continued to teach ideas that had long since been discredited in the West. In addition, doctors were not taught how to think carefully about patients' illnesses; the art of developing a differential diagnosis, the possible diagnoses a patient might have based on their symptoms, physical exam, and laboratory tests, was not vigorously taught.

The teaching began—as did the learning. Our doctors learned how to confidently diagnose and treat common illnesses such as congestive heart failure and pneumonia. They learned how to do neurologic and gynecologic exams and how to use ophthalmoscopes and otoscopes, instruments normally reserved for specialists.

Our doctors learned how to do breast exams, but when they found a lump there was no mammography available to help make a diagnosis. If we wanted to obtain a computerized axial tomogram (CAT scan) to rule out a brain tumor as the cause of a patient's headaches, the patient had to go to Yerevan, site of the country's only CAT scanner. If routine examination revealed an enlarged thyroid gland or suspected abnormal thyroid function, there were no tests we could order to help us with our diagnosis. X-rays were of inferior quality and laboratory results could not be fully relied upon. Most of the routine blood tests that are taken for granted in the West were unavailable in Armenia.

This was the level of medicine the newly independent republics like Armenia had inherited from the Soviet Union, a world power that put the first satellite into outer space. Daily at the clinic I was angered and frustrated by these conditions and by the lack of any acceptable technology. The irony was maddening:

in a country with a wonderful symphony orchestra, an outstanding opera house, almost 100 percent literacy (including every last villager in the most remote mountains), and a population boasting one of the highest proportions of university graduates and advanced-degree holders in the world, Armenian doctors and nurses labored in primitive facilities hampered by inadequate training. It was hard to understand and even harder to accept.

Patients came from all over the city and surrounding villages with various medical problems and in all stages of severity. It did not take long to realize that two of the most common and serious health problems facing the adult population in Gyumri were severe hypertension and chronic gastrointestinal ulcer disease.

On many days patient after patient came to the clinic with blood pressures in dangerously high ranges: as high as 250/140 mmHG, normal being 120/80 mmHG. Some of these patients were young, even in their twenties. I can only speculate about the reasons for these high readings: years of eating a diet extraordinarily high in salt and fat, and years of living with extraordinary stress, made worse by the earthquake, the blockade, and the war. Soviet medicine had not paid attention to prevention issues; there were no strategies aimed at smoking cessation, reducing salt and fat intake, or developing exercise programs. Even when hypertension was diagnosed it was treated inadequately. There was (and still is) the widely held belief among the general population that high blood pressure is dangerous only if it gives you symptoms—such as headache or dizziness. And then, it is important to bring the pressure down only to a level that relieved the symptoms.

Therefore, few patients took medication prescribed by their doctor on a regular basis and many were not adverse to trying those of a neighbor or a friend. Practices such as putting ones feet in hot water to reduce an acute elevation of pressure were deemed adequate. The medical profession did little or nothing to counter these beliefs and practices, cut off from the major advances being made in the field of cardiovascular medicine, and our understanding of illnesses like hypertension.

We had to convince our patients that high blood pressure, even if "silent," was dangerous and that these common practices should be changed. The nurses interacted with patients in a new way, for the first time working as an adjunct to the doctors. They learned to greet patients, talk with them first, and then record their vital signs and alert the doctors if someone's pressure was dangerously high. They learned to discuss changes in eating habits and to review how the patient was to take the medicine prescribed. Patients who were asked to return for follow-up came and began to understand the importance of surveillance and tight control. Often they only interacted with the nurses on these follow-up visits; consequently the nurses began to feel more responsible for the care of the patients.

Slowly, with close follow-up, and on a daily regimen of medication and with salt reduction, we began to see lower blood pressures in our patients; they were as gratified as we were.

Ulcer disease was the other major medical problem many people who came to the clinic had. Their complaints were variations on a theme: years of suffering with abdominal pain, recurrent ulcers, or gastritis nonresponsive to the usual acid-lowering therapies. Some patients even had surgery in an effort to cure the problem, only to have their symptoms and ulcers recur.

Fortunately the discovery that most ulcers are caused by the bacterium *Heliobacter pylori* led to a new antibiotic treatment in the West and offered the possibility of cure to these patients. Word quickly spread about the new "miracle" treatment and hundreds of patients came from all over the region. Cure was something they had never thought possible, but three to four years later the vast majority of these patients are still symptom-free.

There is an hereditary disease that afflicts Armenians as well as Sephardic Jews and Arabs, called Familial Mediterranean Fever (FMF). Armenians call it the "Armenian Disease." It is characterized by periodic attacks of incapacitating abdominal pain and high fevers. There is no cure for FMF, but the drug colchicine can make the attacks less frequent and less severe; it also prevents the development of kidney failure, the one terrible consequence affecting some patients. Young people known to have the disease are often rejected as a potential marriage partner. It is thought that one in seven Armenians carries the gene for FMF. Obviously, the practice has not been effective.

Regularly, either at the Primary Care Center, or privately, patients would seek my opinion about this disease; whether I thought they had it or not, or if they were already diagnosed with it, what treatments were available in America. The following case is illustrative of the kind of problem FMF can present both to the patient and the doctor:

An 18-year-old woman was brought to the clinic by her mother-in-law. After the usual preliminaries, the two women came into the consultation room where Maro, one of our doctors, and I were seeing patients. The older of the two women started, "She has pains in her stomach. I think she must have the Armenian disease," and looking directly at me, ignoring Maro, she asked, "What do you think?" She was the young woman's mother-in-law.

After a few introductory words on my part, I explained that our practice was to see patients alone and asked the mother-in-law to leave the room. Despite being upset by this departure from the norm, she complied. The young woman sitting in front of us looked sad and frightened. After her mother-in-law left the room, she told us through her tears that the woman had accused her of hiding her abdominal symptoms until after the wedding and was threatening her with divorce. In fact, the stomach pains she was experiencing had started only a few months ago. She loved her husband and did not want a divorce. We tried to be reassuring.

When we finished taking her history and examining her, the cause of her stomach pain was not clear. The history she gave was full of inconsistencies, and combined with her physical exam that was normal, we had little to go on. The patient agreed to have blood tests and to return with her husband. In the meantime, for lack of anything else to offer, I suggested she try a milk-free diet and explained exactly what she had to avoid eating. She agreed.

A few weeks later the young woman returned with her husband and without her mother-in-law. None of the staff recognized her at first; she was bright eyed, smiling, and carefully made-up. She felt much better on the milk-free diet and had not had any more abdominal pain. She planned to stay on the diet. The couple had come to seek advice about getting pregnant!

Too often the outcomes of these encounters were not as happy as this example. Many patients with FMF suffer because of their inability to face the diagnosis. Even for those who do, the disease progresses because there is not enough colchicine to take regularly. Colchicine costs pennies a pill in the United States, but in Armenia it costs as much as one dollar a tablet. Some clinics that specialize in FMF distribute the pill free of charge when they have it, but there is not enough for the more than 7,000 registered FMF patients.

In the past few years, the gene carrying FMF has been identified and a blood test is now available for making an accurate diagnosis. Whether people like the patient I have just described will be willing to take the test remains to be seen.

The Primary Care Center in Gyumri continues to operate today providing free care to the residents of Gyumri. Ruben hopes that someday all of Gyumri's polyclinics will be patterned after our model. That day is still in the future.

· PART IV ·

HOMECOMING
1994-1997

*Tea with Dr. Lilit Boghosian and her daughter Nara
in their "garage" home.
Gyumri, 1992*

CHAPTER 14

About Surviving

For nearly twenty-five years Dr. Lilit Boghosian has worked at the Maternity Hospital serving the residents of Gyumri as its chief obstetrician; but never as the chief doctor of her hospital. On the day of the earthquake she was scheduled for surgery at 11:30 a.m. The hospital's chief doctor offered to take her place, knowing that Lilit had a pressing personal problem to which she needed to tend. Lilit left the hospital and had just reached the street at 11:40 when the earth started to shake. She turned to look back at the hospital, only to see it collapse. The chief doctor was killed while she stood poised at the operating table, taking Lilit's place.

Lilit's husband had died of leukemia years before the earthquake, leaving her to raise their three daughters alone. In Armenia, if a widow's husband has a brother, he must support her as best he can; if he is not married, he is obliged to marry her, according to the old custom. Few widows are otherwise able to marry and are left very much alone. Women did not go to public places alone, such as cinemas, theaters, concerts, or even a relative's wedding. When widowed, they were expected to remain at home despite isolation and loneliness. Some of these attitudes changed after the earthquake, because many men were left without wives and were unable to take care of themselves or their children. They needed to remarry, and the women who had been widowed were logical choices.

Lilit, however, had no one to help her after her husband died and her three daughters became her sole responsibility. She devoted her life to them and to her profession. Lilit's two older daughters were married and lived in Gyumri at the time of the earthquake. Nara, her youngest daughter, still lived at home. They all survived the earthquake.

Afterward, Nara and Lilit made a home out of a freestanding garage in a courtyard of their apartment building, which had been destroyed by the earthquake. When they were given a domic, they pulled it up along one side of the garage to serve as a bedroom. The garage itself was divided into a small living room, a kitchen, and a bathroom. Lilit was seldom at home when there was electricity or water. She worked long hours at the hospital and was often called there in the middle of the night; Nara had to perform many of the household chores created by the earthquake and the blockade.

Water had to be collected in pots and large pails whenever the central water was turned on. One of Lilit's sons-in-law hooked up a system of pipes and tubes that provided her with indoor plumbing in the bathroom. When water flowed from the central system all she had to do was connect a hose to the faucet and collect the water in her pails. This was a luxury, since most people had to go outside their houses to a central location to get their daily supply of water.

Once she became comfortable in our friendship and realized that I understood the conditions under which she and Nara lived, she invited me for dinner, then insisted I stay with her when I was in Gyumri.

I would meet her at the hospital and together we would walk home. Usually Nara had already started dinner and Lilit would add the finishing touches. But first she would pull back the carpet covering the kitchen floor, exposing a latch on the floor boards. Then she would pull on the latch to lift some of the heavy floor boards made into a door that led to her underground storage area. Here she stored apples, potatoes, and onions, as well as the foods she and Nara had preserved during the summer harvest season. Lilit would descend into the darkness, holding a candle, and start to pass various things up to me—a *mouraba* along with a bag of onions and say, "Let's try this one. It's a special cherry mouraba. We'll have it with our tea." The best was always brought out for me, her guest. She kept homemade brandy and liqueurs down there too, and sometimes she would hoist herself back up from her underground hiding place holding up a special bottle—"Let's have a drink together tonight!" In the dark, with a single kerosene light burning, we would sit in her kitchen sipping our drinks and tell stories about our families. I told her about my mother and father coming from Kharpert, how life was for Armenians in America; she told me about her father and grandfather, who escaped from Erzerum in eastern Turkey and came to what became Soviet Armenia. When our eyes could no longer take the strain of the kerosene light, or when we felt too tired or cold to go on, we went to bed. But first we washed, using water Nara had stored in the pails piled up on one side of the bathroom.

More than once, when we started to move the heavy pails of water around, Lilit suddenly looked up, put the pail down, threw her hands up, and laughed. Maybe it was the liquor that caused our giddiness, or the image of two women, physicians at that, in their nightgowns, in a bathroom of sorts, trying to manage these pails of water. Together we laughed the endless laughter of children at play. Lilit would say, "*Inch a-nenk? Ahs e mer gyanke.*" (What can we do? This is our life.) And we'd laugh some more, in the middle of the night, by the light of the kerosene lamp.

The winters of this era were extraordinarily severe and Lilit's garage home was very cold. During the winter of 1992 she said Nara and she would get into bed fully dressed, sometimes with even their overcoats on, "hugging each other for warmth, with tears in our eyes from the cold, hoping we would not freeze to death during the night, hoping for sleep so that we would stop feeling the pain."

After graduating from school Nara announced her engagement to Vachig, the young man she had been dating for several years, and the wedding date was set. I could see a sadness creep into Lilit's eyes behind the happiness they showed for her daughter as Lilit faced living alone. When I brought up the question of where Nara would live after she was married, Lilit said, "She will go to live with her husband's family." I pressed the point, "You are all alone, you need her. There are many people in his family. You should not be left alone. Why can't they live with you?" When she refused to consider the possibility, I continued, "His family is understanding, surely they would accept this." She looked at me sternly and replied, "They cannot live here. That is the way it is and the way it must be." I never broached the subject again.

The day of Nara's wedding came. It had been scheduled so that I could be present.

All weddings in Armenia adhere to the same traditions, and Nara's was no different. On the day of the wedding, with groom in tow, the boy's mother, father, sisters, brothers, aunts, uncles, grandparents, godparents, and close friends came to the bride's home. As they danced through the streets carrying gifts in brightly wrapped baskets overhead for all to see, musicians playing ancient instruments heralded their procession. Inside, the bride waited in the bedroom, bathed and ready to be dressed, for it was the women who were arriving, the women with whom she would live the rest of her life, who would dress her in the bridal clothes they have brought with them. Only these women would enter her room. Her dowry was on display in another room, a measure of her worth for all to examine. From the time she was a little girl, her mother had been preparing the dowry, teaching her traditional Armenian embroidery to adorn the pillow cases, sheets, and tablecloths now laid out for all to admire. Regardless of how much or how little education she had, whether she lived in Yerevan or in the remotest village of Karabagh, no matter anything, this was the way.

While the women were in the bedroom dressing the bride, the men from both families gathered in the living room around a table filled with food and drink. The toasts began. At this happy time, special care had to be given to these rituals lest a slight be felt, a dishonor that would never be forgotten. Each man and woman had to be recognized in the appropriate order; each family honored the other. The toasts were elaborate, filled with praises, listing accomplishments, accounting hardships overcome. But before any of this could continue, the man leading the festivities raised his glass in solemn remembrance of the earthquake's victims and those who died fighting for Karabagh. All eyes were lowered, glasses held low, and then raised and extended toward each other, but turned at the last moment, so that hands touched each other, avoiding the noise the glasses would make.

The men then drank to the health and happiness of the new couple and, most important, to the new generation the union will create, to the continuation of the family and of the nation, to the sons who will be born.

Daughters leave their parent's home and become an asset to someone else's family. Daughters cost the family more than they can give back, unless they never marry. Sons, on the other hand, take over the responsibility of protecting the family, supporting it, bringing honor to it. Sons will marry and bring to the family dowries and women, who will bear children and shoulder the burden of physical work.

When the women were finished they brought Nara into the living room to stand next to the groom. They will not speak to each other until nearly the end of the day. To the joyous music of the ancient instruments, the families escorted the couple to the church where the marriage ceremony was performed.

Although most couples now have a church wedding, during the days of communism few dared to do so. Instead, they simply appeared at the government marriage office to register their status as husband and wife. In many places—particularly Karabagh, where churches in outlying regions have no priests—this is still all that is done. Sometimes, even this cannot be done by the wed-

ding day. In that case the families announce the couples inten-
tions, name the day, and their relatives then follow the traditions.
The family, in a sense, performs the marriage itself.

The family gives the marriage its sanctity, and the family keeps
the marriage intact. Family honor is at stake on both sides. The
family intervenes when there is trouble. It is the family that prevents their daughters from returning home and the family that
forces sons to keep wives they no longer want. Although divorce
was easy to obtain under Soviet rule, it was reserved by Armenians for the most dire of circumstances. Unfortunately, divorce is
more common today as families are coming under increased economic pressure.

There were no wedding celebrations in Gyumri for more than
a year after the earthquake; then weddings took place, but without any music. Now, weddings again have all the trimmings.
Nara and Vachig's wedding dinner was held in his parent's home.
Tables and benches filled the large living room, and Lilit and I
squeezed in next to each other, close to where the bride and
groom would sit. (There are no table numbers or carefully determined seating arrangements at Armenian weddings.) I turned to
Lilit and asked—unfortunately at a moment when the room was
silent—"*Davajana ov e?*" She looked at me in horror! "What did
you say?" she asked me in Armenian. I repeated my question.
"What are you trying to say?" she pressed me, neither of us yet
understanding my mistake. "You know, the '*davajan*,' the man
who runs the reception, makes all of the toasts, and so on..." I
explained. It then became clear to her that I had confused the
word for toastmaster, *damadan*, with the word for traitor, *davajan*!

Nara and Vachig spent their first night together in the room
prepared for them by his mother in the family home. Although I
never asked, I am sure that Nara's mother-in-law did exactly what
must have been done to her and to all of the other women in her
family. The morning after their wedding night she would have
come to the newlyweds' room and taken Nara's nightclothes and
the bed sheets. The next morning the women of both sides would

gather to inspect these, not only to confirm the bride's virginity, but also the groom's virility.

After forty days of married life, Vachig took Nara back to her home with Lilit. Nara stayed a few weeks and then returned to her husband and his family. However, she could have stayed for up to several months. This is the period when the final decision is made: the groom has the option of not going back for his wife, and she has the option of not returning. Most Armenian families in Armenia continue to follow this very interesting custom. I wonder how this would work in the United States?

❦

The number 40 (*karasoun*) is special in Armenian tradition, no doubt coming from the many references to it in the Bible. In the Old Testament Solomon and Saul reigned for 40 years, Moses spent 40 days in the desert and was called by God at the age of 40, Noah spent 40 days in the ark before landing on Ararat. In the New Testament, Jesus was presented to the Temple 40 days after his birth, he was tested in the wilderness for 40 days, and ascended into heaven 40 days after the crucifixion.

As I have described, forty days after marriage the *hars*, the daughter-in-law, returns to her family. For forty days after child-birth Armenians consider the mother's life to be in danger and the baby susceptible to bad omen and infection: men are not to look at newborn infants during this period of time. For Armenians, forty days is the official period of mourning after someone dies; on the fortieth day there is a special service of remembrance called the *karasounk*.

I came to understand that traditions like these were the real rulers of life in Armenia. They preserved Armenian society through the seventy years of communism—not always such bad years, but often brutal and repressive. Family traditions, poetry recitation, singing, music, all reflect centuries of Armenian history and culture. Even the way women keep house and certainly the way a guest is treated are rooted in this ancient sense of what home is and the dignity attached to it, be it a shanty in Gyumri or an elegant apartment in Yerevan.

At first some customs appeared repressive, even misogynistic, to me. I would argue with my female friends. Why sleep with the light switch in the "on" position and get up at 2 or 3 or 4 a.m. to iron when the electricity comes on? Why must bed sheets that no one else will see, pillow cases, dish towels, and tablecloths be ironed to perfection under these conditions?

In Gyumri's Maternity Hospital, amidst the mud and squalor, the table is set for tea with a freshly ironed tablecloth spread over it. I beg the nurses, please do not do this for me, at the same time wondering how they manage to get everything so clean without hot water or soap.

Strong traditions govern food and serving guests. Why must I eat even when you do not have enough food. How can I know that you have not sold your shoes or your coat so that the proper table is set. Why are you insulted if I refuse your invitation?

These traditions have kept society together through terrible years when life was turned completely upside down, when nothing could be relied on to be there or to function as it should. Tradition has been there to provide some sense of stability and continuity and I was beginning to understand how important these things were.

It was a cold Monday in November 1994. I was back in Gyumri to spend another week at the clinic. After work I made my way through the city to Lilit's new apartment. Tonight, Lilit was on call and would not be coming home. Her downstairs neighbor expected me and let me in. I unpacked and washed up, using the water in the familiar buckets in the bathroom. For dinner Lilit had left a pot of stew sitting on the kerosene burner, but unable to get the wicks to burn, I heated a package of freeze-dried soup over a can of sterno that I had with me.

By seven o'clock the streets were desolate and the small apartment was beginning to get cold. I put my overcoat on, lit a candle, and started to write about the day's events in my journal. It got colder and colder. Although I did not want to use Lilit's wood, I had no choice but to light a fire in the wood-burning stove she had recently installed. I tried again and again, doing what I had seen others do—layering small pieces of wood underneath a few bigger logs, then igniting it with the help of a benzene-doused cotton ball. The kindling would burn for a few minutes and then extinguish. Nothing I did worked.

I dialed Lilit at the hospital to ask advice, but could not get through. Walking to the hospital in the dark was out of the question; hungry dogs roamed the streets at night and were known to attack people.

A feeling of isolation and loneliness came over me. I lit all the candles I could find, but the feelings did not go away. Despite layers of woolens, my overcoat, and the vermag I had wrapped around myself, I was shivering.

I had to find help. And then it occurred to me: call the downstairs neighbor! Why hadn't I thought of it earlier?

The neighbor, her husband, and children invaded Lilit's apartment the minute I knocked on their door. They quickly lit the wood-burning stove and fixed the kerosene burner and asked if there was anything else they could do for me.

I had experienced only a few hours of being cold, in the dark, alone and unable to see the obvious solution to a simple problem. What was it like to have this experience every day, month after month, with no way out? How can people rebuild their communities and their lives under these conditions? I wondered.

In the morning Lilit came home to make sure I was OK. The night had gone well for her—several deliveries had taken place without any complications. Nara and Vachig will be coming for dinner, she told me, and will bring their newborn baby. Did I want a bath? "Tonight, we'll heat the buckets!" she said, smiling in good humor.

I wondered—how does she do it? How does she survive? Perhaps that too was part of her tradition—to survive! Tonight, I thought, I will drink a toast to Lilit's ability to survive.

Professor Gourgen Melikian with the children of Matchkalashen.
The sweaters they are wearing were knit in Yerevan using
wool donated by a generous family in Massachusetts.
Artsakh, 1996.

CHAPTER 15

A Man for All Mankind

It was 1996. We were sitting around the table in the Melikians' humble apartment, about to eat dinner. Gourgen lowered his eyes, asked God to bless the food, crossed himself, and passed one of his wife Laura's delicious salads to me. While we ate, Laura and their daughter, Mary, complained to me about Gourgen's long hours of work and how stressful his days were. At Yerevan State University, where he is Dean of the Faculty of Oriental Studies, an unending flow of humanity came to his office looking for help. His family was concerned about his health. He had been having chest pains again. How long could he hold up under the stress of everyone else's problems? After all, he had his own problems too. I agreed. Gourgen became annoyed with our conversation and told us the following story:

I was sitting at my desk late this afternoon doing some paper work, getting ready to leave, when a woman in her late twenties opened the door and asked if she could speak with me. At first I wanted to say to her, "It is too late, come back tomorrow," but she looked so poor and sad that I told her to come in. She took a seat at the table in the center of the office. I sat opposite her. She said, "You do not know me, but I remember you from the days when you took your students to the summer camp in Dilijan. I remember that you were always a good man and now I have come to you because I have no place else to go. My husband and I are separated. I have no work. I have a son who is 6 years old. I have no other family. Three days ago I went to the bridge. There is no alternative for me. I am not the kind of woman who can sell her body. What is there left for me to do? But my child's face came before my eyes and I could not jump. I said to myself, 'Hold on for a few more days to see if something might change.' Then I remembered you and so I have come to you for help. You are my only hope."

Gourgen was shaking by the time he finished his story. He gave the woman what money he had in his pocket and promised to help find her a job. "What do you want me to do? What would you have done?" he shouted, his rare moment of rage brought on by the frustration he faced every day, torn apart by the depth of the problems people brought to him. No one answered, and the four of us tried to continue eating, seated around the little coffee table in their living room. We were all thinking about the woman, hoping that we would have done the same thing he had done.

Gourgen had visibly changed over the past two years. Despite the cease-fire in Karabagh, his big eyes were sadder now, the lines around them deeper, and his shoulders were beginning to droop. Day after day they came to him, refugees from Karabagh, wounded soldiers, students with special needs and even other professors, sometimes so many that the anteroom to his office was filled. They brought their needs, their anguish, their sorrow, but rarely their joy. Later I spoke privately with his wife. "What can we do to help him?." "Nothing, there is nothing we can do," she replied, and I knew that she was right.

He asked something for himself only once. He inquired if there was any way to make someone confined to bed more comfortable, to prevent their skin from breaking down and getting sores. "Who is it for?" I queried, "Forget it, forget I said anything," he replied, embarrassed that he had hinted at some personal need. I persisted, and finally he told me it was for his dying father, whom he was caring for at home. By coincidence, I had a few foam mats shaped like upside-down egg cartons that were designed specifically for that problem. I rolled up one of the pads and insisted that he accept it. The exchange took place during one of our many meetings in the warehouse of the Poly-Technique Institute where I first met him. By 1992 we were working very closely together and in 1994 he and his wife invited George and me to live in the apartment next door to theirs, which had belonged to Gourgen's father.

After each of our meetings at the warehouse I always wondered whether it would be the last. Without divulging details, he would hint at the danger of some of the things he did for the Karabagh movement. His involvement was deep, his commitment was total. He believed that the Armenians of Karabagh, despite the overwhelming odds against their success, would someday be free of Azeri rule.

In those days, when all land routes to Karabagh had been cut off by the Azeris, many of us did not believe that an area with only 150,000 Armenians and a handful of freedom fighters could win on the battlefield against seven million Azeris. But when the man with the mustache said, "We will win," none of us dared point out the obvious. We did what we could to help with medical supplies, food, and clothing. The Armenians of Karabagh were suffering greatly; their call for help was just as compelling as the call from the earthquake victims. It was the struggle of these Karabagh Armenians, after all, that had mobilized us back in 1988, before the earthquake.

Gourgen had many close encounters with death on the road to Karabagh. He dodged missiles as he traveled back and forth, delivering supplies during the war, and he had some near misses when the bombs were falling on Stepanakert. He always points out one spot in particular, on the main road passing through the center of Stepanakert. "See that hole in the side of that building? I was standing there talking with Saco when an old woman came running over and told us not to stand there because a missile was about to hit it. Sure enough, we moved and that was exactly where the missile hit a few seconds later." He never saw the woman again and to this day he is convinced that God sent her to save him.

One day when we were coming back from Karabagh during safer times, traveling that same road, our thoughts turned to our close encounters with death. Each of us told a story in turn. When Gourgen's turn came, he did not recount any of his close encounters in Karabagh, but instead one he had in the United States. It happened in 1984 on one of his first trips to California while visiting friends.

One hot sunny August day, shortly after he arrived, his friends decided to take him for a swim in the Pacific Ocean, a special treat for someone from a landlocked country. The group headed for one of California's beautiful coastal beaches. Ignorant of the riptides and strong currents that often occur in these waters, and delighted to have a swim, Gourgen headed into the ocean as soon as they arrived. When he finally stopped to catch his breathe, he saw that he was far from shore and separated from the others. He tried to swim toward them, but the harder he tried, the farther away they seemed to be.

As he told the story sitting there in the car, he waved his arms overhead, showing us how he waved to his friends, trying to catch their attention. His voice conveyed the fear that came over him as he realized that he could not swim toward shore. His friends finally saw him and got a lifeguard from down the beach who had a small boat. But the lifeguard, despite several attempts, was unable to reach him. The waves were getting larger, and Gourgen was now very far from shore. The waves started to pound the back of his head, propelling him down deep into the water. He could not feel bottom. (He slapped the back of his head, showing us just where the waves hit him.) Slap and down he would go, pulling himself back up to the surface with all his might, only to be slapped by the next wave propelling him down again.

That very day Gourgen's only son was taking his final oral exams at Yerevan State University. All he could think of as the waves hit him was that his death on the same day would forever mar his son's success and forthcoming graduation. Our friend had tears in his eyes as he continued; we did too!

As his strength was waning, he looked up at the blue sky. He thought how beautiful the color blue was and how sweet life was. He then said to himself, "This is the last time you will see the sky." As he looked up, his mouth filled with water and the next wave hit.

At that moment he heard a voice yell to him, "Hey mister, do you need help? Hold onto my board. Just hold on and I'll get you into shore. OK?" The young surfer had been out riding the waves, enjoying himself, when he saw a man's arm flailing between the waves. Then he saw nothing, and then he would see the arm again. In that vast ocean, the boy was as surprised to see Gourgen as our friend was to see him. The surfer knew just what to do. Sensing the swimmer's panic he did not touch him, but just pushed the board toward him. "Mister, can you hold on?" "Yes, yes, I can, I can," our friend said, gripping the surfer's board with newfound strength. Together they rode the waves into shore.

We shivered with fear as the story unfolded—not only for Gourgen, but for ourselves. Had he died on that day, our lives would have been very different, and we would never have known it! We would not have been on the road from Karabagh to Yerevan and probably would never have come this far. Gourgen was a man who changed people's lives and influenced the course of events by his intense dedication to a cause.

⚜

Gourgen's father was born in Armenia, but fled in 1933 when word reached him of his impending arrest on trumped-up charges. He made his way across Armenia's southern border into northern Iran, where he lived for many years. Iran had a large Armenian population, numbering close to 200,000. Many were the progeny of the Armenians brought to Iran by Shah Abbas I early in the 17th century as he withdrew his forces from Armenia, leaving for the advancing Turks nothing but ravaged, burned villages.

Gourgen's father settled among the Armenians there, married, and had three children. Gourgen remembers vividly the day he came home and confessed that he had eaten a free meal at school. His mother was furious. He had disgraced his family she said, and the next day, he was made to return the equivalent amount of food to the school. It was his mother who taught him to pray before eating a meal and before setting out on a long journey. She had taken him to attend services at the Armenian Apostolic Church as a child. The Armenian church chants, the *sharagans*, that he heard there would be ingrained in his memory forever.

One day I asked Gourgen, "How is it that you are so religious yet were a communist? I don't understand." He looked at me totally puzzled and asked, "What has one to do with the other?" I explained that I thought part of communist doctrine was denial of a Supreme Being. "How could I not believe in God? I am Armenian, it is in my blood. It is a part of me. It is in my tradition," he tried to explain. Then he added, "It is what my mother taught me."

Gourgen's mother died of cancer when she was forty-nine years old when he was a teenager. His only solace, he says, was that she did not live to see him imprisoned by the Shah for his communist activities. In his youth, he had embraced Communism, believing it would end human poverty and suffering and protect his people. Shortly after her death, the first of several arrests took place. Not wanting to spend the rest of his life in the Shah's prisons, he fled in 1958, reversing his father's route and returning to Armenia. The rest of his family followed over time.

Gourgen had planned to be a doctor but when he finally entered Yerevan State University it was as a student of Persian and related languages. (His particular area of specialty is the new Persian grammar system and the new Persian vernacular dialects.) In the years that followed he refused the promotions within the party offered to him, fearing that he might be corrupted by power as he had seen others corrupted. He was an idealist about communism, but not about communists. He knew corruption existed, but he believed in the ultimate goodness of the system.

It was during those early years at the university that his extraordinary love of nature developed. He became an environmentalist at a time when few had given thought to these issues, either in Armenia or elsewhere in the world. Gourgen knew that Armenia's mountains, now mostly brown and bare, had once been covered with vast forests. He dedicated himself to replanting the trees of Armenia and later of Karabagh as well. Over the next 30 years, he organized the planting of over 100,000 trees in Armenia on special planting hikes he took with his students. After he finished his university studies he took a position at the State University of Yerevan, where he still teaches—not just academic subjects, but also by example about life, integrity, dedication, and hard work.

He seems to intuitively understand the trees and the plants we see growing in the wild along the roads and on the mountains. He knows their names, growing needs, flowering time, fruit, sun and water, medicinal qualities, and histories.

Entering his office one day, I found Gourgen showing some students a twig he had planted in a pot on his windowsill. It looked quite dead to us, but we all knew that soon, as if by magic, without benefit of special plant foods or rooting powders, it was sure to come to life. He cared for it, even talked to it, and patiently waited for the twig to respond. Each time I went to his office over the next few weeks, when I looked at the hopeless little plant he would say, "You'll see. It will be beautiful." And then, as if the little twig wanted to please him, it gave out small buds that turned into leaves. "It will flower soon," he said with great pride, and we all knew he was right.

One day just before the winter of 1993, when the blockade was still choking Armenia, we were on our way back to Yerevan from a small town where we had visited a sick soldier. Gourgen took a detour off the main road to see a grove of walnut trees he had planted nearly twelve years earlier with his students. He parked the car on the side of the road and slowly got out. Something was very wrong. The trees had been cut, only stumps remained.

As the magnitude of the destruction struck home, Gourgen ran from stump to stump, hugging them as if they were his injured children. His eyes filled with disbelief and rage, his arms spread out, his fingers wide apart, he cried, "Look at this! Look at what has happened here! Look! These were the walnut trees we planted, my students and I." His body shook, his voice rang with horror as he repeated over and over again, "look at this one, and this one." His large nostrils moved in and out rapidly with each breath, the tears slipped out of his eyes down onto his long thick mustache, his famous mustache.

"It takes years before a walnut tree bears fruit," he explained. "They produce a few walnuts after five or six years, but after 10 to 15 years, they bring forth tremendous amounts of walnuts and continue to do so for many years. These were ready, and now they will never give fruit." He had been sure that no one would ever cut these trees for firewood because they were about to bear their fruit, precious walnuts.

Thousands of trees were chopped into firewood during the blockade. The devastation is visible everywhere. Drive through Armenia's countryside; only the stumps of once beautiful poplars and sycamores line the roadways. Walk through one of Yerevan's parks; the trees are gone, and only the concrete posts of wooden benches remain. Look through windows that no longer have their sills, into homes that have given up their floorboards. People have burned their books too, one by one, as well as the wooden shelves that once held them.

It was too much to ask now, as another winter approached, that Gourgen's trees be spared yet again. With no other fuel to burn, the energy held in these fibers would be needed to warm a family. Blockaded, with no gas coming in and often no electricity for days at a time, what choice did some poor father have other than to cut these trees to provide heat for his children?

It was hard for Gourgen to accept.

Gourgen made his first trip to Karabagh in 1985 and then again in 1988 as president of the University-sponsored organization called *Hyrenashen* (building the fatherland) to plant trees with his students and to examine historic Armenian sites within the enclave. From that time forward, he has thought about and lived for nothing other than the freedom of the Karabagh Armenians. Once the most devout of communists, he was among the first to revile them after Sumgait and Gorbachev's handling of the Karabagh Armenians. "We lived poor on the Party's promise of a better future, but they deceived us."

Karabagh has become for him not just the symbol of everything Armenian, but the essence of the human struggle. "You know," he said one day, "When I started to plant trees with my students I did it to make the world a better place, not just Armenia. When I fight for the rights of the people of Karabagh, I fight for the rights of all people to live freely. When Karabagh is truly free it will be a great victory over injustice for all the world."

The old women of Matchkalashen.
Their lives have not been easy. Artsakh, 1994.

After examining patients, I am fed fresh fruits and vegetables from the
garden. Vera is on my far right, Manoushag is behind me.
Matchkalashen, 1995.

CHAPTER 16

Matchkalashen Revisited

Each time we went to Karabagh with medical supplies, though exhausted by the arduous journey from Armenia, a day or two had to be set aside for a trip to the village of Matchkalashen. Although it is only about 30 miles from Stepanakert, the capital city of Karabagh, the trip always took more than 2 hours because of the poor roads. We went because this village was among Karabagh's poorest and suffered greatly through the war. The village is on the border with Azerbaijan.

The road becomes little more than a path once it enters the environs of the village. It passes through a grove of mulberry (*toot*) trees with their thick trunks and twig-like branches that spread out, touching one another like hundreds of open umbrellas. The mulberry trees once served as the nidus for a silk industry in this region; now they provide delicious fruit not only for eating, but for the brewing of a pungent powerful vodka, called "*tooti oghi*." The road passes over a stream where women come to fill jugs with water. The women, with years of practice, are adept at carrying these heavy jugs back to their homes. It looks so easy, the heavy jug seemingly weightless, as they blithely scamper up the hillside from the stream, never faltering under its weight.

The village houses now appear, one after another, built of rock, crude but sturdy. A few children are playing in the roadway under the watchful eyes of the old women who are always sitting on the stone walls in front of their houses. An assortment of pigs lying around the sides of the roadway snuggle into puddles of mud, oblivious to passing goats and cows, and to our car as it turns into the main area of the village.

On our last trip we made our usual first stop at the kindergarten to unload the food we had brought as part of the support we give to this kindergarten. Then, before heading up to home where we will spend the night, we went to the medical dispensary to make arrangements to meet the *feldsher* in the morning and see patients with him. Since there is no telephone communication with the village, we were never able to let the villagers know when we would be arriving. Sometimes they would get news that we were in Stepanakert and would assume that we would come to the village in a day or two. Patients from miles around would come and wait for me at the medical post. Unfortunately, delays often occurred and we didn't arrive as expected.

In Matchkalashen we always stayed at Armik and Vera's home. Armik is one of the village leaders. Vera, his wife, is a school teacher. Both are university educated. During the years of active fighting, Vera shouldered all the work to keep the family fed and clothed and their small farm going while Armik served with the military protecting the nearby border. He was gone for weeks, if not months at a time and now, for his valiant efforts, he enjoys the respect of the other villagers.

Keeping the land fruitful and the farm animals healthy is back-breaking work. At 5 a.m., before Vera goes to her teaching job, she feeds the pigs, ducks, and chickens, and milks the cows and sets them out to pasture with the goats. She makes cheese, butter, and yogurt with her own hand, using the milk fresh from her cows.

Vera's kitchen is a covered patio, outdoors, that she uses year round. She carries water to the house from a spring several hundred yards away. There is no indoor plumbing. They do not have refrigeration because electricity is intermittent, I suspect, as it has always been. And yet, despite the proximity of the farm animals, the ever present mud, and the lack of any conveniences, Vera manages to keep the patio and their home clean.

From the center of the village I would often make my way on foot up the steep road that led to Vera's home, high on one of the hills that cradled the village. The road was made of large cobblestones that were unevenly placed to provide some footing. This was appreciated most after it rained when a thin layer of mud made the stones slippery. Sheep and pigs used the road too. I was always afraid of falling.

One night after dinner at Vera's, her youngest sister, Manoushag (the name of a flower, similar to a violet), took me to her home along a path through the orchards. It was a quarter-mile walk down a rock-strewn, muddy path alongside a stream. The night was very dark, and the path was hard to negotiate. Manoushag wore high heels; I sported loafers. She seemed to float over the rocks and small streams, avoiding the mud, never missing a step. I did my best to keep up with her and she did her best to slow down, frequently turning to ask, "Are you all right?" Despite my great care to place each new step I took on a firm surface, my right foot slipped off a rock into the soft mud. As I pulled back, my foot came out of my shoe, which was now firmly stuck in the mud.

I tried to balance myself on my other foot, my shoeless foot in the air, while Manoushag extricated my shoe from the mud. There she was, attractively dressed, her make-up tastefully applied, in heels, without a bit of mud on her, while I, in jeans and loafers, had mud all over my shoes, splattered up to my knees. We laughed so hard that I lost my balance again, barely able to keep from falling completely into the mud. Understandably, my friends in Matchkalashen pray that there will be no rain for several days prior to my visits.

On the way up to Vera's, women sat in front of the houses that lined the road. Some were knitting, while others spun the yarn from a spindle that they dangled and twirled from the raw wool. Chickens and ducks scurried around them along with the children in their charge. Some of the women just sat with their hands folded, looking very old and very tired. As I passed by, each stopped her work to give me a welcoming hug. They gathered around me; other women came out of their houses. Some offered an invitation, "Come in and have a cup of tea in my home." Others asked, "How long are you staying?" and then, "Will you see patients later?" "Can we come to see you later?" Invariably the question came, "Did your husband come with you?"

Over the years, as they got to know me better, the women would gather around me and touch my clothes, curious about how someone from America can be so plain—no make-up, a simple hairdo, and simple clothes. My "penny" loafers attracted much attention. My wash-and-wear shirts received what I now know were admiring looks. As time went by, the questions became even more personal: "Is this how you always dress? Does everyone in America dress this way? What kind of house do you live in? How many rooms does it have? Do you drive a car? Is it true that women in America don't cook and don't clean their own homes? Are there really machines that wash your clothes and dishes? Do you preserve vegetables and fruits for the winter? Do you have a garden? Does your husband help you? Was your marriage arranged? Did you have a dowry? Why didn't you have children? How can you sleep on sheets that are not ironed? How much money do you earn?

The fact that I had higher education and was a doctor did not surprise these village women at all; they never asked questions connected with my professional life. Even these village women are encouraged to obtain a university education, like Manoushag, Vera, and her daughters. After all, it is they who are responsible for the education of their children.

On our last trip, Vera's yard was a frenzy of activity by the time we arrived. When our car was spotted entering the village, news of our arrival spread quickly. Vera's mother and sister-in-law left their homes, climbed through the backyard's of the village to Vera's, to start the preparation of the evening meal even before Vera arrived. When she arrived, Vera changed from her school clothes into the colorful housecoat Armenian women customarily wear at home. The other women in the yard wore black, the color they will wear for the rest of their lives in mourning for their sons who have died in the war. An assortment of chickens and ducks scrambled around the yard, the dog barked and grunts emerged from the pig stall as we opened the large gates and entered the yard. It was a wonderful scene.

Over the wood fire Vera placed a thin metal sheet on which she would bake bread. Working quickly, she divided a large ball of dough into small rounds, flouring each and covering it with a damp cloth. Her work table stood next to the fire. Her mother-in-law, a cheerful woman despite being completely bent over by age, kept the fire going, feeding it with the twigs gathered from the fields. They worked rapidly. One by one, Vera rolled out each of the rounds of dough. She skillfully hung the large, round, very thin sheets of dough over a long dowel-like stick, then flipped it onto the red-hot metal surface. Her sister-in-law completed the baking by flipping the bread over and rapidly turning it around to make sure it cooked evenly.

I had seen many women baking bread in this region over the years, but never this particular type of bread. Speaking to them in Armenian I said, "In America, my grandmother and my mother made bread exactly this same way on a wood fire, just like the one you have made. We had a thin metal sheet, just like the one you are using, which was special for baking this bread. We still have one and we still make this bread. We call the sheet a *saje* and the bread *saje-a-hatz* (hatz means bread.) Vera looked at me with a big smile, equally amazed, and said in Armenian, "We call this a saje, and we call this bread saje-a-hatz too." And then she added with a big smile, "*Shad ooragh em.*" (I am very happy).

I told her how special this bread was for me while growing up in New York City. The baking of this bread was a big event. My grandmother made it only in the summer when we were at our cottage in the country, the only place that a wood fire could be made. I had to be out of bed by 6 a.m. if I wanted to eat the bread as she took it hot off the saje—which I did, with butter and honey. Vera ran to her storage bin and brought out the honey she had collected from their beehives and the fresh butter she had made. The rest of the baking could wait. She took bread hot off the saje, and together we ate it just as I always had as a child, dripping with butter and honey!

When Vera said, "I am very happy," I understood what she meant. Up to that moment, despite our both being "Armenian," I was as much a foreigner to her as she to me. But now we had a different kind of bond. People far beyond her land, their experiences foreign to her, but people she longed to know made the same bread, on the same fire, using the same *saje*. We are the same people. We had found something more of ourselves by finding this bond with each other.

"Can you imagine," I said, "that ten years ago I did not even know that there were Armenians who lived in a place called Nagorno-Karabagh? I had never heard of it, and I did not know that Armenians like you existed." Vera replied in a very serious tone, "And what about us? What about me, living in this village? I had no idea that Armenians like you existed. It is more amazing to me that YOU exist, not that I exist." I had never thought of it that way.

One day while Vera and I sat cleaning vegetables in her kitchen on the patio, I asked her to tell me about her life. How did she manage to do so much hard work, teach school, and take care of her family? Vera is a small, strong woman, with clear skin, dark eyes, thick black hair cut short, and white teeth you see when she smiles her big, warm smile. She has a dignity that comes with knowing exactly who she is. These are her words as I recorded them in my journal that night:

"My life here is very pleasing to me. I am happy to be in my own home, which I will never leave again, even if there is more fighting. I would rather die here than leave and live somewhere else. Yes, my life appears hard to you, but for me every task I perform is with great pleasure and love, even though there are times when I am exhausted and wish the smell of the cows would leave my body.

"My husband is a good man and has always done what is best for us. He works very hard too. When the fighting started this place was terrible. The planes would come in low and there were tanks not too far

away from here. Grad missiles were being fired at us. We carved out a cave in the stone behind our house. That is where we hid. Our house was hit by a Grad and the second floor was ruined. We have just finished rebuilding it. The government sent word that the village must be evacuated; the fighting men stayed, but all the women and children had to leave. We went to Yerevan to live with our relatives for 7 months. This was the worst time of my life. They were very nice to us, but we were guests and I could not bear it.

"One night for dinner our cousin opened a bottle of her own green beans. We all ate it. After a few hours, I started feeling sick and experienced double vision. I had read about botulism and knew that was what my two children and I had. I asked to be taken to the hospital. It was late at night, and the doctor refused to believe it was botulism. Maybe he was insulted because I was so insistent. So we went to another hospital and another, until we found a doctor who understood that we had botulism and that we were very sick. I was the sickest of the three of us.

"I said to the doctors, 'I know that there is an antidote—please, please try to find it for us, otherwise we will die.' I knew this because I had read about it also. [A mark of this women's intelligence: where, in the midst of a war, in the back villages of Karabagh did she find something to read about botulism?] The doctors called from place to place and our relatives went from hospital to hospital, searching for this medicine. Time was running out. Finally, the medicine was found at the Children's Infectious Disease Hospital. There were only a few doses, and they were supposed to be saved for children at that hospital: they gave it to us because we were the family of a freedom fighter from Karabagh."

Tears came to the edge of my eyes as I listened to Vera. The timing was right, the place, the hospital—it all fit.

"Vera, who would believe this? I think that the antidote you were given was from doses we brought from America. Ara Asoian, the chief doctor of that hospital, had given me an account of how the 50 doses of antidote donated to us by Connault Laboratories of Canada that we had given to him had been used. He told me that 7 doses went to another hospital for a family from Karabagh!"

Vera and I have a special affection for each other. The fact that supplies I brought from America helped save her life has made all the work, the pain, the risk, and the frustrations worth it. Sometimes I think that if there had been no other benefit to any of my efforts over these years, this one single act would have sufficed. And I might never have known of it had we not shared those few quiet moments together.

But what if she had not been the wife of a fighter? How would the story have turned out? These were indeed hard times that dictate hard decisions.

⁘

Matchkalashen's medical post was located in the center of the village opposite the two-story school house. It was a small building of stone with an old wooden floor similar to the other medical posts I had seen in many of Karabagh's villages. It was also a place, I imagined, that could be any of a thousand places on earth where people are so poor that if you give them an aspirin they will remember you for the rest of their lives.

"*Parev, parev, Doctor-jan*," the old feldsher said as he came around his desk somewhat reticently. I would be asking questions again, and in front of the patients he would take a secondary role; both made him uncomfortable, I was sure.

The nurse started to bring the patients in one by one as she had on my other visits. Near the end of the day she ushered in a little boy named Antranik with his mother and father.

Antranik stood in the center of the small medical post, his feet spread apart slightly, his hands at his sides, with the biggest smile he could make, as if to say, "Here I am world!" His eyes sparkled and his ears, well his ears came out just enough to make this little boy one of the cutest I have ever seen.

He was six years old and complaining of belly pain. I asked his parents a series of questions about Antranik, running through a mental list of possible diagnoses that might cause a little boy to have stomach pain, but none of their answers seemed to fit. I asked Antranik to go behind the white curtain and lie on the cot so that I could examine him. His mother followed close behind him. He pulled up his shirt; it was then that I saw the scars on his belly. His parents had neglected to tell me that Antranik had picked up a colorful ball one day, one that had come out of a cluster bomb. He was lucky to be alive. He had undergone six operations in an effort to reconstruct his insides.

I looked at the mother baffled, but then realized that Antranik's parents were coping with the reality of what happened to their son by denying it. They were trying to treat Andranik as if he were just like any other child.

The cease-fire had been in effect in Karabagh for over two years, but the dying and the mutilation went on. Not only were skirmishes continuing along the borders, but land mines and cluster bombs continued to maim and kill. It seemed that every time we came to Karabagh, we heard about another person who had died from one of these demons. The news of these explosions rips through the entire population of Karabagh, passing from village to village, from mouth to mouth, each new injury recalling injuries from the past, and in some ways, producing casualties that are harder to accept than those from the war itself.

All I could offer Antranik were some simple suggestions—medicinal herbs to soothe his stomach and intestines, perhaps another consult with the surgeons; with time, he might be better. Hopefully, there would be no more surgery.

It had been an exhausting day, the last patients I had seen were still lingering on the small porch in front of the medical post. I thanked the feldsher for his help and told him that I would be back in the morning to review my treatment plans for the more difficult cases we had seen. He smiled and everything seemed to be all right between us.

I washed my hands one more time at the small sink while the nurse poured water for me. Manoushag arrived just as I was finishing and told me that everyone was waiting at Vera's house to have dinner. Then with a smile she added, "A car is coming to take us or would you prefer to walk up through the back path?"

We laughed and laughed again as we remembered that night while making our way through the mud. We needed to laugh and we did, as hard as we could.

The village called Damala, north of Armenia,
in the Republic of Georgia, 1995.

CHAPTER 17

Damala and Women's Hands

For several years my friends Tigran and Ida, the doctors who had given Garbis and me their apartment in Ashotsk after the earthquake, have been inviting me to Damala, the village where Tigran was born and his parents still live, in the southern part of the Republic of Georgia. Finally in the fall of 1995 we arranged to make the trip one weekend before the snows come and block the road to Ashotsk.

On a Friday afternoon early in November, Tigran and Ida picked me up from the Primary Care Center in Gyumri. My cousin Iris, who was in Armenia at the time, joined us. Together we drove back to Ashotsk.

The following morning, before leaving for Georgia, Ida and I made rounds at the hospital she and Tigran worked in. It was a modern hospital built by the Caritas Christi of Italy, a gift of the Pope. It cost 12 million dollars and was completed in less than two years after the earthquake. The facility was beautiful: clean and warm, with its own 24 hour supply of electricity. The Italians continued to support the hospital and maintain control of its administration.

Many of the patients were from Akhalkalak, a region in southern Georgia that we will pass on our way to Tigran's village. Populated entirely by Armenians—numbering nearly 100,000, if not more—its medical care was so poor that many people came to Ashotsk for treatment despite the difficulty of the journey. Others went on to Gyumri or even to Yerevan if they had relatives with whom they could stay.

Ida, a neurologist, was eager to review her patients with me. She lamented that she was alone and had no colleagues with whom she could exchange ideas. She also did not have sufficient textbooks in her field. (Later I arranged to get her a book on clinical neurology and Harrison's *Principles of Internal Medicine*.)

A few weeks earlier I had introduced Ida to the use of an ophthalmoscope. It turned out that the hospital had one, but no one knew how to use it since there was no ophthalmologist in Ashotsk. Ida hoped she could become proficient enough in its use so that she could perform the eye exam necessary for her patients who had suffered strokes. This would save the cost and the difficulty of sending them to Gyumri to be seen by the ophthalmologist there.

Once under way we reached the border with Georgia in twenty minutes. Tigran made the trip often and was well-known since he was second in command at the hospital. The guards waved us on without any problem. The road, in good condition for a few miles, deteriorated rapidly and never improved. For the next 4 hours we journeyed over rocks with little relief from the jarring jolts. Only a donkey was meant to travel this way; how the cars survive was beyond my comprehension. My thoughts turned to the severely ill patients we had just seen. How did they endure the trip?

After the dissolution of the Soviet Union, the status of Georgian-born Armenians deteriorated significantly. The republic was already dealing with two ethnic minorities struggling for independence (the Ossetians and Abkazians); hints by some Armenians in the Akhalkalak region that they wished to break away and be united with Armenia simply made the government nervous about another of its ethnic groups. Azeris had been known to kidnap Georgian Armenians and take them to Azerbaijan as hostages for ransom or for exchange with Azeri prisoners of war. For a time, the capital city of Tiflis, now called Tbil-isi, was considered a dangerous place for Armenians. Yet Tigran assured me it was safe to make the trip.

We passed many villages, each either Russian or Georgian, easily identified by the differences in architecture. Turks once lived here too, but Stalin had rooted them out. There were no Armenian villages until we reached the region of Akhalkalak. It was Saturday and the streets of the city were filled with cars, peo-ple, and children. The houses, mostly made of brick, looked like the semi-attached two-and three-story structures common in the old parts of many European cities. To the casual viewer, things did not look too bad here. But the hospital told another story, and I understood why the people of Akhalkalak made the difficult journey to Armenia for medical treatment.

We found the hospital on the outskirts of the city. The large, flat grounds and several buildings, unkempt and worn, showed the signs of years of neglect. A nurse on duty directed us to the building where the patients were, its entrance door, long since broken off its hinges, hanging by a single screw. We entered and went up to the first floor. The stairs were crooked and half-bro-ken. The walls were wet from leaking pipes; the ceiling's paint peeling, its plaster chipped. The windows to the outside were cracked and shattered. We went from floor to floor, through the freezing corridors, looking for the patients. Maybe there were none: maybe this was not really a hospital. Maybe, just maybe, someone was playing a practical joke on us. But it was no joke, it was a hospital and we finally found the patients.

Tigran and I did not speak as we walked through the halls. Tigran had not been in here for a long time and had grown accustomed to his new hospital; he was stunned by the squalor, as was I. We encountered another nurse, who took us to the patient rooms on the floor above. There was no doctor on the premises, she informed us. It was Saturday afternoon and the doctor had gone home. She would call him if we wanted. We declined the offer.

The first room we entered was like all of the rest; large, with a high ceiling, no electricity, and with a small wood-burning tin stove in the center. The patients' families brought wood from home to keep the stoves burning. The rusted metal beds that lined the rooms looked barely able to hold the weight of even a small woman. There was no running water. To my surprise, however, the rooms were very clean. Colorful vermags brought from their homes covered each patient, softening the stark poverty of the surrounding room. I held back my tears again, touched by their efforts to maintain their dignity.

In these terrible conditions I expected the patients to be grim. I did not think I could face them. What would they ask for? What help could I offer them? As I turned to leave, the nurse who had accompanied us introduced us. Greetings and warm smiles erupted in every corner of the room from under every vermag. The welcome we received simply for being there was neither guarded nor shy.

Ida and Iris joined us, and in each room, we introduced ourselves, chatted with the patients for a while, even took pictures together. Then we gave each patient the only gift we had with us, a box of Band-Aids. At the last minute before leaving Yerevan, Gourgen Melikian had given me 100 boxes of Band-Aids, the only thing that was immediately available and that could be transported easily. "Don't go empty handed," he had said. "The people there are very poor. Have something to give them." How right he was! Their gratefulness for this small gift could not be measured.

We continued on to Tigran's village, Damala. The first settlers of this village were Armenians fleeing Turkish massacres in the late 1800s. Five families came first from the city of Erzerum just across the border. They carefully selected the village site for maximum protection from neighboring Turks: it was behind the mountain, completely out of view from the road until one actually arrived—thus the name, Damala, which means "hidden" in the Georgian language. Some of the villagers returned to Erzerum when things quieted down, but then came back to

Damala in the early 1900s. More families came in 1915. The village now had 500 families.

When we arrived on the outskirts of the village, Iris and I walked the rest of the way, following our car, which moved slowly through the streets. We wanted to savor the mountain air and get a feel for the village. It was late in the afternoon, and many of the village women were on their way home from the fields. Dressed in long skirts and aprons of bright prints, wearing thick, colorful socks and soft shoes, they maneuvered easily over the rocky uneven dirt path that served as the village's main road. Vivid scarves covered their hair, pulled back and knotted at the nape. Some carried big baskets, filled with the fresh harvest from the fields, on a hip or balanced on a shoulder. As we walked through the village, we were pleased not to be greeted with suspicion, but with friendly smiles, offered by the women as they peeked at us for just a moment as they passed by.

Within a few hours the entire village knew that Tigran and Ida had arrived from Ashotsk with an American doctor. In the early evening people started coming to the house for medical consultations. These Armenians had even less medical care available to them than those living in Akhalkalak. They were grateful for any help we could give.

Some of the patients needed X-rays and blood tests; Ida asked them to come to the hospital in Ashotsk, where she could arrange for these. Most said that they could not come: it was the harvest time, or there was no one to leave the children with, or they did not have a car to make the trip in. There were no complaints, no demands. Nor did they express anger over these difficulties.

We had the chance to meet and talk with many of the women we had passed earlier. We even sat around a *tonir* as they baked bread. We were impressed by how strong they were both physically and mentally. They seemed to bear adversity as if it were a crotchety old friend. They have no self-pity and no expectations from life for themselves; they hope only that life will be better for their children.

The women of Damala performed the labors traditionally assigned to them and the work of men as well. Life here was always hard for Armenians, an ethnic minority within another republic. For many years the men left Georgia for other republics to earn better salaries. They lived and worked in these other lands for months or years at a time (some even had second families), then returned to their Armenian homes, only to leave again.

Armenian tradition is strict with regard to the division of labor in the village. The man builds the house, the woman tends to the duties within it; he holds the ox and plows the field, she sows the seeds. He cleans the barn, she milks the cow; he cuts the wood and the hay, she cooks the food and serves. The woman holds the keys to the house and often the keys to the money box as well. She stays at home and raises the children, overseeing their education; he goes wherever he wishes so long as he provides the money needed to keep his family housed and fed.

The women of Damala long ago put aside these traditions in the face of hard economic times. They held the ox and plowed the field, cut the wood and the hay, cleaned the barn and milked the cows, kept the home clean, the children fed and clothed, managed their wants and often those of the mothers-in-law with whom they lived, waiting for their men to return.

The largest women's hands I have ever seen belonged to these women. The fine motor muscles of the palm and fingers, the thenar muscle of the thumb, and even the bones of the hand were enlarged and overdeveloped, telling the story of the hard work they did.

They came reluctantly with their medical complaints that night in Damala. They came about their bleeding hands, the skin thickened and cracked, red with irritation from rubbing, eczematous, and with chronic dermatitis. Some complained of severe pain and color changes in the fingers and toes; many had suffered frostbite and infections. There were no rubber gloves to wear for protection from the cold water in which they washed the clothes, sheets, and towels, day in and day out; their large hands and thickened skin were so accustomed to the cold that they no longer felt it—like so many of the other women I met in the villages of Armenia and Karabagh. I remembered a woman who had come to our clinic in Gyumri.

⚜

It was her first visit. She was young, according to her birth date, but the heaviness in her eyes and the sad lines around her mouth made her look much older. She kept her coat on, the small kerosene heater in the corner had not yet warmed up the clinic. Her hands, hugging each other, were tucked in the folds of her coat. She started to talk. Her eyes lowered, she smiled, and for a fleeting moment we saw her big black eyes sparkle. She thanked me and my colleague, Maro, for seeing her and for the clinic, looking for things to talk about other than the real reason she has come.

"How can we help you ?" Maro finally asked. "The nurses have written here that you have a problem with your hands."

"Maybe you cannot help, but when I heard the doctor was here from America I thought I would come and ask about my hands." There was silence.

She did not take her hands out from under her coat. Maro continued the questioning: "What exactly is the problem with your hands?" The young woman told us about the sores on her hands and the pain.

"May we see your hands?" She looked from doctor to doctor, searching for some way out. Slowly, she took them out from under her coat and laid them on the table, as though her hands belonged to someone else.

The skin was raw, with color variations from purple to blue to red. A few of her fingers were white and swollen. Some areas were bleeding, others were crusted and had pus oozing from them. We felt pain, just at looking at her hands. Maro and I exchanged glances. How did this woman live with this condition? How much pain must she experience each time she put her hands in cold water?

I had seen many such patients over the years. A woman or a man would reveal a serious medical problem they had lived with for months, even years: an infected wound, devastating migraines, swollen joints, even chest pain. They ignored physical pain and medical problems as long as possible. There was no time for illness: the villager's work came before everything else. The cows could not wait to be milked, the fields had to be plowed, the harvest reaped, the yogurt made, the bread baked. Their determination to continue working despite pain and significant physical problems would be considered deviant to an American, but for an Armenian villager, it was simply what was expected.

Maro and I continued the questioning, trying not to sound accusatory. She told us she had suffered with this condition for nearly two years. She had not seen any doctor because she lived far away and had too much work to do. Her mother-in-law, a good woman, helped with the children, but is old and could not work in the fields.

Her eyes were pleading, but she turned in her chair as if the visit were finished. I reached out and touched her arm and told her we would try to help. My prayer is silent: "Dear Lord, don't let me fail her."

We described frostbite and asked if she had ever had anything like that. She thought so, perhaps two years ago. I explained that her problems started with damage to her skin from frostbite. Now, both the cold weather and the cold water in which she washed the family's clothes exacerbate the condition. She could have an infection caused by bacteria, or a fungus, or both. Several treatments might have to be tried before finding the one that worked. We made no promises of cure or even of improvement. We gave her antibiotics to take by mouth and creams for her hands. Did she have gloves to wear in the cold weather? Could she heat the wash water even a little? Would she use the medicines we gave her? We wanted to see her in one week to monitor her progress. She promised to take the medicine and to return.

Two weeks passed and she still had not returned. Every time I thought of her, my spirits slumped. I assumed she had not kept her follow-up appointment because there had been no improvement in her condition. Then, one day she appeared with loaves of bread she had baked, apologizing for being unable to come earlier. She was much better and willingly showed us her hands now. She hoped we would enjoy the bread. Could I take some of it back to America?

The village of Bertadzor. Artsakh, 1994.

CHAPTER 18

A Fragile Fortress: Bertadzor

The mountains and valleys, and all the land that stretches out before you with magnificent beauty, give meaning to their lives, generation after generation. Even before you and I became urban nomads, we could not have understood their devotion to this land just as we never understood the real meaning of the land to the American Indian. We cannot understand why a man is willing to die for a small village high up on a mountaintop.

November 1994

In the morning when we arrived in Bertadzor (which means fortress above the canyon) Vigen, the region's chief doctor, left me off at the medical post to spend the day working with the village *feldsher*. Vigen and the two men who had come with us were continuing on to the next village to attend a funeral. Sveta, the feldsher, and two nurses were standing at the medical post when we arrived. The three women greeted me with hugs and kisses as though I were an old friend returning home after a long absence. Any anxiety I had about Vigen's leaving me alone quickly left me.

One nurse appeared older than the other and seemed to be more in charge of running things. Both wore white lab coats, gray and frayed from years of washing. They rushed back and forth, in and out of the medical post. The older one gave instructions to the people beginning to line up outside the door, trying to reassure them; everyone would be seen—the American doctor had said so. Patients who were older or very sick would be seen first. They would organize everything. Before the first patients could be seen, however, the three women insisted that I rest from the journey and have a cup of coffee. Later in the morning they brought food from home to be sure I had enough nourishment for the day's work.

Fortunately, Sveta, a woman in her early fifties, spoke a form of the Armenian language close to what I spoke, making it easy for us to communicate with each other. She had been a feldsher for many years, and by the way she talked about her patients and their demeanor toward her, it soon became obvious that she cared deeply about them. She was smart too and, eager to learn, she kept asking the right kinds of questions when I pointed out important physical findings such as heart murmurs, enlarged livers, and abnormal lung sounds.

The first patient Sveta was anxious for me to examine was a 14-year-old girl recovering from pneumonia. Her father was a *fedayee* and considered a hero. Sveta wanted to be assured she had done the right things medically; my confirmation would raise her status in the village. She seemed nervous as I took the history and then examined the girl while her mother watched. Based on Sveta's evaluation and the history the young girl's mother gave, pneumonia seemed to be the correct diagnosis; the medication and dosage she received appeared appropriate. There was no evidence of pneumonia now, and I concurred that the girl was cured. Sveta was delighted.

In order to wash my hands, I had to go out to the hallway where the next patients were waiting and the village children stood watching. Each time, those gathered about us would hush their voices, and all eyes would stare intently as the old nurse ceremoniously poured the cold water from a pail over my hands while I lathered with the soap I had brought. The nurse had put one of the children in charge of guarding the soap. She had been stern in her instructions: "The doctor's soap is your responsibility," she said. "It will be a dishonor on the village if it disappears."

When we had finished seeing all the patients, this old nurse, whose height was half that of mine, stood as tall as she could at the edge of the hill next to the medical post. With the mountains her backdrop, in a loud voice, she made a speech. She asked me to thank all of the Armenians in America and Europe, and wherever else they are, for their support. "It is because of their help that we breathe this air freely today," she said, waving her arms for extra emphasis. "It is because of their help, and the help of all the good people in the world and the Red Cross, that my son, who is in a prison in Baku, will someday be free." Her Armenian was thick with the local dialect. There was a split second lapse between her words and my ability to comprehend what she said; it was like reading a ticker tape, waiting for each word to come through to understand what she was saying.

Was my brain translating correctly? Did she say her son is in prison in Baku? This poor woman, wearing her grayed white lab coat so proudly, working diligently with us all day, never once showed the burden she carried. We all knew what that meant: she would probably never again see him. The International Red Cross, in whom she placed so much hope, was not allowed to see the Armenian prisoners. Did she know this? I put my arms around her and told her I would tell America exactly what she wished and we parted.

Vigen had returned and together with Sveta we climbed up the hill from the medical post toward a house with a small balcony carved of wood that overlooked the valley below and the snow-capped mountains surrounding us. The air was thin and I climbed slowly. It had been a long day and I was tired, but there was one more patient to see. In the yard below the house a group of men were waiting for us. As greetings were exchanged with them and introductions made, a woman came out onto the balcony and invited us in. She was the patient's daughter.

We entered through the front door, which opened into a long narrow room with shutter-like windows extending the full length of the outside wall above the yard we had just been in. It is the room of windows, the *shushaband* (literally, wall of windows). From the outside the shushaband gives a distinctive architecture to an Armenian home. Its design captures the sun's heat and light and insulates the other rooms from the winter's cold. It is a place for drying fruits, herbs, and vegetables; to grow decorative plants and even lemon trees; and a place to read or drink tea with a guest in the late afternoon.

Inside, next to the front door, there was a sink and a work table. A few steps into the room was a wood-burning stove with a long overhead pipe vented through the wall of windows, a dining table with some chairs, a chest of drawers, and two worn club chairs. At the far corner of the room was a metal frame bed, where our patient lay, buried under her vermag.

This room served as a family room. It had once served as the Azeris' main headquarters when they captured Bertadzor. There were a few old prints on the walls, placed to cover the deep burns and holes the occupiers had made in the stone. From over the hills and up the mountain road the Azeri's had entered the village in 1992, destroying the ancient bridge that leads to the group of villages in these mountains. The signs of war we saw when we entered the village in the morning were everywhere: burned houses, caved-in roofs, bullet holes in the cement foundations, and broken windows not easily repairable.

Many men died here in the fight to protect this village; the few who were left faced certain death and fled into the hills in the moments before the Azeris entered. They had no choice but to leave some of the women behind, hoping they would be spared. Among them were the women of this household.

One of the Azeri soldiers had held a knife to the throat of the patient's daughter, demanding to know where the men were hiding. Her mother had pleaded with the Azeri saying, "There are no men here. If you kill her, who will raise her children?" A second Azeri came in and confirmed that there were no men in the village and the two women were spared, miraculously. Many hardships followed.

But that was in the past; and today there was cause for celebration. Their mother had survived a major heart attack 10 days ago and was now getting better. When her chest pains started, her son drove to Shushi to find Vigen and bring him back to Bertadzor. It took six hours to get to Shushi, find Vigen's home, help him get the medications and equipment he needed from the hospital, and make the return trip. The road they traveled, the same unpaved rocky one full of potholes, winding through the mountains, was the same road we took today to reach Bertadzor from Shushi. It was a well-traveled road, much of it backtracking along the main route from Armenia to Karabagh before taking the turn that leads to Bertadzor. The potholes, made by missiles during the active fighting, were the size of craters. Heavy mountain rains that caused rocks and mud to slide down onto the road made conditions even worse. Driving here required stamina and expertise.

Sveta had already been at the patient's side for several hours, monitoring her blood pressure and pulse when the son arrived with Vigen. She had also administered nitroglycerin before he arrived, the only medicine she had for someone thought to be having a heart attack. Vigen had never worked in a modern cardiac intensive care unit, with its monitors of every imaginable kind and every conceivable medication immediately available, delivered and administered to the patient with the writing of a few lines in the order book. He did not even have the benefit of an electrocardiogram; he had brought one with him, but there was no electricity with which to run the machine. Vigen had to trust his clinical skills.

Although the patient was only 58 years of age, Vigen's findings convinced him she was having a heart attack. Bertadzor's small medical post, where I had worked all day with Sveta, had only a few cots for beds and absolutely nothing else in it; transferring the patient there would not offer any advantages. Moving her to Shushi over the mountain roads was unthinkable. She would have to remain at home. Despite the difficulties, and without the benefit even of supplemental oxygen, Vigen managed to stabilize his patient. He would have to leave her in the care of her family and the feldsher, as he had done with so many patients before her. Neither Vigen, Sveta, the patient, nor the family contemplated any alternatives. Everyone accepted that the mother would be nursed by her daughters, while Sveta, who sat with us now, proud of her part in the patient's care, would monitor her condition, reporting back to Vigen when she went to Shushi for medical supplies.

Debilitated and confined to bed, the mother's strength nonetheless could be felt. Her hair, a deep bronze color, was thick, pulled back and braided. Her features were strong without being stern; she had large brown eyes with thick lashes and brows, and high cheekbones. I could imagine how impressive she had been on the day the Azeris arrived, wearing her traditional colorful smock and pleading for her daughter's life. From the Armenian she spoke with me now, I knew that she was educated. Her pleading would have had a certain elegance to it, her pride in who she is would have come through to the Azeris, she would have known the kinds of words that would touch them. At the moment at which both of these women could have been killed, she was able to save them. The daughter and the other women in the household served her now with graciousness and love. They revered and honored her; she accepted it, though obviously made somewhat uncomfortable by her confinement and forced dependence. They came and tucked the pillows under her head and the vermag around her body, wanting her comfort to be complete. One felt the bond that went beyond the mother and daughter relationship; after all, together they had confronted their enemy and lived.

Based on the electrocardiograms Vigen had finally been able to record, it was evident that a large portion of the mother's heart had been damaged by the heart attack; I was surprised she had survived. Seated by her next to the big bed, we started our evaluation. She seemed to be tolerating the medications Vigen had given her; there were no identifiable side effects. She still had not walked more than a few feet within the room; her low level of activity seemed commensurate with the damage she had sustained to her heart. She'd had no further chest pain, nor problems sleeping or eating. Vigen asked me to do the exam—it would be an honor for the family. The women who had come into the room and were gathered around the bed now withdrew. I proceeded with the physical examination: vital signs, head, neck, pulses, lungs, heart, abdomen, and extremities. I found no abnormalities. There were no signs of congestive heart failure or arrhythmia, which might have complicated a heart attack. There were no laboratory tests to review. There was no cholesterol value to shake a finger at!

We discussed with the patient the possible causes of her heart attack. She did not have diabetes or a history of high blood pressure, nor was she overweight. We postulated that the heart attack might have resulted from all of the stress she had undergone during the war. We tried to reassure her that with time and rest, and without any recurrence of similar stress, she would slowly heal and be able to resume her normal activities. We decided to continue the same medications with some minor changes in dosages; one aspirin every other day was added to the regimen. I encouraged her to eat as many vegetables and fruits as possible, to use oils made from sunflowers and olives, and to avoid fats from animals. Interestingly, this discussion about what to eat raised many questions from the women who had now gathered around us again. They had heard something about cholesterol and wanted to know more. I explained that fats from animals should be avoided for their families' good health and made suggestions for ways of doing so. Unfortunately, dairy products, their only source of calcium and often of protein, were straight from the cow or goat to the table. There were no low-fat varieties I could recommend.

While we talked, our patient's daughters were busy moving back and forth between their mother's bed and the kitchen area, preparing for the celebration that was to follow. Not only was their mother getting better, but the doctors who had helped her were now here. The family would show their gratitude by setting a table with generous servings of fruits from their orchard, tomatoes from their garden, preserves from the family's winter reserves, cheese, yogurt and, of course, freshly baked bread. The men had slaughtered a pig for the celebration and were preparing it for the barbecue. They started a large fire with twigs gathered from the fields. The pork would be seasoned and cooked just right, and I would be offered the best pieces to taste hot off the fire, even before we sat at the table. I was the honored guest; this banquet was for me, the doctor from America, the one who months before had given Vigen some of the very medicines used to save their mother's life.

From her bed the mother could gaze out the long wall of windows to the mountains surrounding the village. From this dominant position in the room she could see, as well, all that went on in the family's life. Our work over, she watched as we gathered around the table and dinner was served. As we ate the men made many toasts, first thanking God for the victory of the forces that gave their village back to them and for the strength of the people of Karabagh. Then, Vigen was toasted for the care he gave their mother, and their mother, for her life and recovery from her heart attack. The men took turns making toasts to me, my work, and the Armenian diaspora. One of the men drank to "the call of our shared ancestral blood," which I heard and which brought me across thousands of miles of oceans and mountains to their little village. Through the ritual of toasting the men could tell what was in their hearts, could speak the things that they could never say to me or to each other directly. It is a ritual to which I have grown accustomed. I am no longer embarrassed by the sentiments expressed or annoyed by the lengthy speeches taking up time of which better use could be made. I have come to understand and respect their need for this ritual.

Through all of this, Sveta sat quietly next to me, still wearing her blue smock, similar to the ones operating room nurses wear. She did not eat any of the food that had been put in her plate, nor had she said one word, even to me.

When the eating was over, the mother asked if she could join us at the table. Vigen and I nodded our approval. With the help of one of the women, she slowly made her way to a chair, which was placed next to me. One of her sons, who had been sitting quietly until now at the other end of the table, started to sing. The melody was familiar, but not the words. His voice was not particularly beautiful, but it had an engaging quality as he wound through a minor scale, singing in quarter tones and halftones as only one who has heard these melodies since childhood can. The lyrics were improvised, humorous at times, inserting the names of family members, telling a story about his mother. After he finished, his sister, who had been leaning against the wall of windows, gazing at the mountains while her brother sang, without changing her stance started singing "*Myrig, myrig...*" "mother, mother," again in a melody of quarter-tones and halftones. Her song was intense and sad. The applause was enthusiastic for both of them. For an encore, she and her husband sang a humorous duet of love while playfully dancing in the center of the room.

We left the village just before sunset, saying good-bye to the family and repeating our instructions to the patient. Sveta and I hugged; I promised to return. The village children in their tattered clothes and worn slippers waved good-bye, running after our car as the last houses of the village disappeared from view. The mountains slipped away as well; the old car rumbled over the rocky road around the steep curves, slowly descending into the valley. The ancient bridge with its stone arches came into view. It had served travelers for centuries but now lay in useless ruin. At the foot of the mountain we crossed over the gully to the next mountain via the makeshift bridge of wood planks the villagers had set on metal piles. As we passed over, we lamented the destruction of the beautiful ancient bridge during the war; the men expressed confidence that someday it would be rebuilt. As I looked back, Bertadzor seemed like a nest perched precariously high up in the boughs of the mountain, a fragile fortress above the canyon. I was glad that I had not turned down Vigen's invitation to come with him that morning. We drove back to Shushi in silence, filled with the events of the day, too exhausted to notice even the road.

Children gathered around the water fountain. Lachin, 1996.

"Just married." Lachin, 1997.

CHAPTER 19

Lachin Revisited

The Lachin Corridor, the region that links Armenia and Karabagh, had been turned into a military base by the Azeris. From this position they prevented travel between the two. In May 1992, Karabagh forces captured the Corridor and opened the road to Armenia once again. The region has remained under Armenian control and it was relatively safe to travel through the corridor although during periods of active fighting it came under missile bombardment from adjacent Azeri-held territory. Though many of us traveled through the corridor before the May 1994 cease-fire, it was only afterward that we could really be sure of the safety to do so.

Before there was a hospital or even a doctor in Lachin, sometime early in 1995 I had the following experience. We had been in Karabagh for several days and were on our way back to Yerevan. We stopped in Lachin to deliver medical supplies, antibiotics, and a variety of other medicines that I had saved for Mariné, the nurse who worked here.

We found Mariné at the medical post, a single large room where she saw settlers who were sick, provided them with first aid, and dispensed medication. She was the only health care person for miles in any direction. That day, when I entered the dimly lit room, it looked just as it always did, rather messy and disorganized. On the wall to the right was a small cabinet in which Mariné kept her most important medicines. Everything else was in boxes scattered in a seemingly random fashion all over the floor. But I knew from past experience that Mariné knew exactly where everything was. There was a large desk in the middle of the room on which the most frequently used medicines were kept handy and a large ledger in which Mariné recorded everything that transpired in the room.

At first the glare from the two small windows on the far wall prevented me from noticing two women standing in the corner on the left, hidden in the shadows, silently wringing their hands. My attention went to Mariné, her back to the door, bent over the patient's extended arm, and to the patient facing me, covered with blood and expressionless. He was a tall man of about 50 years of age sitting very straight in a chair that Mariné had set close to one of the windows. His right arm was stretched over the back of the chair, allowing his injuries to be illuminated by the daylight as much as possible. Mariné, wearing a disposable surgical gown, had already injected the man's hand with anesthetic and had applied pressure in an effort to stop the bleeding. With a young friend assisting her, she was preparing to place the first sutures as I walked in.

Mariné told me that the man severed his fingers on a saw that he was using to cut wood for the house he was building. She seemed delighted at the timing of my arrival and asked if I would help. I nodded and slipped into another gown that her friend pulled out of one of the boxes on the floor. I looked the situation over, examined the patient, and looked up at Mariné. My mind was racing, but I knew I had to think slowly and carefully. A man's hand was at stake, maybe his life. Should we send him to the nearest town two hours away? Doctors there might not try to save his fingers, Mariné said. The man did not want to go either; he preferred that we take care of him.

It seemed we had no choice but to continue what Mariné had already begun. In my mind I went down the checklist of Emergency Care 101:

Control blood loss and prevent shock: Mariné had already applied pressure to control the bleeding, but blood was still coming out of the multiple areas of open wound. There was no way for me to know how much blood he had lost. Blood loss, along with a possible nervous system reaction to his pain and general condition, could cause a drop in his blood pressure. If this happened in his seated position, he would pass out. I suggested that he lie down, but Mariné pointed out that this would make it impossible to get sufficient light on his hand. The room had no portable table; there was no lamp. Seated he remained.

Prevent infection: The man's hand had black dirt encrusted with the blood deep in his wounds. We could assume that the saw he used was old and carried the threat of tetanus. No vaccine was available, and Mariné had no antibiotics left at the medical post. Fortunately, I had brought a big supply with me. Before we did anything else, we selected several different antibiotics and asked the man to take them now before we continued. I knew I was practicing unacceptable medicine, but like Mariné, I was doing the best I could. I prayed that one of the drugs we gave him would prevent a major infection.

Before washing his hand and fingers I asked for a pair of sterile gloves and noticed for the first time that Mariné was working bare-handed. "Mariné, you must not do this. You are putting yourself and your patient in danger." She told me she could not work wearing gloves and tried to reassure me by adding that she had washed her hands thoroughly. There was no time to argue.

I proceeded with washing the patient's hand for several minutes, using the blue bar soap Médecins Sans Frontières workers had provided for the medical post. It was impossible to get all of the dirt off. The skin was deeply lacerated in many places. The index finger had exposed bone at the middle joint, and the terminal portion of that finger was dangling by a tendon. After working out a plan for how to approach the suturing, we started trying to put the man's hand back together. Mariné placed the sutures while I held the skin together, giving her directions as to where to insert the needle for each suture as we went along. She was good. The situation had not frightened her. Mariné had confronted this kind of emergency before.

It took us nearly two hours. The man never passed out and he never went into shock. We gave him additional antibiotics and instructions on how to take them. The women standing in the corner took him home, his hand bandaged and wrapped in gauze, cradled in a sling fashioned out of one of their scarves. He agreed to return the next day to have his hand examined for infection. He thanked us and left with the two women.

We told our patient to rest for a few days, but we both knew that he would probably go right back to work building the house for his family. He had arrived two days ago in Lachin, a refugee from Shahumian, one of many Armenians who had been driven out of their homes.

The patient had signed no papers, given no written consent, had no insurance. There was no record of what we had done, save a single line Mariné wrote in the big ledger: severed fingers sutured, antibiotics dispensed. A man's hand: I never even knew his name, and I never saw him again.

I found Gourgen and George waiting for me by our car in the warm sunlight. "You two really missed a lot of excitement. You should have come with me." They both rolled their eyes to indicate that they had no desire to get involved with severed fingers if they did not have to. I was about to joke about their leaving the real work to the women when I thought better of it; they might call on me the next time we had car trouble on the road!

Later that same year, in October 1995, I headed for Karabagh with my mother's youngest sister, affectionately known as Aunt *Hassie*, and our friends Gourgen and Gavrosh. We decided to break the ten-hour journey by staying in Lachin overnight. The regional officials had prepared a place for us to stay—the very best that there was to offer then.

We arrived in the city about 10 p.m. and went directly to the government headquarters. Officials directed us to one of the multilevel buildings we had just passed on the main road as it wound up the mountainside on which Lachin was built. There were no signs of life, the buildings blackened by fire, without windows and gutted to the core. We drove back down the road and on closer look saw that one of the buildings did have a few window frames in place covered with plastic sheeting with a dim light coming from behind them. There were also lights coming from a few other places scattered around the hillsides, an indication that indeed people were living in the ruins. We pulled in behind a four-story structure. The yard was strewn with twisted metal and concrete blocks; the scene reminded me of Gyumri. Hassie and I exchanged questioning glances. We made our way through the rubble, up the stairs to the second floor. The apartment we were to use had two rooms. A man and a young boy were seated in one of the rooms playing backgammon, *nardi*. They disappeared as soon as we entered the rooms. I was not sure whether they were just waiting for us or whether this was where they actually lived. Later we chided ourselves for not giving the boy a present. We had been so exhausted it had not occurred to any of us.

There were two beds in each room; the one in which my aunt and I were to stay, where the man and boy had been, also had a table and a small hutch. The first thing we wanted to do was to "use the facilities" and wash up before cutting into the bread and melon we had purchased from a farmer along the way. As it turned out the "facilities" were simply the out-of-doors; and because there was no water, washing was accomplished with the prepackaged wipes that we always carried.

We ate our bread and melon, said good night, and the men retired to the adjoining room. My aunt, always a good sport, promptly donned her nightclothes, pulled back the covers of her small bed, exposing the gray but clean sheets, crawled in and went to sleep. I had more trouble settling in. A mouse had visited our room earlier and continued scratching in the walls through the night, giving me visions of further invasions. Dogs barked incessantly in the street below, perhaps from hunger or maybe to ward off wolves and coyotes.

My aunt's even breathing through it all assured me that she was getting a good night's sleep. At 3 a.m. I needed to use the outdoor facilities again! I opened the front door as quietly as I could and made my way through the half-destroyed building, down the narrow cement block stairs into the night. I was not sure whether I should be afraid or not. If I was, what should I fear: thieves, lurking Turks, random violence, wild animals, the hungry dogs? Instead I decided to enjoy the night air.

It was a glorious night, cool and clear, high up in the mountains, the sky packed with stars shining more brightly than I had ever seen. The clean air refreshed me and made me forget how tired I was. Sitting on the top stair leading into this battered, broken-down, half blown-up building, I thought about the events that brought to this place such an unlikely quartet: my aunt asleep upstairs, so far from her Madison Avenue apartment, surrounded by rats and barking dogs, in someone else's bed; the two men in the adjoining room, former Communists, now activists, who had become such dear friends, and me, sitting on these stairs in Lachin in the hours before dawn. Lachin, the city that not so long ago was an Azeri stronghold from which the road to Karabagh was effectively blockaded. How far from home this is. Or is it? I wondered.

In the morning my aunt confessed that she had not heard a single noise; she didn't even realize I had left the room during the night. The men too had slept soundly. With the benefit of daylight, we found latrines on the main road and then made our way to a water fountain in the center of town. Here we quite publicly washed our faces and brushed our teeth along with several other people who seemed to have appeared out of nowhere to do the same. We exchanged greetings, but not much more. I think everyone was too embarrassed, or possibly too shocked, at performing these personal tasks in the company of so many.

That was nearly two years ago. Each time we approached Lachin on our way to Stepanakert, Gourgen asked, "Do you want to stay in Lachin for the night?" My answer was always the same—No—but we frequently stopped for an hour or so to deliver supplies to Mariné or to make arrangements with the chief administrator for the delivery of relief supplies for the villagers.

By the spring of 1997, with the cease-fire still holding, a hospital had been set up in a renovated building and a surgeon, a veteran of the war, had taken over as chief of the region as well as of the hospital. Gourgen introduced me to him on the front steps of the new hospital. His name is Artsakh, the ancient Armenian name for Karabagh that he adopted as his own. On hearing that I was from Boston, the surgeon said, "Boston? There was a woman doctor from Boston who visited our field hospital on the front lines in Drmbon when Lady Cox was there. I never knew who she was or what happened to her. I remember that she took my picture." I looked at him more closely, in his trim white doctor's coat, out of army fatigues, now older with deep lines creasing his face, I had not recognized him—I should have, because he, like Gourgen, had a distinctive mustache.

We wrapped our arms around each other as if we had been friends for many years. "But the woman I remember had long hair," he said looking at me sternly. "What happened to your hair?" It was less a question than a statement.

Over coffee in his small office we reminisced about that day in Drumbon in 1993. The fighting on that front had not yet started when Lady Cox, Zori Balayan, Gourgen, and an entourage of journalists and interested others arrived. The mountains were quiet, giving no hint of what was to come later that afternoon. The group, relaxed and casual, dispersed in several directions. Lady Cox made sure that the journalists talked to the doctors and villagers from the area. I wandered off with the unit's nurses, chatting about their work here. Each was no more than 20 years of age and had volunteered for this duty, they told me. They traveled back and forth to the interior, moving from location to location, depending on where the fighting was the heaviest. They were not ignorant of the dangers they faced and what would happen to them if captured by the Azeris. The work was hard, and they were proud of what they did.

They showed me around the small house that had been converted into a field hospital. The first room was a receiving area for the wounded. The next had two operating tables, two freestanding lamps, and an anesthesia machine. Then there was a small room lined with cots, one next to the other with no space between them. The last room held all the medical supplies. There was no activity in any of the rooms. It was as still as a theater set waiting for the actors to appear.

It was when we came back outside, where everyone else was gathered, that I took a photo of the surgeon. About that time the relaxed, almost jovial atmosphere that had developed among our group and the medical staff and the soldiers was shattered by the booming sound of a cannon not too far away. The fighting had resumed.

In a matter of minutes a military vehicle raced toward us. In it were the first of the day's wounded. They were carried into the receiving area on stretchers and transferred to the examining tables. The men, grim-faced, then left, only to arrive shortly afterward with more casualties. The doctors and nurses, one minute standing around chatting with us, were now transformed into a unit of professionals with only one goal: to save the lives of the young soldiers entrusted to them.

The scene was not pretty. The men, some young, some old, were brought in a few at a time. The nurses worked as fast as they could, cutting away uniforms to expose bullet-ridden legs and chests, cleaning the wounds and preparing those who would go to surgery. The doctors were evaluating the injured: who should be transported back to Stepanakert, who needed surgery immediately.

Gourgen pulled at my arm. It is time to go. I agreed. My skills were not needed here. To remain would be to play the role of a tourist. Gourgen was right, it was time to leave. My only satisfaction was knowing that we were among many who had helped to provide the supplies these doctors and nurses were using.

Now, four years later, we met again, in a safer time, a safer place. The surgeon invited me back. "Please come and stay with us for a few days, a week, a month. We can learn a lot from you." I knew that this was true. The region now had five doctors, and the hospital had received a lot of medicine and equipment they did not know how to use. "Where would I sleep if I came to stay?" I asked, the memory of my sleepless night here in 1995 still vivid. "You'll stay right here in the hospital. We will give you your own room." I promised that I would come back to stay.

When I returned a few weeks later, my first night in Lachin was spent in the newly built guest house, quite comfortable but too far from the hospital. In the morning I moved to the hospital as Artsakh had suggested. There I could be more involved with the patients, workers, and with the hospital routine. The facility was renovated by the government and equipped by Agape, a humanitarian organization sponsored by the United Methodist Church in the United States. Beds, mattresses, medicines, and basic medical supplies had all been provided by them. Thus I and the 22 patients had very comfortable beds on which to sleep. The rooms were warmed by radiators filled with water and heated by electricity. The hospital lost electricity on that first day; on the second and third, there was no running water. To meet such emergencies, water was stored in a large tank alongside the hospital. Pails of water from this tank were brought into each of the washrooms and were kept filled by the housekeepers. Water for drinking was brought in from the main mountain spring that was the water source for the town.

By the time the doctors made their rounds at 9 a.m. the hospital rooms, hallways, floors, and washrooms had been thoroughly cleaned by the two housekeepers, who refused to be stymied by such trifles as a lack of running water. A bathhouse in the adjoining building contained a shower connected to a water tank that was heated by making a fire under it. Several times a week the fire was made, and the hospital's patients and employees were welcome to bathe in turn. It was a little inconvenient, but no one was complaining!

At about 11 p.m. on my second night the nurse's aide on duty called me to the maternity area. A pregnant women who had come from a faraway village a few days before was now in the last stages of giving birth. By the time I got there Artsakh, the nurse on duty, and one of the other doctors were cheering on the screaming mother, exhorting her to push and push again. The baby's head came out, and without any apparent difficulty a little girl was born. The placenta was delivered and examined; all seemed routine. We were congratulating the mother when quite unexpectedly she started to hemorrhage.

Artsakh, experienced on the bloody fields of war, quickly sutured the pulsating artery when another opened up. He tied it off, but the blood kept coming. The young woman became pale, her blood pressure was inaudible. It began to seem possible that she might bleed to death in front of our eyes. The room was narrow, with barely enough space for the table on which the young mother was lying. We asked the nurse to get an IV pole, solution, and catheters. Medicine that would maintain her blood pressure by constricting her blood vessels was not available; neither was there any blood for transfusion.

The young woman looked up at us with her big eyes, wide open throughout the delivery and now showing the pain of each suture as Artsakh placed them as fast as he could. "Don't worry, everything is going to be just fine," he kept saying. The young woman closed her eyes, losing consciousness.

I thought we were headed for real trouble, but Artsakh was right. Much to his credit, he managed to finally get control of the situation. When he was fairly sure that the young mother's bleeding had stopped, he came to the side of the table where I had been standing, slipped his arms under her, lifted her off the table, and carried her to her room, gently placing her on the bed. He looked at me and said, "What can I do? We don't have any other way to get the patients back to their rooms. I carry everyone after surgery."

In the morning, much to my surprise I found the young mother sitting up in bed, breast feeding her baby. She barely recalled the events of the night before.

⚜

I spent the rest of the week sorting through the hospital's supplies, reviewing medications with the staff, and answering their many questions as best I could. They were excited to learn about the new antibiotic treatment for ulcer disease that I had introduced to doctors in Gyumri and Stepanakert; fortunately, the needed medicines were all in their stockroom.

On the weekend, Artsakh took me on a tour of the region to see the newly resettled villages where Armenian churches dated as far back as the 11th century. The most beautiful of these was *Dzeedzernag-a-vank* in the village of *Dzeedzernag-a-tagh* (a *dzeedzehrnag* is a swallow). Half of the roof had been destroyed, exposing the church interior to the elements. On one wall the faint but clear image of a once gilded fresco could still be seen. The church had been used as a shelter for farm animals by the Azeris. The villagers hoped some day to have enough money to make the necessary repairs. (In Turkey as well it is common practice to house animals in Armenian churches and historical sites leading to their destruction.)

We went from village to village talking with the villagers, asking how they were doing and specifically about their medical needs. Artsakh told them that medical posts would soon be established in these regions so that they would not have to travel to the hospital unless very ill. The villagers had no complaints and expressed only hope for the future. I could see, however, that the villagers who were thriving and happy had resettled here with large families: husbands, wives, parents, children, and grandchildren all living under one roof or close-by to each other. Those who were less happy had small families or had come alone.

When it was time to leave Lachin I promised to return again. My visit had been meaningful not because of what I brought, but because my presence created a bond with the world beyond these villages. And what did they give me, these villagers and these doctors living a frontier life? I cannot explain it; I do not clearly understand it myself.

⚜

Gourgen and Ashot picked me up on their way to Karabagh. By the time we left Lachin it was snowing heavily, but the roads were not icy and visibility was fairly good. It took three hours to reach Stepanakert; we arrived after midnight, exhausted but happy to be in the small apartment we had built near the center of town. No longer did we have to impose on our friends for a place to sleep, although in true Karabaghtsi style we could knock on even a stranger's door and find it open to us.

In the morning we went to the Arpen Center for Expectant Mothers that we had opened in December of 1995, in memory of my mother. Many women in Karabagh who were having abortions really wanted to have their babies. We hoped that assistance through their pregnancy might help them to do that. Each month nearly 500 pregnant women come to the Center to receive several kilos of food, cooking oil, vitamins, soap, shampoo, laundry detergent, and clothing. More than 2500 mothers have received assistance through the Arpen Center; each has had a baby!

The small warehouse behind the Center was packed to the ceiling with the food and clothing we had brought from Yerevan by truck; there was no room for even one more box. Sarkis, who runs the center, told us about some of the problems he had with foodstuffs. The 50 kilogram sacks of sugar, like the ones we just purchased at the new wholesale depot in Yerevan, tended to lose about 5 kilos of weight after being in dry storage. Sarkis was concerned we might think he was stealing the sugar! He insisted we take an unopened 50 kilogram sack of sugar and weigh it together. We did: he is absolutely right—it weighed 45 kilos.

The next day we visited the pediatric hospital where we were funding the renovation of the Intensive Care Unit. On entering through the ground floor doors, the first thing one sees is a poster with pictures of land mines and various types of cassette bombs children might come in contact with; another reminder of the war's bitter legacy.

Up on the second floor the old intensive care area had been totally demolished; walls, windows, doors, and tile floors were under construction. The builder promised to have five of the rooms finished by May 2. We were skeptical. When George visited the unit a few weeks later he was impressed by the quality of the workmanship and the attention to detail, and the fact that the builder had kept his promise.

Our last night in Stepanakert one of our friends asked me to see two members of his family who were sick. Both, it turned out, had Familial Mediterranean Fever. Fortunately, I had some colchicine to leave with them. I would see both again on my next visit.

Early the next morning we started back to Yerevan. On the way we made several stops, including one at the village of Leesagor, in Karabagh, about a half hour before reaching Lachin. Leesagor is not really a village yet, but a settlement of refugee families. We stopped to distribute clothing and shoes donated to our organization through the UAF. While the distribution was carried out, with each family coming forward and signing for what they were receiving, Gourgen lectured them about the need to believe in each other, to be honest, and to help each other through these hard times. Speaking in a loud voice so that everyone who was gathered around us could hear, he preached: "If your neighbor dies of hunger and you die of gluttony, what good is it to anyone? You have both died. It is only through helping each other that we will all survive."

On the way home we had to stop several more times because of construction. A new road was being built through the Lachin Corridor, one that would make the journey to Karabagh safer, shorter, and definitely more comfortable.

Just outside the city of Lachin, as we waited for the construction crew to open up the road, a man we did not know approached our car and started to talk to us. He was about 30 years old, a refugee from Getashen, he told us. He was on his way to the mountains to bring home a wild pig his brother had killed. "Please come stay the night with us. We have added a second floor to our house, and we have room for you. Everything is very good now. I have no complaints. Praise God." Then he told us his children were sick with the *grippe* and his cow had wandered into some electrical wires and had been electrocuted. All this he said with a smile! Just as we were getting ready to move on, he offered the invitation again. "Please come and stay the night with us."

On the way home we stopped to plant trees along a portion of the road that had been completed. Gourgen had brought five walnut saplings from Yerevan. Each was planted in someone's name: one for George, one for Gourgen, one for Ashot, one for me, and one for Monte Melkonian, the extraordinary *fedayee* from Fresno killed in Karabagh. George and I had met Monte just three weeks prior to his death in June of 1993. We were taken by his down-to-earth personality, his energy, youth, knowledge, and commitment. Songs memorializing him were already being sung by the children of Karabagh.

It took Ashot and Gourgen at least a half hour to pick the site—taking into consideration the sun, protection from mountains slides, drainage, and water—and another hour to plant the saplings. I sat on the side of the mountain and thought about all that had happened since Dick and I made our first trip after the earthquake nearly ten years ago.

The nuclear plant, Medzamor, was up and running; there was electricity once more in Armenia, and life was a little bit more comfortable, if not easier. Most people still lived at the poverty level or below it.

Ruben had been elevated from the city level to the position of Regional Director of Public Health for Shirak region and had also been elected a member of parliament. Armen moved his young family to Yerevan, where he is the director of internal medicine and intensive care at the Malatia Hospital. Over the course of the past year, his units have taken their place among those most respected in the city.

Lilit was still living in Gyumri and working at the Maternity Hospital. Her daughter Nara had moved to Germany with her husband and was now expecting their second child. These are still hard days for Lilit. Unfortunately, the city of Gyumri has not changed much since the first six months after the earthquake. Half destroyed buildings are still evident everywhere and a significant proportion of the population still lives in temporary housing. The reasons are myriad.

Gulnara left her job with the City Council to work for the United Nations in the Office of Migration. She and her husband organized two non-government organizations, one to study political parties in Armenia and the other, gender issues. They have published several pamphlets on these topics working out of their small apartment.

Gourgen's responsibilities at the University have increased as Dean of a growing department with 400 students enrolled. He was nominated for the Nobel Prize in Literature (1997); the gold-engraved letter telling him of his position among the last group of finalists was quite impressive to see. He continues to be the right arm of the Armenian Health Alliance in Lachin and in Karabagh where many changes have taken place. We have watched with great satisfaction, for example, as the city of Stepanakert has undergone a transformation during these past few years. The destruction caused by the missile attacks and aerial bombings had left not a single roof intact, nor a pane of glass in place. Now, hardly a trace of this destruction remains.

And I had changed too. My hair had turned gray, there were more wrinkles on my face, a little rise in my blood pressure, more aches in my bones, the not-so-subtle hints that time was moving on, even when we were too busy to notice.

After the planting was finished, they joined me on the roadside. Gourgen asked God to bless our food; and then we ate the cheese, eggs, and *jengalov hatz* that had been baked especially for us.

We sat there and enjoyed breaking bread together on that warm Sunday afternoon, on a new road, where not so long ago the missiles and the snipers would have made it impossible. We toasted our families, we toasted George, his parents and my parents, showering blessings up and down through the generations.

The mountains surrounded us, as they had for three thousand years. The sun shone and we breathed the air of freedom, so sweet, despite the hardships and the suffering. How true was the inscription on Artsakh's famous monument: *Menk enk mer sarere*. "We are our mountains." It surely felt as though I were home.

Children waiting for their mothers at the Arpen Center.
Stepanakert, 1996.

Epilogue

I t was 1992.
The telephone startled me at
6 a.m., and when I heard
Rose's voice I was sure she had bad news. "We're OK. Mom is
OK," she immediately reassured me, then explained that the desk
clerk at Mom's residence had just called her. Mom had been
standing at the front desk for more than 15 minutes in a state of
panic. The desk clerk had apologized for calling so early in the
morning, but she did not know what else to do. Rose spoke to
Mom but had been unable to calm her.

"The Turks are after me." she cried to Rose over the telephone. "They have set my room on fire. They will kill me if I go
back in there. We have to get everyone out. Please help me." She
was filled with fear. "Mom," Rose pleaded, "There are no Turks.
There is no fire. Please go back into your room. You are safe,
don't worry." Nothing she said helped, and after ten minutes of
trying, Rose told the desk clerk she would dress and come right
over. That would take at least 40 minutes: would I call and try to
calm Mom?

"Mom always listens to you," she added. After I had earned my
M.D., it seemed to be true. I had become the final authority on
issues that were disputed between Mom and Rose, who was now
her primary caregiver. They would agree to put the question to
me, whatever it was, and after I gave my opinion, Mom would
say, "Well, if Carolann says so. . . ."

It wasn't always like that. She was always instructing me on how to do things, how to iron a shirt starting with the collar, how to hold a wooden spoon when mixing a batter, how to punch down the dough and knead the bread for the *saje-a-hatz* she learned to bake from her mother, Rosa. Despite many hours of helping her, I never could get it quite right. My *kufta*—big stuffed meatballs with onions and spices that Mom served in hot broth, Kharpert style—were never as delicious as hers. Nor could I make her famous *yalanchi*—grape leaves stuffed with rice and pine nuts—come out the way she did, tender and tart with just the right amount of lemon.

Our family looked forward to these delicacies on special occasions. Mom would make them after coming home from her part-time job at Macy's Department Store in the Bronx. No matter how hard she had worked that day or how tired she was or whatever else she was committed to doing, she made these delicacies because she knew we loved them so much. She would phone just before she started to prepare the stuffing, "Will a hundred *yalanchi*s be enough?" Whoever got the call would assure her that seventy-five would do. "I'll make a hundred anyway, just to be sure."

Not having enough food was a fear my parents shared. At the last minute before guests arrived my father would come into the kitchen. "Arpen, do you have enough food?" he would ask, his thick eyebrows tensed over the issue. "Al, this is a fine time to ask me! What do you think?" She hardly showed her annoyance at the intrusion as she was hurrying with her final preparations, putting the finishing touches on the dining room table, spread with a fine cloth and set with our best china.

Dutifully, Mom would stop and run through the list of all that she had prepared over the past two days. Without fail, Dad would say something about not having enough bread and at that last minute would disappear down the stairs out of our second floor apartment before Mom could stop him. He would come back a half-hour later laden with bundles of bread and fruit.

After enjoying a wonderful meal the family would sit around the table and chat for several hours and invariably exhort me to play a piece or two on the piano. "Why are we paying for lessons if you won't play for company?" Mom would argue. After the relatives were gone, Mom and Dad would discuss the state of the leftovers. If too much of a particular dish was left over, Mom would feel that her guests had not liked it; if the leftovers were scant, Dad felt that Mom had not made enough. There was no winning that one.

I heard Rose's voice again, "Are you there? Please call the residence right away." I dialed the number, and the desk clerk who answered gave the telephone to Mom. She was still standing there, in her nightgown, the clerk had said, but they had put a blanket over her shoulders. "Hello, Mom? This is Carolann. Do you know who I am?"

"Don't be funny," her voice was strong over the telephone. "Of course I do. You're my daughter in Boston. You're the doctor." Then she added, with the spunky sarcasm that had become characteristic of her in old age, "You're the doctor who knows everything." I didn't mind. She seemed to be a little calmer. "Mom, what are you doing at the front desk?" She told me about the Turks. She went on to explain that she had seen them last week in the dining hall of the residence. A group of them had moved in and were trying to burn her out of her room. There was no longer any panic in her voice, and I knew that I could get through to her.

Despite her susceptibility to hallucinations and delusions, which we thought was caused by the medication she took for her Parkinson's disease, the disease that would slowly take her life, she was still a practical person above all else. I knew I could appeal to that part of her personality to bring her out of this crisis. "Mom, where is your roommate?" "In our room." she answered. "Well," I reasoned, "how could there be a fire in the room if she is still sleeping in there?" That did it. The hallucination vanished, but not the Turks.

The fact is, the Turks have never vanished for any of us since they marched into ancient Armenia in the 15th century. Maybe my mother would have had some peace in her last years before her death if the Turks had at least acknowledged what they had done to her and to her people over the centuries. But that acknowledgment is yet to come. Some countries—like the United States, it pains me deeply to say—have also never officially acknowledged what happened to the Armenians during that era as genocide. Turkey holds strategic interest for the West, and the Azeris hold the rights to the oil fields of the Caspian Sea.

But Karabagh stands as a thorn in the side of the big powers. Little Karabagh, about the size of the state of Rhode Island, has said: We have had enough of Turkish-Azeri domination. We have had enough burning and plundering in the night. We want to be free and will fight to be free of Turkish domination. Perhaps if the Genocide of 1915 had been recognized, the world powers today might be more understanding of the plight of the Armenians of Karabagh and their unwillingness to continue living under Azeri domination.

This is where my journey has finally taken me. It has been ten years since the earthquake propelled me into the relief effort and brought me back to Armenia over and over again. I have made friends with people I never dreamed existed— Gourgen and Lilit, Gulnara and Ruben, and Armen and Vera too. I have been to places I never expected to see—the earthquake devastated cities of Armenia, the war ravaged cities and villages of Nagorno-Karabagh. I have dared to do things that I could never have imagined attempting.

Perhaps Armenia and Karabagh are not my home, but they are my ancestral homeland.

Today my mother smiles down from her photograph on the wall opposite the entrance to the Arpen Center, established in her memory. Some day soon we hope that the women the Center serves will not need our assistance, that life will return to normal for them, that peace will become a reality for our people and for all the people in this region who have suffered so much.

On one of my recent trips there, just after we had hung Mom's picture on the wall decorated with cheerful decals, one of the pregnant women who had come for assistance asked me about it.

I told her that it was a photo of my mother, Arpen, who herself had been a refugee. The young woman, her growing belly obvious under her thin dress, sweetly and simply said, "Tell her thank you from all the women of Karabagh. Tell her thank you."

. . .

PICTURES FROM MY
PHOTO ALBUM

My grandmother's and father's passports issued in Constantinople, March 16, 1921.

Shortly before their deportation: my father, looking up, is to the right of his mother, behind his cousin. Abraham and Araxie are on her left. Kharpert, 1915.

My favorite photo of my mother
Arpen, taken right after she and
dad were married.
New York, 1935.

My mother's and
grandmother's passport
issued in Canstantinople,
May 31, 1920.

Armenian Legionnaires.

George's father, Neshan Najarian,
in his Legionnaire's uniform somewhere
in Europe or the Near East,
around 1918.

My dad and me on Easter Sunday. 34th Street in New York City, 1950.

Three generations lined up for some fun. Left to right: Grandmothers Elizabeth (4th) and Rosa (8th), Araxie (11th), Mom (13th), and my cousins. I'm first, apparently giving directions to the photographer. My sister Rose is next. New York, 1946.

My grandmothers as I remember them—Rosa (on the left) and Elizabeth. New York, 1967.

*Our meeting with Dr. Andrei Sakharov. On his right are Jirair Libaridian
and Robert Najarian. On his left are Michael and George Najarian.
My aunt Hassie Yankelovich and I are between them.
The little girl is Sakharov's niece.*

*One of several demonstrations by diasporan Armenians, in front of
the Soviet Embassy. New York City, 1988.*

Dick and I ready to board the cargo plane at Logan Airport.
Boston, January 2, 1989.

Senator Edward Kennedy, one of several speakers at our send-off. Governor
Michael Dukakis is on his right and Speaker George Keverian on his left.
Boston, January 2, 1989.

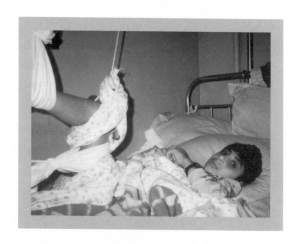

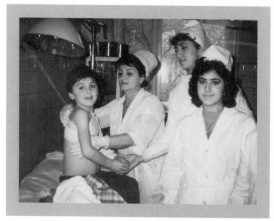

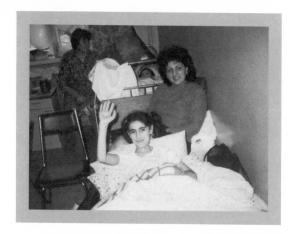

Earthquake injured children in Yerevan hospitals. Armenia, 1989.

An unusually large tent to house the homeless after the earthquake. 1989.

"Domics" came in a variety of shapes such as water tanks (right) and boxcars (below).

The view from Rosa's doorway, Gyumri, 1993.

Some of the destruction we saw. Gyumri, January 1989.

*Only the façades
of these buildings
withstood the
earthquake.
Gyumri, 1989.*

*A master stone cutter
rebuilding his own home
in Gyumri's traditional
style. 1997.*

Drawings made by the children Garbis and I were working with. Ashotsk, 1989.

Children offering crocuses to Garbis (standing in the rear) and me. Ashotsk, 1989.

Doctors Sarkis, Ida, and Tigran are to my left (in white coats), their chief is to my right. Ashotsk, 1989.

*At the Pediatric Infectious Disease Hospital doctors keep
intravenous fluids warm under a wood-burning stove
while a patient's food is cooking on top.
Yerevan, 1993.*

*Gulnara Shahinian
holding one of our
banners: No Heat,
No Water, No Light.
Yerevan, 1993.*

An example of Armenian church architecture, Amasia, a few miles from Gyumri. 1996.

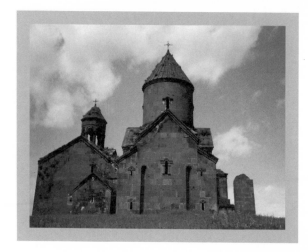

One of Armenia's most beautiful churches, Saghmosavank, built in the 13th century. 1987.

"Khatchkar" (cross of stone), traditional carvings commemorating events and honoring people. There are thousands of khatchkars in Armenia. Each carries the artist's mark. (A few khatchkars are found in Ireland.) 1987.

The dramatic memorial to the victims of the 1915 genocide.
The "eternal flame" went out in 1992 due to the blockade of natural gas.
Yerevan, 1989.

One of Yerevan's impressive sculptures.
This one is of Gomidas, the celebrated priest-composer. Armenia, 1995.

Taken with the crew after our landing in Stepanakert on my first trip to Karabagh. Our pilot Raffi is on my left. May 1992.

The boy scouts and girl scouts in Shushi on Victory Day. May 9, 1996.

*Prof. Gourgen Melikian with Monte Melkonian, freedom fighter and hero,
taken three weeks before Monte was killed.
Stepanakert, May 1993.*

*Monte Melkonian followed by children singing a tribute to him.
Lady Caroline Cox and Zori Balayan are to his far left. May 1993.*

A woman carrying water to her home. Matchkalashen, 1996.

Baking bread in a "tonir," this one built above the ground. Karabagh, 1995.

Women spinning yarn on a spindle. Matchkalashen, 1994.

*The rock on which Shushi is built. The village of Karin-Dak
("under the rock") was subjected to flaming tires hurled from above
by Azeris. Undaunted, the villagers lived the war out in their cellars.
Karabagh, 1993.*

The children of Karin-Dak. Karabagh, 1993.

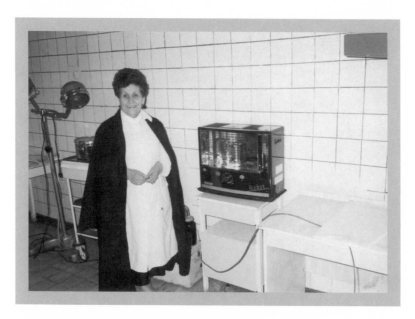

Maternity Hospital chief, Dr. Brina Marutian. The kerosene heater was donated by a group of young New York Armenians through the Alliance. Stepanakert, 1993.

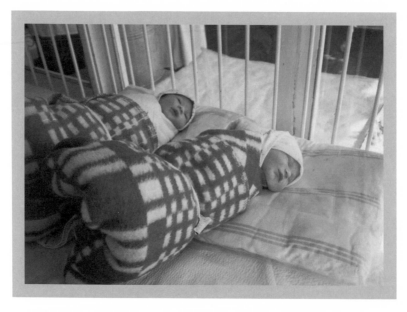

Newborns: swaddling continues to be the custom. Stepanakert, 1994.

"Please say 'thank you' to Arpen." Stepanakert, 1997.

Opening festivities at the newly renovated pediatric intensive care unit, funded by the late Nazik Tilerian, 1915 genocide survivor. Stepanakert, 1997.

Shushi's famous cathedral, Ghazantchetsots, where the
Azeris stockpiled missiles. Photo taken one snowy
morning before returning to Yerevan.
Karabagh, 1993.

My Aunt Hassie and me posing with Karabagh's famous
monument called, "We are our mountains."
Karabagh, 1995.

Dr. Armen Pirouzyan, his wife
Nara, and their children.
Gyumri, 1996.

Drs. Ida and Tigran with their
children on the way to
Damala, 1995.

At the United Nations,
the 11th century khatchkar,
a gift from the Republic
of Armenia. Left to right:
Drs. Asoian, Khatchatrian,
Marutian, and Pirouzyan
with Dr. Louis Najarian
(of New York).
July 1995.

Dr. Vigen Khatchatrian, his wife
Gayanne, and their children.
Shushi, 1995.

Prof. Gourgen Melikian
with his wife Laura.
Yerevan, 1995.

One More Word
from the Author:

There is an old joke about an overzealous mother who buys two shirts for her son and hangs them in his closet. The following morning, wanting to please his mother, the son puts on one of the shirts and appears at the breakfast table. Upset, his mother asks, "Didn't you like the other shirt?" In writing this book many decisions had to be made about what material to include from my journals and memory. Some of my trips to Armenia and Karabagh were left out entirely as were several Armenian Health Alliance projects; thus many people who were active with the Alliance also are not mentioned. These were choices that had to be made—I had to select some stories but not others. It was also impossible to mention all the projects others undertook in response to the earthquake; those that I refer to were part of the story line. The following updates seem appropriate because these people were part of my story:

- Hrair Hovaguimian, M.D., who performed Gagik Altunian's heart surgery, eventually saw his dream come to fruition: the establishment of a pediatric heart surgery center in Yerevan. Over 1000 babies and children at this state-of-the art center have had heart surgery performed by Dr. Hovaguimian and by the Armenian doctors he has trained.

- The Mental Health Outreach program established by Armen Goenjian, M.D., continues in Gyumri with the assistance of

Louis M. Najarian, M.D., Madeline Tashjian, Ph.D., and others. The Armenian psychologists they trained now staff this center. Garbis Moushigian has remained active in Armenia as well.

- Richard Aghababian, M.D., who went to Armenia with me on the first trip after the earthquake, has continued his work in Armenia as part of the Boston University-Armenia Medical Partnership Program designed to improve emergency medical services in Yerevan. The partnership with Yerevan's Emergency Medical Center was spearheaded by Dr. Aram Chobanian, M.D.

- Raffi Manjikian, whom I met at the Second Children's Hospital, helped found the Armenian Children's Milk fund which continues to regularily send soy infant formula to Armenia and Karabagh.

Sources

Adalian, Rouben P., ed. *Armenia and Karabagh Factbook*. (Washington D.C.,Armenian Assembly of America, 1996).

Armenia: Report of a UNICEF Mission, March 1992.

Autier P., Férir, M.C., and Hairapetien, A., et al. "Drug Supply in the Aftermath of the 1988 Armenian Earthquake." *Lancet* 1990; 335: 1388–1390.

Bournatian, George A. *A History of the Armenian People*, Vols. I and II. (Costa Mesa, CA: Mazda Publishers, 1993).

Centers for Disease Control. "Emergency Public Health Surveillance in Response to Food and Energy Shortages in Armenia, 1992." *Morbidity and Mortality Weekly Report* 1993; 42 (no. 4): 69–71.

Farmer, R.G., and Chobanian, A.V. "Health Care In Armenia Today." *Western Journal of Medicine* 1994; 160:331–334.

Hovannisian, Richard G., ed. *The Armenian People From Ancient to Modern Times*, Vols. I and II, 1st ed. (New York: St. Martin's Press, 1997).

Goenjian, A.K., Najarian, L.M., Pynoos, R.S., Steinberg, A.M., Petrosian, P., Setrakyan, S., and Fairbanks, L.A. "Postraumatic Stress Reactions After Single and Double Trauma." *Acta Psychiatrica Scandinavica* 1994: 214–221.

Malkasian, Mark. *"Gha-ra-bagh."* (Detroit: Wayne State University Press, 1996).

Mirak, Robert. *Torn Between Two Lands*. (Cambridge, MA: Harvard University Press, 1983).

Morgenthau, Henry III. *Mostly Morgenthaus*. (New York: Ticknor and Fields, 1991), pp. 152–172.

Najarian, C.S., and Najarian, N.L. "Two Years After the December 1989 Earthquake in Armenia: A Relief Worker's Perspective." *A Journal of International Affairs* 1991; 48–51. (Publication of Georgetown University).

Shahmuratian, Samuel, ed. *The Sumgait Tragedy, Pogroms Against Armenians in Soviet Azerbaijan*, Vol I. Eyewitness Accounts. (Cambridge, MA: Zoryan Institute for Contemporary Armenian Research and Documentation and New Rochelle, NY: Aristide D. Caratzas, 1990).

World Bank. 1996. "Armenia: Confronting Poverty Issues."

Suggested Reading

Arlen, Michael, J. *Passage to Ararat*. (New York: Farrar, Straus & Giroux: 1975).

Balakian, Peter. *Black Dog of Fate: An American Son Uncovers His Armenian Past*. (New York: Basic Books, 1997).

Dadrian, Vahakn N. *German Responsibility in the Armenian Genocide*. (Cambridge, MA: Blue Crane Books, 1996).

Emin, George. *Seven Songs About Armenia*, trans. Mkrtich Soghikian. (Yerevan: Sovetakan Grogh, 1983).

Kricorian, Nancy. *Zabelle: A Novel*. (New York: Atlantic Monthly Press, 1998).

Marsden, Philip. *The Crossing Place: A Journey Among the Armenians*. (New York: Kodansha America Inc., 1993).

Miller, Donald E., and Miller, Lorna Touryan. *Survivors: An Oral History of the Armenian Genocide*. (Berkeley: University of California Press, 1993).